DALE

ALKA DEV

SERGE SALAT

MARCELLO DI PAOLA

THE QUITO PAPERS AND THE NEW URBAN AGENDA

UN-HABITAT
WITH RICHARD SENNETT
RICKY BURDETT AND SASKIA SASSEN
IN DIALOGUE WITH JOAN CLOS

ANITA BERRIZBEITIA

GILES SMITH

JANE HARRISON

ADAM KAASA

LOEIZ BOURDIC

HENK OVINK

AMICA DALL

GIANPAOLO BAIOCCHI

SHLOMO ANGEL

JOHN BINGHAM-HALL

NEW YORK UNIVERSITY

UN⊕HABITAT
FOR A BETTER URBAN FUTURE

Routledge
Taylor & Francis Group

LONDON AND NEW YORK

First published 2018
by Routledge
711 Third Avenue, New York 10017

and by Routledge
2 Park Square, Milton Park, Abingdon, Oxon, OX14 4RN

Routledge is an imprint of the Taylor & Francis Group, an informa business

Disclaimer: The designations employed and the presentation of the material in this publication do not imply the expression of any opinion whatsoever on the part of the Secretariat of the United Nations concerning the legal status of any country, territory, city or area, or of its authorities, or concerning delimitation of its frontiers or boundaries, or regarding its economic system of development. The analysis, conclusions and recommendations of the report do not necessarily reflect the views of the United Nations Human Settlements Programme, the Governing Council of the United Nations Human Settlements Programme or its Member States.

Library of Congress Cataloging-in-Publication Data

Names: United Nations Human Settlements Programme.
Title: The Quito papers and the new urban agenda / UN-Habitat, with Richard Sennett, Ricky Burdett and Saskia Sassen; in dialogue with Joan Clos.
Description: New York: Routledge, 2018. | Includes bibliographical references and index.
Identifiers: LCCN 2017046378| ISBN 9781138572065 (hardback) | ISBN 9780815379294 (pbk.)
Subjects: LCSH: Sustainable urban development--Developing countries. | Urban policy--Developing countries. | Urbanization--Developing countries.
Classification: LCC HT169.E8 Q58 2018 | DDC 307.7609172/4--dc23
LC record available at https://lccn.loc.gov/2017046378

Typeset in Frutiger

Publisher's Note: This book has been prepared from camera-ready copy provided by the editors.

THE QUITO PAPERS AND THE NEW URBAN AGENDA

CONTENTS

x Preface: Why *The Quito Papers*?

Richard Sennett and Ricky Burdett

1 Introduction

Joan Clos

1
Forces Shaping 21st Century Urbanization

3   Introduction

4   The Universe of Cities

6   **1.1:** Growing differences in population dynamics require focus- and speed-differentiated approaches to good urbanization

18 **1.2:** A massive loss of habitat is accelerating and driving new flows of migration

26 **1.3:** Large-scale urban land acquisitions could de-urbanize cities and undermine public control

32 **1.4:** Lack of access to water and the risks caused by an excess of water require a rethinking on the place and shape of future urbanization

42 **1.5:** If democracy is to survive it will have to resist internal populism and embrace external cooperation

48 Who Owns the City?

Saskia Sassen

2
The Science of Urbanization and the Open City

LIST OF ILLUSTRATIONS

ACKNOWLEDGEMENTS

Overall supervision
For UN-Habitat: Dr. Joan Clos, Under-Secretary General and Executive
Director of the United Nations Human Settlements Programme
(UN-Habitat)

For New York University: Richard Sennett, Professor of Humanities, New
York University, Professor of Sociology, The London School of Economics
and Political Science

Editors
Filiep Decorte, UN-Habitat
Andrew Rudd, UN-Habitat

Authors of main papers (in alphabetical order):
Ricky Burdett, Professor of Urban Studies at the London School of Economics
and Political Science and the director of LSE Cities and the Urban Age project
Saskia Sassen, Robert S. Lynd Professor of Sociology at Columbia University
Richard Sennett, Professor of Humanities, New York University, Professor
of Sociology, The London School of Economics and Political Science

Authors of other selectively abridged papers (in alphabetical order):
Shlomo Angel, Gianpaolo Baiocchi, Anita Berrizbeitia, John Bingham-Hall,
Loeiz Bourdic, Amica Dall, Alka Dev, Marcello Di Paola, Jane Harrison, Sara
Hertog, Dale Jamieson, Adam Kaasa, Marco Kamiya, Jean-Louis Missika,
Henk Ovink, Serge Salat and Giles Smith

Layout, illustrations and photographs
Marshall Allen, Paola Chapdelaine, Akanksha Chauhan, Sophiya Khan,
Muhammad Saleh, Shanshan Tao and Wouter Verstraete

Thanks also to Dominick Bagnato of Theatrum Mundi for his assistance
and support and Matthew Skjonsberg and Clay Strange for their initial
research inputs.

Cover
©SubMap by Attila Bujdosó, Dániel Feles, Krisztián Gergely and Kitchen
Budapest. SubMap is a distorted, subjective city map showing Budapest
from 'our point of view'.

PREFACE
WHY *THE QUITO PAPERS*?

RICHARD SENNETT AND RICKY BURDETT

Like many of the participants who took part in the Habitat III conference held in Quito in 2016—an epochal event that occurs every 20 years—we knew that something good would come out of it. We watched with interest as thousands of urbanists, policymakers and scholars engaged with the lengthy process of agreeing on the manuscript for the New Urban Agenda. We queued in the sun alongside 30,000 others in Quito to witness the adoption by 167 signatory nations of a document that will now shape the debate in global urban policy for decades to come.

But we also knew that this historic event was an opportunity to engage in a parallel process: to radically re-think the way we talk about and make our cities. We shared with Joan Clos—Executive Director of UN-Habitat and the inspiration behind Habitat III—the belief that the physical and the social are deeply connected in cities, but that somehow the fragile connection was broken by the principles of the modern movement enshrined in the 1933 Charter of Athens. This manifesto, conceived on a cruise-ship in the Mediterranean by the leading modern architects and planners of the day, still influences the shape and the dynamics of urban form 80 years after its formulation. From 'towers in the park', to the 'separation of cars and pedestrians' and the 'zoning of different uses', the Charter provided technical answers to the complex problems of the mid-20th century city.

The built reality of this rationalist vision is palpable in cities and peripheries globally. Regularly spaced high-rise towers, separated by dead space and wide roads into rigid functional zones define the instant cities of Songdo in South Korea, Gurgaon in India and the new urban realities of Kigali and Luanda. Similar typologies mark the dormitory towns on the edges of Istanbul and the centrally planned metropolitan uber-region of Jing-Jin-Ji (120 million people around Beijing) and the economic hubs of the Yangtze and Pearl River deltas in China. These landscapes are familiar, even commonplace in different geographies of the urbanizing world.

We felt there was an opportunity, which Dr Clos and UN-Habitat

Fig 1: Towers in the park, Mumbai
© Matthew Niederhauser and John Fitzgerald with support from the MIT Norman B. Leventhal Centre for Advanced Urbanism

embraced, not to offer a 21st century version of the Charter, but to start a discussion that both challenged the status quo and opened up new lines of enquiry. *The Quito Papers* are just that: a collection of statements, considerations and observations that emerge from discussions coordinated by Richard Sennett at NYU with a number of individuals and institutions from different disciplines and professions. The content is intentionally broad, ranging from architecture, planning and urban design, to land ownership and regulation, water management and environmental philosophy. Together, the contributions form a multifaceted assembly of perspectives that critique the

identify new trends and propose new insights on contemporary urbanization.

UN-Habitat has also contributed new research to provide a more complex and complete picture of patterns of global urbanization, focussing on the way cities are expanding without control and highlighting the risks associated with weak leadership and chronic under-investment. The document importantly underscores Dr Clos' belief that the nation-state plays a critical role in addressing the problems and opportunities of cities across the globe and that we need to re-learn how to plan cities with well-designed public space as a

Unlike the 1933 Charter of Athens, *The Quito Papers*, which were drafted in 2016, do not propose a manifesto made up of simplistic slogans and recommendations. This is intentional. The urban condition of the 21st century is more fragile and more complex. It requires a different approach.

The Quito Papers offer a mirror to cities today. They reflect the potential for wider and more inclusive debate made possible by advances in technology and sharing of information. They recognize that urbanization is incomplete, messy and organic and that the new urban discourse needs to be reflexive of these technologies and

Many of the 94 recommendations of the 1933 Charter of Athens still determine the generic forms and physical organization of the 21st century city.

Ricky Burdett

The ideas presented in this document are intended to provoke greater imagination, not propose policies and solutions. Central to this effort is a re-examination of the strict functionalist separation of activities that still dominates planning practices worldwide. It argues in favour of clustering over segregation and isolation. It promotes a line of thinking that recognizes the importance of context and time in city-making. And it encourages the embracement of a broader time horizon, with openness to the past and the anticipation of an uncertain future. It embraces the concepts of flexibility and resilience, accommodating heterogeneity and change, in ways that allow people to re-appropriate spaces and places. Unlike the temporal and spatial certainties of past models, the emerging discourse on cities acknowledges experience, temporality and surprise as central to the choreography of city-making.

Ultimately, *The Quito Papers* recognize that urbanization is a necessarily open process that is both iterative and incomplete – just like the cities where most of the world's population will live in a few generations from now. We see this document as a complement to the *New Urban Agenda*. One of the key legacies of Habitat III should be to mark a paradigm shift away from the rigidity of the technocratic, generic modernist model we have inherited from the Charter of Athens towards a more open, malleable and incremental urbanism that recognises the role of design and space in making cities more equitable. We hope that *The Quito Papers* can contribute to this collective effort.

Fig 2: Future of suburbia
© Matthew Niederhauser and John Fitzgerald with support from the MIT Norman B. Leventhal
Centre for Advanced Urbanism

Fig 3: Night lights map
Data courtesy Marc Imhoff of NASA GSFC and Christopher Elvidge of NOAA NGDC.
Image by Craig Mayhew and Robert Simmon, NASA GSFC.

INTRODUCTION
JOAN CLOS

The New Urban Agenda adopted at Habitat III in Quito is an important milestone. The concrete commitments from Member States allow us to move beyond the limitations of Habitat I and II—which focused predominantly on the problems associated with urbanization and the role of local governments, respectively—and ensure that urbanization is a driver of inclusive development. For the first time, and building on the Sustainable Development Goals, urbanization and its challenges and opportunities are at the centre of global policy making.

The Quito Papers and the New Urban Agenda outlines some of the emerging challenges facing cities, including for global governance and urban democracy. This publication also com-plements the New Urban Agenda by pushing our collective reflection on the urban future, as issues and urgencies evolve. Based on a series of dialogues and position papers initiated by me and commissioned by Richard Sennett, *The Quito Papers and the New Urban Agenda* has several distinct entry points. Part One outlines the overall challenges facing cities in the 21st century and Part Two offers a number of concep-tual frameworks and approaches for dealing with those challenges. Each Part is also composed of a body of illustrated arguments, synthesized from selectively-abridged background papers from over 15 commissioned authors and interspersed with in-depth papers.

The debate should not stop here. This publication will stimulate further crit-ical thinking on the key challenges of our rapidly evolving urban world and inspire policy makers, practitioners and engaged citizens. It draws on a rich, ongoing dialogue I have had the pleasure of taking part in over the last years with thought leaders such as Richard Sennett, Saskia Sassen, and Ricky Burdett from the London School of Economics Cities Programme and Urban Age series and Shlomo Angel of New York University.

The success of the New Urban Agenda depends on actions taken by national governments and the pact they make with local governments through their national urban policies. It is a conversa-tion I hope we can broaden and use to prioritize our actions and lead to ever holder political commitments.

FORCES SHAPING 21ST CENTURY URBANIZATION

INTRODUCTION

Population dynamics have enormous impacts on national and global development and pose particular challenges to urbanization now and in the future. There is an unprecedented diversity of demographic structures across the world, including age distribution and population growth. The growing differences between Europe, Japan and the Land-Rich Developed Countries and Sub-Saharan Africa require focus- and speed-differentiated approaches to good urbanization.

At the same time the world faces new challenges related to emerging and accelerated streams of migration, new geographies of control over rural and urban land and a stressed relationship with water, representing a 'new' history in the making. They have the potential to reshape the urban world as they will surely alter its ongoing trajectory. And as these challenges are supranational in nature, they will require a shared vision and responses that are more flexible than they have been in the past.

A massive loss of habitat is accelerating and driving new flows of migration. Emerging flows of migration point to structural changes in the areas of origin. A sharp increase in rural land acquisitions is feeding the loss of habitat, with debt servicing part of the logic of extraction. These represent a new phase of advanced capitalism. As a consequence, new and emergent flows of migrants in search of a bare life rarely have an option of return.

Another accelerating phenomenon is large-scale urban land acquisitions which are already de-urbanizing cities and undermining public control. In particular, the corporate buying of urban properties and land is taking on worrying new features.

Water is the last substantive commons on the planet. All the same, the risks caused by an excess of water require a rethinking as much as the lack of access to water. There is at the same time too little and too much water. Urban development can no longer just assume that water can be simply extracted from the ground and moved to where it is needed. There seems to be a paradoxical relationship between water-stressed cities and availability of rain, which should be recognized as a resource. But time is running out fast—radical transformative innovation is needed to fend off disaster.

The reach of human activity is now pervasive, challenging traditional notions of liberal democracy. Clearly democracy needs to evolve if it is to survive; however, new agents and non-agents are complicating the cooperation that would be required for this evolution. They are also making responsibility increasingly difficult to assign and creating a preponderance of 'veto players', all of which are leading to governance gridlock. Ultimately this means that liberal democracies the world over are experiencing a crisis of legitimacy. If they are to survive it, states will have to muster the internal coherence to resist populism and the external coherence to be more cooperative.

This section extracts from and synthesizes recent work by Alka Dev, Saskia Sassen, Jane Harrison, Henk Ovink, Dale Jamieson and Marcello Di Paola.

Fig 4: The universe of cities of more than 100,000 inhabitants

© UN-Habitat / Shlomo Angel, NYU

Land-Rich Developed Countries

Latin America & the Caribbean

Europe & Japan

Western Asia & North Africa

Sub-Saharan Africa

Southeast Asia

East Asia & the Pacific

South & Central Asia

The UN Population Division divides the world into two mega-regions: More Developed Countries and Less Developed Countries. The classifications that appear above and throughout this book subdivide the mega-region of the More Developed Countries into two (Land-Rich Developed Countries and Europe and Japan), to create groupings with similar land availability, and the mega-region of the Less Developed Countries into six. The relatively similar urbanization patterns of the resulting eight world regions of the sample facilitate monitoring and reporting.

Growing differences in population dynamics require focus- and speed-differentiated approaches to good urbanization

Population dynamics are closely linked to development challenges, including urbanization

While the total number of people in the world is growing more slowly than in past decades, future population growth will be older and almost entirely urban. In 2016, there were 7.4 billion people in the world, having grown by 2 billion since 1990. According to the United Nations projections, the world's population could reach 9.7 billion by 2050.

Alka Dev notes that, overall, both education and life expectancy have improved on average; people lived up to 70 years during 2010-2015, which was five years longer than two decades earlier. Increasing longevity and declining fertility have also led to an aging population. In 1990, people over 60 years of age

comprised 9% of the world's population; in 2016, they comprised 12% and by 2050 they are projected to reach nearly 22%.

The world will also certainly become more urban. Nearly all of the future growth of the world's population will take place in urban areas. In 2016, more than half of the world's population resided in urban areas, compared to 43% in 1990. By 2050, over two-thirds of the world's population will be urban. Essentially all population growth in the future will be in cities: the urban population is projected to grow to 6.4 billion by 2050 while the rural population will remain around 3.3 billion. The largest increases will occur in less developed countries in Asia and Africa.

Sub-Saharan Africa (SSA), in particular, will experience the most rapid growth in terms of its total population (and, by extension, its urban population) posing huge challenges to cities. Between 2016 and 2050 in SSA, the urban population will grow 45% faster than the total population; 3.25% per year as compared to 2.25% per year. Translating these average rates to doubling time equates to the urban population of SSA doubling in just 21 years, compared to 31 years for the total population.

The next largest rate of change in total population growth will be in the countries of Western Asia and Northern Africa (WANA) which will add 1.28% more people to

Fig 5: Canaan in Croix-des-Bouquets and Thomazeau on the outskirts of Port-au-Prince, Haiti
Following the 2010 earthquake, the national government made land available 10 km outside of the capital for the emergency relocation of an urban camp at risk, though without having planned it beforehand. People invaded the area, which in four years mushroomed into an informal town of around 150,000 people.
© UN-Habitat

Fig 6: Aerial view of Jefferson Chalmers neighbourhood, Detroit
Due to the weakening of its automobile industry, the city has suffered a major economic decline and lost 64% of its population between 1950 and 2013.
© Bing Maps (Microsoft Product Screenshot reprinted with permission from Microsoft Corporation)

its overall population each year while growing moderately more urban. However, in the countries of South and Central Asia (SCA) and Southeast Asia (SEA), the urban populations will grow more than twice as fast as the total population. In contrast, in Europe and Japan (E&J), the total population is projected to shrink modestly by 2050, but the urban population of the region is projected to grow, albeit at a very slow rate. A similar pattern is predicted for China. Land-Rich Developed Countries (LRDC) and Latin American Countries (LAC) will also grow moderately more urban while adding to the total population.

The process of urbanization, or 'urban transition', describes a shift in a population from one that is dispersed across small rural settlements in which agriculture is the dominant economic activity towards one where the population is concentrated in larger, dense urban settlements characterized by industrial and service activities. Historically, the urban transition has been linked closely to economic development. In Europe and Northern America, rapid urbanization over the late nineteenth and twentieth centuries was observed to accompany the industrial revolution and rapid economic growth. A similar, although generally weaker, association between urbanization, industrialization and economic development has been observed more recently in many parts of Latin America and the Caribbean and Eastern Asia as well. The urban transition and economic growth have been linked in part because economic development fuels urbanization. People are drawn to cities that offer varied opportunities for education and employment, particularly in the industry and services sectors. Urbanization, in turn, generally has had a positive impact on economic development and poverty reduction.

Cities concentrate diverse pools of labour that businesses need in order to grow. Furthermore, the density of people and businesses in cities facilitates knowledge and information sharing, fostering new enterprises and technological

innovation. As hubs of commerce, government, and transportation, cities provide crucial links with rural areas, between cities, and across international borders. Approximately 80 per cent of global gross domestic product (GDP) is generated in cities.

Recent trends in developing regions, particularly in sub-Saharan Africa, have challenged long held notions about the association between urbanization and economic growth. While a dearth of data on urbanization in the region complicates any inference about trends, the available evidence suggests that the urbanization process continued in sub-Saharan Africa between the 1970s and 2000,

despite economic contraction in the region over the same period. Demographers note that the urban transition observed in sub-Saharan Africa in recent decades, while not consistent with economic theories of urbanization, is consistent with the demographic transition experienced in the region.

The demographic theory of the urban transition posits a 'pre-transition' period characterized by high birth and death rates. During this period a given country's (or region's) population is mostly rural and mortality rates in urban areas tend to be much higher than those in rural areas owing to the heightened risk of death from infectious diseases that spread easily in densely

populated areas that do not have good sanitation. Moreover, urban birth rates tend to be lower than urban death rates such that the urban population is sustained only by continuous replenishment through rural-to-urban migration. However, with improvements to public health, death rates begin to decline faster in urban areas than in rural ones and eventually the number of urban deaths falls below the number of urban births. This means that the urban population grows not only because of rural-to-urban migration, but due to natural increase as well. In most regions, including in sub-Saharan Africa, the process of urbanization has tended to occur in tandem with the declining mortality and fertility rates

Fig 7: Cartogram showing projected annual rate of urban population growth
© UN-Habitat based on data from Yannick Savina

- Land-Rich Developed Countries
- Latin America & the Caribbean
- Europe & Japan
- Western Asia & North Africa
- Sub-Saharan Africa
- Southeast Asia
- East Asia & the Pacific
- South & Central Asia

that characterize the demographic transition, lending support to the notion that the urban transition is better explained as a demographic phenomenon than strictly as an economic one.

The consequences of the rapid pace of urban growth present many development challenges as they are projected to result in disorganized cities with large proportions of people living in unplanned and illegal settlements. Countries in SSA—and to a slightly less extent in SCA and SEA—are poised to bear the brunt of urban demands. The lack of basic public infrastructure and housing tenure or land rights combined with substandard living conditions may become one of the biggest public health disasters of the century. Not only can this phenomenon eliminate the urban opportunities that drive development and economic growth, they can also create extremely inaccessible pockets of poverty where people live in far worse conditions than rural areas.

Fig 8: Population pyramids 2016-2050

© UN-Habitat based on Data from UN DESA

Population pyramids visualize the most fundamental demographic characteristics of human populations: age and sex. In aggregate, they indicate the number of people in a population who are going to engage in any predictable demographic behaviour such as schooling, marriage, employment, family formation, migration and so on. Pyramids sized in proportion to their respective regions' share of world population.

Land-Rich Developed Countries

Western Asia & North Africa

Southeast Asia

Latin America & the Caribbean

Europe & Japan

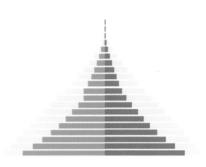

Sub-Saharan Africa

There is an unprecedented diversity in demographic structures across the world: age distribution and overall growth

The world's regions differ markedly in terms of the demographic changes they are currently experiencing. Population pyramids visualize the number of people in a population who are going to engage in any predictable demographic behaviour such as schooling, marriage, employment, family formation, migration and so on. They are an important tool for understanding population level needs for specific types of public and private resources.

Historically, they had the shape of a pyramid: there is a large group of young people at the bottom, fewer and fewer people in each succeeding generation and a small number of older age groups at the top. Current populations around the world vary from being quite youthful, as in SSA, to being much older, as in E&J. The diversity in age structures across the world is also indicative of different rates of fertility, mortality, and population growth. Three categories of population dynamics that can be understood broadly help explore the potential regional impact of population growth on urbanization.

SSA and WANA countries are in the first category, which is characterized by high fertility rates, high rates of mortality and low life expectancy; these contribute to a more traditional pyramid shape. SSA has a wide pyramid base, typical of a rapidly expanding population with a large number of births and a large number of people in the younger age groups. Children under five are the most numerous segment in 2016 (16%) and will remain so in 2050 (12%). In the next three decades, SSA countries will add 90 million children under five years to their population; from 160 million currently to nearly 250 million in 2050. The large numbers of new residents that will SSA cities absorb will be disproportionately young. In 2016, there were nearly as many youth aged 0-14 years as working age people 15-64 years in SSA, meaning a very large dependency ratio of youth compared to the productive population. By 2050, over half of the population will still be in the younger age groups but the working age population will

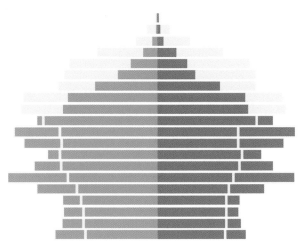

East Asia & the Pacific

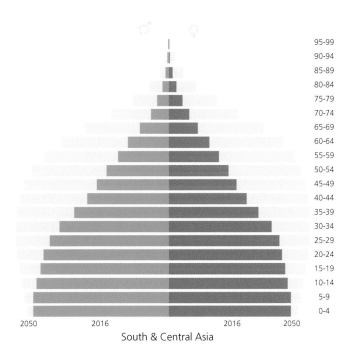

| 95-99 |
| 90-94 |
| 85-89 |
| 80-84 |
| 75-79 |
| 70-74 |
| 65-69 |
| 60-64 |
| 55-59 |
| 50-54 |
| 45-49 |
| 40-44 |
| 35-39 |
| 30-34 |
| 25-29 |
| 20-24 |
| 15-19 |
| 10-14 |
| 5-9 |
| 0-4 |

2050   2016   2016   2050

South & Central Asia

have grown from 527 million to 1.3 billion. If today's youth are given sufficient education, training, and job opportunities, then this increase in the proportion of working age people could lead to a 'demographic dividend' for SSA. If instead they are unemployed or underemployed in subsistence agriculture, the growing number of unskilled working age people will pose a challenge to the achievement of sustainable development.

Similarly, children under five are the largest segment of population in WANA now (12%) but a declining birth rate will slow the proportion of this population to 8% by 2050. WANA countries will also have a large population of youth (nearly

120 million youth under 14 years old), but also a comparably large dependent population of people over 64 years. WANA countries will need critical resources for education, employment, housing, and security for its youth, especially since most of them will be competing for resources in urban settings. However, resources will also need to be directed to an aging population.

The second category consists of the most developed countries; both land-rich ones such as the United States and others that are not, such as Japan and European nations. In both, the population structure follows more of a dome shape rather than the traditional

pyramid. A steady fertility decline in these countries has led to a more rectangular shape typical of low fertility countries as the high fertility bulge of the past has moved to the middle working ages, representing a large portion of the population between 15-64 years. Rather than an expansion of the population, land-rich developed countries (LRDC), European nations and Japan will face a shrinking workforce, due to lower birth rates, and a considerable aging population, given lower mortality and longer lifespans. By 2050, in Europe and Japan the proportion of people between 15-64 years will have decreased from 65% (currently) to 56%, and the proportion of people 65 and older will have

Fig 9: 'Arab Spring', Egypt, 2011
© Saleem Al Homsi

increased from 19% (currently) to 29%. Similarly in LRDC, there will be a 6% decrease in working age segments and an 8% increase in people over 65 years. In both regions, the proportion of children and youth will remain relatively stable. The needs of people in these countries will require reallocation of resources to support a large group of the elderly but also strategies to sustain economic growth with lower proportions of working age people.

Finally, the pyramids for the Latin American Countries (LAC), South and Central Asia region (SCA), and Southeast Asia (SEA) region show their passage through the demographic transition—fertility declines began in the 1960s and early 1970s due to introduction of fertility reduction programs and accelerated rapidly into the early 1980s, resulting in a slowing down of population growth. The population structures of these countries are also represented by a wide base. Until fertility rates decline and the births and deaths become equal, substantial population growth can still take place due to high fertility conditions of the past that led to larger proportions of people in reproductive age groups. Depending on their place in the demographic transition, the high fertility bulge of the past will move into the older ages resulting in increasing shares of older age groups and a moderately stable working population. In LAC, for example, there will be a decrease in children and youth under 14 years, from 25% currently to 17% in 2050. The proportion of working age people (15-64 years) will also decrease by 4% while the proportion of those 65 years and older will increase from 8% to 20% by 2050. The countries of SEA, some of which entered the transition early, will also see a 7% decline in the population under 15 years but an increase of 10% in those 65 and older. The working age groups will decrease slightly from 68% to 65%. In SCA countries, which experienced a fertility decline later than LAC and SEA, the younger populations will also decline, although the working age popula-

tion will increase slightly from 65% to 67% and there will be a smaller increase in the proportion who are over 65 years.

The pyramid for the EAP region largely represents the situation in China where high fertility from the past can be seen as a large middle bulge of working age people who will form a large proportion of older age groups in the next decades. The working age population will decrease significantly from 73% in 2016 to 59% in 2050, while the shares of those who are 65 and older will increase from 10% to 28% over the next three decades.

Fig 12: Location of urban agglomerations with at least 500,000 inhabitants, 2014
© UN-Habitat based on Data from UN DESA, 2014

Small Cities
(500k - 1 million)

Medium Cities
(1 - 5 million)

Large Cities
(5 - 10 million)

Mega Cities
(10+ million)

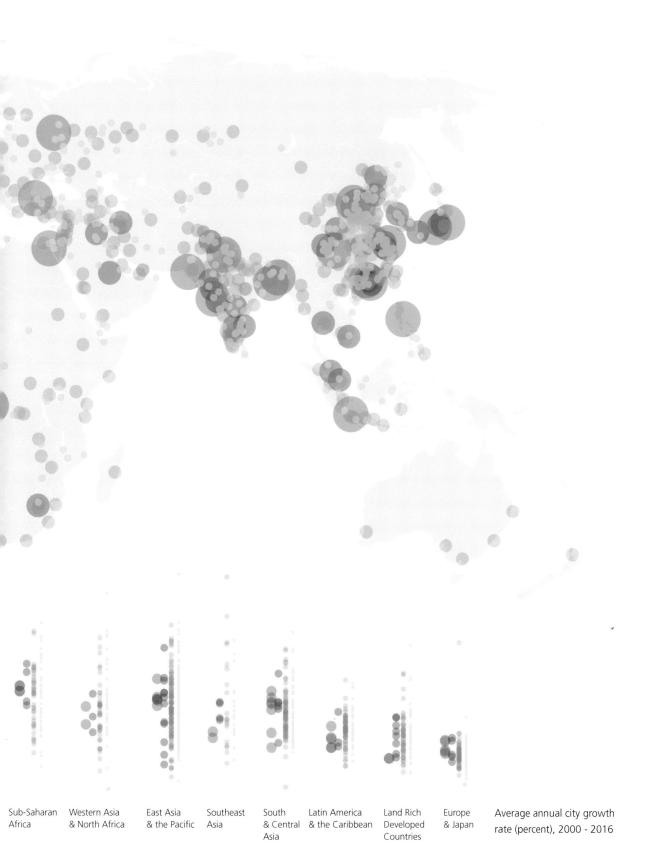

Sub-Saharan
Africa

Western Asia
& North Africa

East Asia
& the Pacific

Southeast
Asia

South
& Central
Asia

Latin America
& the Caribbean

Land Rich
Developed
Countries

Europe
& Japan

Average annual city growth
rate (percent), 2000 - 2016

**Fig 13: UN-Habitat's global
sample of 200 cities**
© UN-Habitat / Shlomo Angel, NYU

Land-Rich Developed Countries

Latin America & the Caribbean

Europe & Japan

Western Asia & North Africa

Sub-Saharan Africa

Southeast Asia

East Asia & the Pacific

South & Central Asia

A massive loss of habitat is accelerating and driving new flows of migration

Emerging flows of migration point to structural changes in the areas of origin

In her current research Saskia Sassen is focusing on a particular set of migration flows that have emerged recently. These new flows are generally far smaller than ongoing older ones but are of interest because they provide clues to their origins and the larger shifting contexts of which they are a part. In this way the migrant can be seen as an indicator of emerging changes in the area where they come from, whose impact over time and at scale is still to be fully understood and visible.

Sassen examines three migratory flows. The first is the sharp increase in the migration of unaccompanied minors from Central America, specifically Honduras, El Salvador, and Guatemala. The second is the surge

in Rohingyas fleeing from Myanmar. And the third is the migration toward Europe, originating mostly in Syria, Iraq, Afghanistan, and several African countries, notably Eritrea and Somalia.

These are three very different types of flows, and the third one contains particularly diverse ones. Yet each points to a larger context in which extreme conditions, rather than economic calculus, provoke chain migration. These conditions arose from situations larger than the internal logic of households and the vagaries of national and local economies, and they operate at city, regional and global geopolitical levels.

The immigrants constituting these new flows are distinct from those of the million-plus immigrants who are mostly modest middle class, increasingly joined by professionals, functioning in the global economy and who have entered through formal channels or become formalized eventually in their new home countries. In contrast, the immigrants constituting these new flows are not the poorest in their countries of origin.

Extreme violence is one key factor explaining their migration. A second factor is thirty years of international development policies, which have left much land dead. Mining, land grabs, and plantation agriculture have expelled directly and indirectly

Fig 14: The Old City of Homs has been destroyed by years of conflict, Syria
© UNHCR / Andrew McConnell

Fig 15: Syrian refugees arriving by boat on the island of Lesbos from Turkey, Greece
© UNHCR / Andrew McConnell

whole communities from their habitats. Moving to the slums of large cities, or, for those who can afford it, out of their home countries, has increasingly become the last option. This multi-decade history of destructions and expulsions has now reached extreme levels of which the vast stretches of dead land and water bodies are a stark reminder. Some localized wars and conflicts arise from this destruction, as part of a fight for habitat. Climate change, through increased droughts and/ or floods, further reduces liveable ground.

These emerging flows point to larger histories and geographies in the making. If not formally acknowledged and proactively prepared for, they could eventually become overwhelming to existing immigration and refugee policy systems, to the mostly urban areas receiving them, and to the men, women, and children who constitute them.

Fig 16: São Paulo stock market representing
the virtual nature of advanced capitalism
© Rafael Matsunaga, CC by 2.0

A new phase of advanced capitalism is feeding the loss of habitat

The geographic expansion and systemic deepening of capitalist relations of production in the global South is nothing new. However, Sassen focuses on recent years, which are marked by a new phase in the loss of habitat due to the scaling up of land and water grabs, expelling smallholder growers for massive expansion of mining and large-scale occupation of land to build modern high-rise environments for the upper middle classes. Furthermore—and insufficiently recognized in standard measures of economic growth—these grabs register as growth in the Gross Domestic Product, in ignorance of the smallholder economies they have replaced.

Much attention has already been paid to the destruction of pre-capitalist economies in the global South via their incorporation into capitalist relations of production. But the post-1980s period makes visible another variant of this capacity to appropriate or destroy traditional capitalism and deepen a type of advanced capitalism dominated by a financial logic. This is critical because high finance is radically different from traditional banking. The traditional bank sells something it has, generally money, for interest. Finance sells something it does not have, so it needs to develop complex instruments that enable it to invade other sectors in order to financialize whatever value can be extracted and then insert it into fin-

ancial circuits. It is this feature that leads Sassen to posit that finance is an extractive sector that, having extracted what is there to be extracted, moves on, leaving behind destruction. These represent new predatory dynamics rather than merely evolution, development, or progress. At its most extreme this can mean the immiseration and expulsion of growing numbers of people who cease to be of value as workers and consumers. But it also means that traditional and petites bourgeoisies cease to be of value.

30 years of international development policies have left much land dead, extracting what is there to be extracted, moving on, leaving behind destruction.

Saskia Sassen

Debt servicing is part of the logic of extraction

Debt servicing has been a key instrument for disciplining and weakening governments by forcing them to pay growing shares of national revenue for interest on their debts rather than economic development (IMF). Whereas countries should be drawing foreign investment to and furthering mass manufacturing by national firms—which can generate a modest but effective middle class—debt servicing has made them susceptible to signing unfavourable deals with global firms in extractive industries.

The extraction of value from the global South and the implementation of restructuring programmes at the hands of the IMF and the World Bank have had the effect of 'recon-ditioning' the terrain represented by these countries for an expansion of new forms of advanced capitalism, including acquisitions of vast stretches of land for agriculture, water and mining. This has systemically weakened and corrupted governments; even resource-rich countries have experienced the immiseration of their people. It is now clear that these programmes did not deliver on the basic components for healthy development. The discipline of debt service payments was given strong priority over infrastructure, hospitals, schools, and other people-oriented development goals, such that many of sub-Saharan African countries have less functioning health and education systems and economies and more destitution than several decades ago.

The primacy of this extractive logic became a mechanism for systemic transformation that went well beyond debt service payment, the devastation of large sectors of traditional economies, including small-scale manufacturing, the destruction of a significant portion of the traditional and petite bourgeoisie, the resulting survival economies of the poor, and, in many cases, the impoverishment and progressive corruptibility of the state.

The gradual destruction of traditional economies has come precisely at a time of extreme financialization and systemic crisis based on a growing demand for those material resources.

Fig 17: The boundary between intact forest and deforested land for palm oil plantations, Indonesia
© Mighty

Fig 18: Deforestation from palm oil plantations in Papua New Guinea. Piles of wood prepared to be burnt by Korean Palm Oil Company Korindo
© Mighty

Sharp increase in rural land acquisitions represents a structural transformation

The weakening and corrupting of governments in the global South described previously has enabled a sharp increase in land acquisitions by foreign governments and firms since 2006. What concerns Sassen is the clear emergence of a new phase of Capitalism, rather than the continuation of a centuries-old practice going back to diverse imperial phases.

One reason for these land acquisitions is rapid development in some parts of the world that is generating a demand for industrial crops, food crops, wood, water and metals. In addition, the financialization of commodities has brought new potentials for profit making to the primary sector, thus stimulating

large-scale speculative investments in land. These investments in land have crowded out investments in mass manufacturing and other sectors mentioned previously. The rise in such investments happened at a time when several countries of the global South were beginning to experience significant growth in mass manufacturing, with increasing amounts of foreign direct investment (FDI) in this sector.

The issue is not one of nationalism versus globalism, but one of complexity: where once there was a prospect of democratic decision-making, now we see an expansion of opaque transnational networks that control the land with a global governance system

geared primarily towards enabling corporations. With this expansion of acquired land, what was once 'national sovereign territory' becomes merely a commodity on sale in the global market. In other words, we see a weakening of a complex entity that at its best can uphold the state's authority and inhabitants' rights while holding the state accountable.

Fig 19: A global web of agricultural land
© UN-Habitat based on data from
The Land Matrix Global Observatory

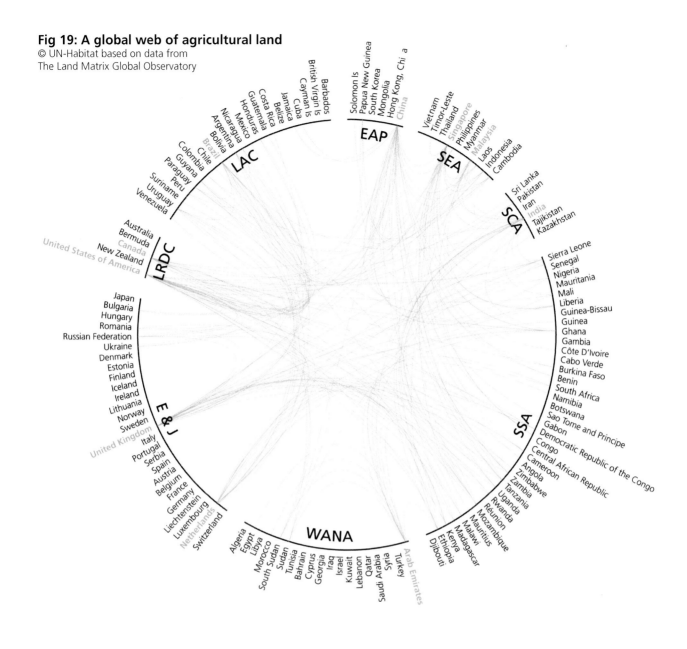

Top 10 land-investing countries:

1. United States of America	6,608,845 hectares
2. Malaysia	3,885,360 hectares
3. Singapore	3,215,852 hectares
4. United Kingdom	2,271,235 hectares
5. Arab Emirates	2,269,687 hectares
6. China	2,241,468 hectares
7. Brazil	2,069,943 hectares
8. India	2,069,483 hectares
9. Canada	1,993,032 hectares
10. Netherlands	1,744,545 hectares

Top 10 land-targeted countries:

1. Papua New Guinea	3,792,653 hectares
2. Russian Federation	3,363,012 hectares
3. Indonesia	3,235,335 hectares
4. Democratic Republic Congo	3,155,258 hectares
5. Brazil	2,745,758 hectares
6. South Sudan	2,691,453 hectares
7. Mozambique	2,448,695 hectares
8. Ukraine	2,404,407 hectares
9. Congo	2,148,000 hectares
10. Argentina	1,582,516 hectares

Syria

DROUGHT

Agricultural policies promote production of
staple crops resulting in overuse of
groundwater

Syria is se▪
in wheat ▪
90% of
used for ▪

WAR

Chandil Dam, India

1978   1981   1982   1990

| CONSTRUCTION |

First rumours of a   *Start of the first land*   *Submerging of first*   Irrigation
dam development   *acquisitions without*   *villages causing first*   not being ▪
project in Chandil   *notice upfront*   *displacements*   because ▪

EXPULSION

The MONYWA project, Myanmar

1978

Mining Enterprise   S&K bec▪
No.1, state-owned,   ventur▪
starts exploiting   ME1 and
Sabetaung &   compa▪
Kyisintaung (S&K)
deposits

Copper wa▪
150 acres ▪
around Ch
River

DEAD LAND

New and emergent flows of migrants in search of a bare life rarely have an option of return: a new history in the making

Wars, dead land and expulsions are producing a vast loss of habitat for a growing number of people. Even though each country has its own specific sources and conditions, Sassen argues that there is a history that weaves itself across this diversity and traces an expanded geography of instability and economic destruction. The current fragility started in the 1980s. The role of rich donor countries has also shifted: overall they give less in foreign aid for development than 30 years ago. As a result, the remittances sent by low-income immigrants are now larger than foreign aid. Philanthropies have also entered the realm once almost exclusive to governments.

As a consequence, a record number of people have been expelled from their homes and are in search of 'bare life', with no home to return to. These new dynamics are enormous challenges to the international system and countries and cities across different regions, including Europe, which until recently had been considered one of the most stable regions.

The histories and geographies shaping the three sets of flows introduced above are varied and complex. As a result, there are no easy solutions. These refugees are not usually the poorest in their countries, even if departing from their home countries leaves them without any resources; many have

advanced educations and started out with not insignificant means. Most are not emigrants per se, but rather refuge seekers. 'Sending them back from where they came' is often not an option because what was once home is now a war zone, a new private gated community, a corporate complex, a plantation, a mining development, a desert or a flooded plain; in short, a space of oppression and abuse.

These particular flows are subsets of larger flows of displaced people, but they stand out by their surging numbers and by the extreme conditions in the areas where they originate. An examination of the areas they are escaping often brings to the fore larger histories and geo-

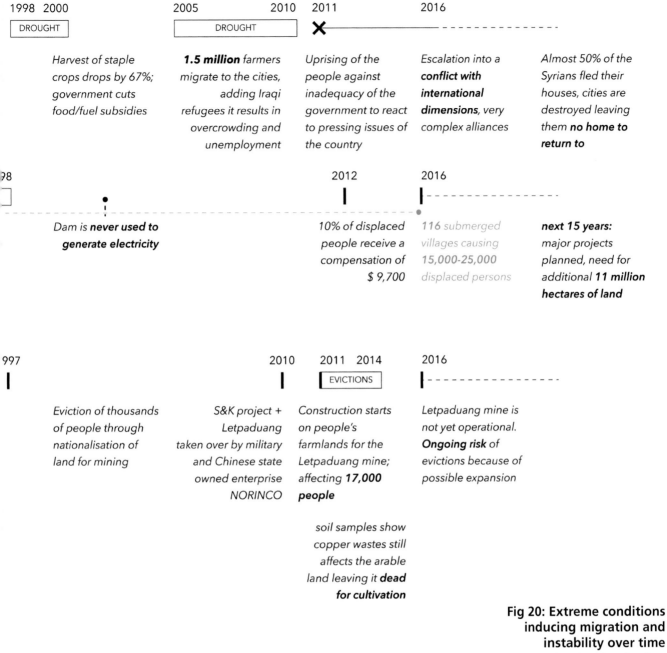

1998	2000		2005	2010	2011		2016	
DROUGHT			DROUGHT		✗ -----		------	

Harvest of staple crops drops by 67%; government cuts food/fuel subsidies

1.5 million farmers migrate to the cities, adding Iraqi refugees it results in overcrowding and unemployment

Uprising of the people against inadequacy of the government to react to pressing issues of the country

Escalation into a **conflict with international dimensions**, very complex alliances

Almost 50% of the Syrians fled their houses, cities are destroyed leaving them **no home to return to**

'98 .... 2012 .... 2016 ----

Dam is **never used to generate electricity**

10% of displaced people receive a compensation of $ 9,700

116 submerged villages causing 15,000-25,000 displaced persons

next 15 years: major projects planned, need for additional **11 million hectares of land**

'997 .... 2010 .... 2011 2014 .... 2016 ----

EVICTIONS

Eviction of thousands of people through nationalisation of land for mining

S&K project + Letpaduang taken over by military and Chinese state owned enterprise NORINCO

Construction starts on people's farmlands for the Letpaduang mine; affecting **17,000 people**

Letpaduang mine is not yet operational. **Ongoing risk** of evictions because of possible expansion

soil samples show copper wastes still affects the arable land leaving it **dead for cultivation**

Fig 20: Extreme conditions inducing migration and instability over time
© UN-Habitat based on data from Amnesty International, IDMC, Carbon Brief

graphies than the immediate and most visible causes might suggest—in other words, not necessarily war per se. They often point to longer histories of oppression and exploitation of a country's population as well as the destruction of its local economies.

These dynamics do not indicate a lack of order—they are the new order, and the departures that signify them are likely to continue. The three extreme flows of refuge seekers Sassen examines are a sort of first indication of a process that is likely to escalate, reshaping our urban world and its population and creating new challenges that will require supranational, national and city level answers.

Large-scale urban land acquisitions could de-urbanize cities and undermine public control

Corporate purchases of urban properties and land exhibit worrying new features

Most buildings in a city tend to be privately owned. While this is not new, the corporate buying of properties in most major cities of the world sharply increased after the 2008 crisis. Many newly-acquired buildings are underused and functioning essentially as a storage space for capital. This has exacerbated another trend in these same cities: the escalating price of modest housing, which is now excluding more and more of the working and middle classes.

It would be easy to explain the post-2008 investment surge as more of the same. After all, the late 1980s also experienced a rapid growth in national and foreign buying of office buildings and hotels. But an examination of the prevalent trends points to a whole new phase in the character and logic of foreign and national corporate acquisitions. Currently the corporatizing of access and control, and increasingly even ownership, has extended not only to high-end urban sites, but also to the land from beneath the homes of modest households and government offices. Corporations are buying whole pieces of cities at an unusually large scale. The mechanisms for these extractions are often far more complex than the outcomes, which are often quite elementary in their brutality. It is too early to confirm whether there is a difference in urban impact between national and foreign investment.

Several new features stand out. First, the buying of buildings has accelerated sharply. In 2016 there were about a hundred cities worldwide that had become significant destinations for such acquisitions (as ranked by the value of national and foreign buying of property in 2013-2014). In these cities, the corporate buying of existing properties reached over US$ 600 billion from mid-2013 to mid-2014 and over US$ 1 trillion from mid-2014 to mid-2015. These cities account for 10% of the world's population but 30% of global GDP, and, even more shockingly, 76% of all property acquisitions. Inevitably, this degree of concentration has also enabled the invention of a sort of real estate 'matching market' that

Fig 21: High-end corporate buildings whose large scale and homogeneity of use are undermining urbanness.

controls a large proportion of the high-end real estate sector.

Second, a whole new market for high-end housing has developed. In the post-2008 period, much of the buying of buildings has been to destroy and replace them with far taller, more luxurious buildings, which are often isolated from their environment and, as they often serve as secondary, tertiary or quaternary residences, are often temporarily unoccupied.

Third, the foreclosing on modest properties has resulted in swathes of underused urban land. In the US in recent years this has led to the loss of home-ownership, along with a significant amount of empty or underused land. The financial instrument involved is perversely brilliant in that it allows investors to use these mortgages in order to build asset-backed securities; it persuades what are in fact mostly low-income households that they can buy a house, asks them just to sign the contract, and not to pay anything for years. Investors made vast profits by selling the financial instrument as an asset-backed security to the high-level investor world. As this instrument can travel globally, it was also sold in Europe where foreclosures are also accumulating.

Fourth, corporations are acquiring whole blocks of underutilized and dead industrial land for site development and the spread of megaprojects. The availability of large-scale, obsolete industrial land and the abundance of unused houses in fairly central urban land due to the foreclosing of modest properties have enabled large-scale land acquisition for site development and megaprojects. Regrettably, the privatizations and deregulations that accelerated in the 1990s across much of the world have only strengthened and enabled this proliferating urban gigantism.

Fig 22: Gated community of Lomas de Angelopolis in Puebla, Mexico
© Sheffield Institute for International Development (SIID) / Emma Morales

Density alone does not make cities— large-scale acquisitions of urban property risk de-urbanizing them

While cities are strongly correlated with density and built-up terrain, Sassen argues that not all densities are the same—some actually de-urbanize cities. For her, the definition of a city is the space where those without power can make a history and a culture for themselves.

The scaling up of acquisitions results in a systemic transformation in the pattern of land ownership in cities, one that could alter their historic meaning. While not new, what stands out is the sharpening and corporatizing of extraction, of access and control, and increasingly even ownership. The large-scale corporate buying of, literally, urban space in its diverse instantiations introduces a de-urbanizing dynamic in that it is not adding to mixity and diversity. This often implants within the urban fabric a new formation in the shape of multiple high-rise luxury buildings. This new set of implants contains within it a logic all its own. It cannot be urbanized in the specific or idiosyncratic terms of a given city—that is, it cannot be tamed into becoming part of the logics of the city where it inserts itself. Such implants keep their full autonomy and essentially give the city their back.

Megaprojects thus raise the density of the city but risk de-urbanizing it, by thinning the texture and scale of spaces previously accessible to the public. In other words, they gener-ate vast footprints that inevitably kill much urban tissue: small streets and squares, density of street level shops and modest offices, and such. Where before there was a government office building handling the regulations and oversight of this or that public economic sector, or addressing the complaints from the local neighbourhood, now there might be a corporate headquarters, a luxury apartment building, or a mall. The overall effect of large corporate private ownership has been a reduction in publicly owned space. These megaprojects also act often as de facto gated spaces that concentrate many people from the same socioeconomic class and lack a dense mix of uses and types of people. Often this type of devel-

The overall effect of privatization has been a reduction in public buildings and an escalation in large corporate private ownership. Density is not enough to have a city.

Saskia Sassen

opment reinforces itself with walls, whether real or virtual.

Cities are at risk of losing their cosmopolitanism if large-scale buying continues. Density matters, but so do complexity and incompleteness: in this mix lies the capacity of cities across histories and geographies to outlive far more powerful but fully formalized systems. This combination also allows those without power to assert 'we are here'. Where the powerless have left their cultural, economic or social imprints—even if mostly in their neighbourhoods—eventually each one of their imprints can spread to a vaster urban zone. None of this can happen in an office park, no matter its density; it is a privately-controlled space where low-wage workers can work, but not make. In contrast it is in large, messy and somewhat anarchic cities that develop over time that the possibility of gaining complexity in one's powerlessness and leaving a historic trace can happen, because nothing can fully control such diversity of peoples and engagements.

Density, combined with complexity and incompleteness, makes cities spaces of innovations, small and large. This includes innovations by those without power because they too produce components of a city, leaving a legacy that adds to its cosmopolitanism. Few places outside of cities enable this. Complexity and incompleteness also facilitate the shaping of an urban subject that overrides the religious subject, the ethnic subject, the racialized subject, and, in certain settings, also the differences of class.

However, rather than functioning as spaces for people from diverse backgrounds and cultures, the global cities of today are expelling people and diversity. Their new owners, often mostly part-time inhabitants, are very international, but that does not mean that they represent diverse cultures and traditions: they represent the new global culture of the successful, which is astoundingly homogeneous no matter how diverse its countries of birth and languages.

HUDSON
STREET

GATED
COMMUNITY

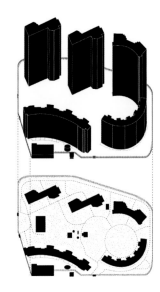

time spent

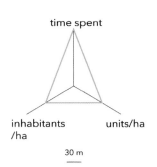

inhabitants
/ha   units/ha

30 m

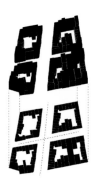

time spent

inhabitants
/ha   units/ha

30 m

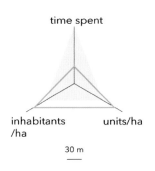

LUXURY
APARTMENTS

time spent

inhabitants
/ha   units/ha

30 m

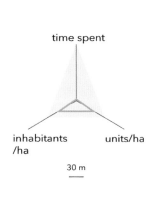

SHOPPING
MALL

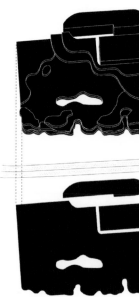

time spent

inhabitants
/ha   units/ha

30 m

Fig 23: De-urbanizing typologies

OFFICE
PARK

time spent

inhabitants
/ha

units/ha

30 m

1.4 Lack of access to water and the risks caused by an excess of water require a rethinking on the place and shape of future urbanization

Water is at the core of everything and at the heart of an uncertain future

Henk Ovink argues that water that is at the core of everything; it is key to all risks and uncertainties, all interdependencies and also all opportunities. It is through water that the world feels the impact of climate change the most. Indeed, water is at the core of many of the most extreme risks related to climate change, including sea level rise, and this is putting pressure on cities, societies and citizens to act soon lest the entire system collapse and leave many victims in its wake. Water is at the heart of this uncertain future.

Water is essential for social and cultural well-being. Its quality defines economic and societal prosperity and its quantity—whether too much or too little—defines societal vulnerability. Water is also critical for food and energy production. And it is an urban matter: an asset if managed right, a severe risk if not. With the world's urban population possibly increasing past 70% in 2050, it is in cities that lives and assets will be at severe risk if not developed with resilience in mind.

Urban water resilience concerns the safety, scarcity and quality of water, and this is as affected by the way cities develop as by the health of riverine basins that support them. Often the intersections between water, ecology and the economy exist at a regional scale. To act effectively at this scale communities, cities and regions worldwide need to change their approaches to be more comprehensive and resilient than in the past.

Fig 24: Water footprint of major cities
© UN-Habitat based on data from UNESCO

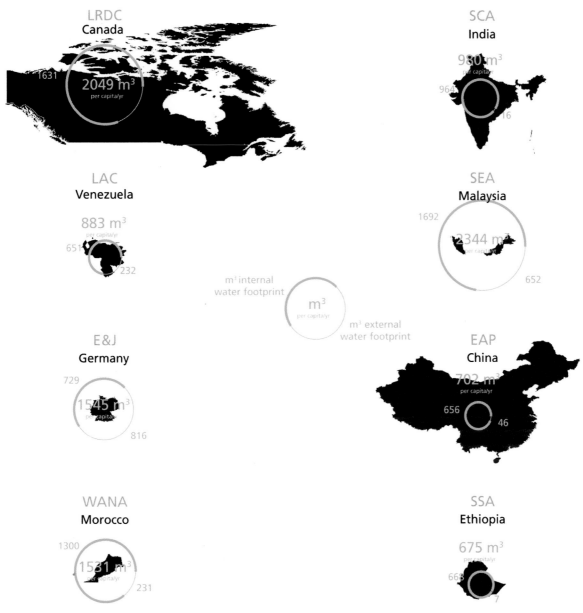

LRDC
Canada
1631
2049 m³
per capita/yr

SCA
India
980 m³
per capita
964
16

LAC
Venezuela
883 m³
per capita/yr
651
232

SEA
Malaysia
1692
2344 m³
per capita/yr
652

m³ internal
water footprint

m³
per capita/yr

m³ external
water footprint

E&J
Germany
729
1545 m³
per capita
816

EAP
China
702 m³
per capita/yr
656
46

WANA
Morocco
1300
1531 m³
per capita/yr
231

SSA
Ethiopia
675 m³
per capita/yr
668
7

Water is global risk number one

The World Economic Forum (WEF) Global Risks Report of 2016 identifies the impact of water crises as the number one global risk for the next decade. Two billion people will be devastated by 2050 if the world continues with its current practices. Of all worldwide disasters, 90% are water related. WEF's Global Risks Perception Surveys show repeatedly that most future risks (climate change, water crises, biodiversity loss and ecosystem collapse, extreme weather events, natural catastrophes, man-made environmental catastrophes, etc.) are increasing in frequency and impact. Many of them are interdependent at the regional and even metropolitan scale. Although this increases their complexity, Ovink believes that this is also the scale at which humankind can adapt to and mitigate these risks most effectively.

In the coming decades climate change will add to the pressure that economic growth and development are already putting on both groundwater and renewable surface water resources. Global water requirements are projected to be pushed 40% beyond sustainable water supplies by 2030. The nexus of food, water, energy and climate change has been identified by the US National Intelligence Council as one of four overarching mega-trends that will shape the world in 2030. The unpredictability of climate change could cause cascading crises, with a decreasing ability to grow food and access water precipitating sudden and uncontrolled population migrations. Already as of 2014, the number of refugees worldwide from environmental or conflict-related causes had reached its highest level since World War II.

The rapid, inadequate and poorly planned expansion of cities in developing countries also risks leaving urban populations highly exposed to the effects of climate change. Many cities are located near the sea or natural waterways where they are more at risk of flooding. Indeed, 15 of the world's 20 mega-cities – those with over 10 million inhabitants – are located in coastal zones threatened by sea-level rise and storm surges.

Fig 25: Projected waterstress in 2030
© UN-Habitat based on maps of World Resources Institute

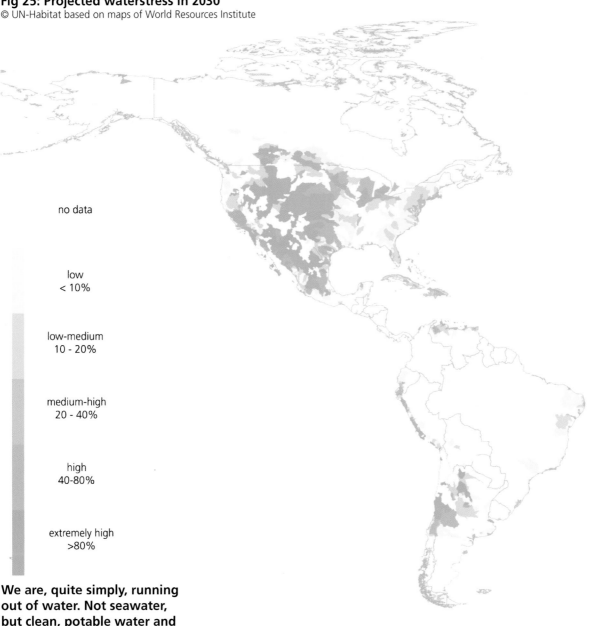

no data

low
< 10%

low-medium
10 - 20%

medium-high
20 - 40%

high
40-80%

extremely high
>80%

We are, quite simply, running out of water. Not seawater, but clean, potable water and this requires fresh thinking as a matter of urgency

Jane Harrison focuses mostly on the world's increasing lack of access to potable water. Securing a reliable supply of clean water has been one of the most important issues throughout human history. There is a fixed water supply on the planet, the global population is expanding and with development and economic growth the world's desire for water continues to increase. Half of the global population—four billion people—is already trying to survive without adequate water for at least part of the year and water use is growing at twice the pace of population growth. By 2025, two-thirds of the world population will be experiencing water 'stress conditions'. While the extent and nature of this stress varies from area to

area, many parts of the world will need to manage their water much more effectively if they are going to sustain their growth, and in some cases, prevent a major regression in welfare. The impact of water stress will be seen across economic sectors, with the potential to generate subsequent crises: In other words, we are already living in the endgame of a water-stressed world.

In the event that populations continue to increase as current predictions suggest and that they—by desire or design—flock to the cities for work and livelihood, they will exacerbate the predicaments of existing settlements and challenge their governments in unprecedented ways. The destabilizing effects

of poverty and lack of access to basic resources such as water, coupled with the impact of climate change, may strain urban conurbations to a breaking point and precipitate a desperate and even sudden disappearance of the civic milieu.

Landmasses have already been divided into complexes of multiple ownerships, seizures of minerals have led to the dissolution of the geologic commons, tracts of sea are limited by nation states, and water rights are the current favourites of the world's prospectors. Water now represents one of the last substantive commons on our planet.

However, given the vast disparities between water appetites of the developed world and water consumption restrictions (particularly outside of the developed world), water has already begun to feel like the currency of the future. Humans are behaving less and less spiritually as they live in ways that consume and destroy the very material they depend upon to survive. The invisible hand of Adam Smith will not ensure that the world's scarce freshwater resources are allocated in a way that creates the highest value to humankind. The world must acknowledge that the wise use of natural resources is not the private territory of the market. Freshwater allocation in particular is primarily within the realm of politics.

Water is one of the last substantive commons on the planet.

Jane Harrison

Fig 26: Where does Mumbai get its water from?
© UN-Habitat based on data from Robert McDonald et al, 2014

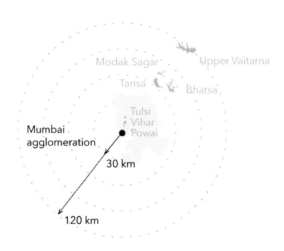

Urban development can no longer assume that water can be simply extracted from the ground and moved to where it is needed

3,220 million litres per day cross-basin transfer for 19,442,000 people

The assumption that water can always be moved from place to place has been the primary ethos of modern urban development. The next few decades will be the most rapid period of urban growth in human history, with 2.6 billion additional urban dwellers expected by 2050. All these new urban dwellers will need water, but surprisingly little is known globally about where large cities obtain their water from or the implications of their associated infrastructure for the global hydrologic cycle.

With their complex networks of urban water infrastructure, major cities, occupying about 1% of the earth's surface, are currently drawing their water across a cumu-

lative distance of 30,000 km from almost 50% of the Earth's surface. By and large this occurs in complete disregard of the impact to those ecosystems.

Consider the deterioration of the infrastructures transporting water to major cosmopolitan centres, the expenditures needed to repair and upgrade, the impressive leakage rates, the escalating water demands of affluent societies, the water footprint of the sum total of goods demanded by a city, the energy required to move the water from its point of extraction to the taps, and the water footprint of the associated costs and the resources required to bring water from a remote location to an ever

increasing population. In sum, these support the projection that by 2040 there will be a $143.7 billion shortfall in the funds required to maintain, upgrade and expand water infrastructure.

Groundwater is currently the primary source of freshwater for approximately two billion people. Groundwater extraction as a method for obtaining water has tripled in the last 50 years. More than half of the world's 37 largest aquifers are depleted. The most overburdened aquifers are in the world's driest areas, where populations draw heavily on underground water. Climate change and population growth are expected to only intensify the problem.

Fig 27: Where does Los Angeles get its water from?

© UN-Habitat based on data from Robert McDonald et al, 2014

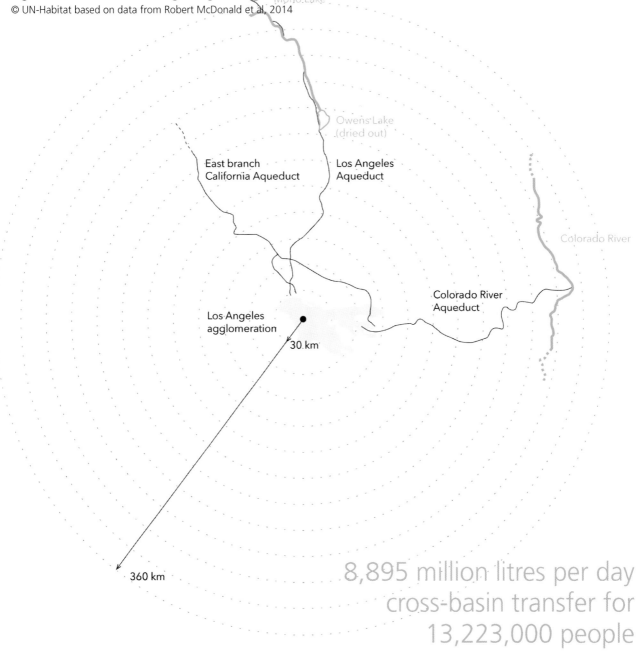

Mono Lake

Owens Lake
(dried out)

East branch
California Aqueduct

Los Angeles
Aqueduct

Colorado River

Colorado River
Aqueduct

Los Angeles
agglomeration

30 km

360 km

8,895 million litres per day
cross-basin transfer for
13,223,000 people

In the 1980s development programs in developing countries focused on groundwater extraction rather than on the surface water systems, based on the assumption that groundwater (underground) was an inherently safer water source for communities than surface water (e.g. rivers, ponds and canals), Surface water is susceptible to problems of pollution and evaporation, and that this shift in focus would reduce problems such as cholera. These advantages, coupled with the relative ease of tapping into a water supply at the point of need, make the extraction of groundwater very attractive. As a result people have come to rely increasingly on the digging of wells and drilling of boreholes as the mainstay of water development and the most popular way of supplying water to people.

But a reliance on boreholes can be extremely problematic. It has been reported that some 250,000 boreholes have been constructed for use in Africa, and, according to the World Health Organization, approximately 60% of these boreholes are broken or have run dry. Moreover, in many instances boreholes are drilled into non-replenishable aquifers, containing water millions of years old. Once depleted these water resources are gone (at least from the perspective of the current era of human existence). In any case, while groundwater supplies have reduced problems with bacteriological contamination, they can have serious problems with toxicity caused by salinity and high levels of fluoride.

LONDON

population:	8.63 million
built up area London:	1572 km²
average per capita water consumption:	164 l daily or 60,225 l annually
annual rainfall volume generated per m²:	600 liters / m²

current area London

5 km

SCENARIO 1:
assuming constant population number 8.63 million
assuming London consumption of 164 liters daily gives
average per capita consumption 60,225 l annually

100 m² of harvesting area per capita required
equivalent to a land area of 1,806 km²

SCENARIO 2:
assuming constant population number 8.63 million
assuming London target of 105 liters daily gives
average per capita consumption 38,325 l annually

64 m² of harvesting area per capita required
equivalent to a land area of 1495 km² < current land area London

There seems to be a paradoxical relationship between water-stressed cities and availability of rain

Jane Harrison points to the interesting paradox of water-stressed cities located in regions that have an abundance of rain. In spite of the increasing awareness of global environmental issues in recent years, the level of water illiteracy in both the developed and developing worlds remains. Of the twenty most water stressed cities in the world, five are in India and six in China. Tokyo is considered the most water stressed city on the planet despite its annual rainfall of 1,530 mm, and drizzling London, with a mere 590 mm of rain a year, is the fifteenth. In 60% of European cities with more than 100,000 people, groundwater is being used at a faster rate than it can be replenished.

In the popular mind, Africa is seen as a dry continent. But overall, it actually has more water resources per capita than Europe.

However, much of Africa's rain comes in bursts and is rapidly swept away or is never collected. The time has come to realize the great potential for greatly enhancing drinking water supplies by harvesting more of the rain when and where it falls. There is enough rain falling on Africa to supply the water needs for 13 billion people—twice the current world. This conundrum reveals a global failure at the intersection of development and the values of the developed world, visible through the ingrained habits of engineering, certifiable greed of governments

and fragile, childlike conviction that humans share in never-ending resources.

If Nairobi, with its 926 mm of rainfall annually, and considerably more than London, were planned to harvest the water required by its inhabitants what would it look like? Based on Nairobi's surface area of almost 700 km² and its population of 3.5 million an inhabitant would need the amount of water harvested from a piece of land about 16 m². If one imagined the area of Nairobi divided neatly and equally, there is 200 m² available per person. And yet there is almost no reliable water supply in the Nairobi slums and the rains pour down doing untold damage and spread-

NAIROBI

population:	6.54 million
built up area Nairobi:	696 km²
average per capita water consumption:	115 l daily or 42,000 l annually
annual rainfall volume generated per m²:	744 liters / m²

Fig 29: Spatial footprint and rainshed of Nairobi
© UN-Habitat based on data from Jane Harrison

current area Nairobi

5 km

SCENARIO 1:
assuming constant population number 6.54 million
assuming Nairobi consumption of 115 liters daily gives
average per capita consumption 42,000 l annually

56.5 m² of harvesting area per capita required
equivalent to a land area of 745 km²

SCENARIO 2:
assuming constant population number 6.54 million
assuming WHO target of 100 liters daily gives
average per capita consumption 36,500 l annually

49 m² of harvesting area per capita required
equivalent to a land area of 696 km² = current land area Nairobi

---

ing disease before they evaporate in the heat and disappear.

Water illiteracy will be the undoing of development unless the world acts quickly. It is essential to develop models of settlement that draw on ancient knowledge and begin to scale up ideas about cities and settlements in relation to the intelligent use of locally-available water sources, an idea known as 'reverse innovation'. The abundance of rainfall in Africa is mirrored by abundance in many of the regions of the world undergoing water stress. Eventually the world's reliance on groundwater and remote surface water systems to satisfy the water demands of dense urban populations will cease to be

viable. The default assumption that desalination is an answer comes with a massive health warning and at great financial and environmental expense.

The world needs to reassess radically the relationship between urban populations, urban densities and scales, and a rather dreamlike reliance upon 'remote' water. Failure to do so means growing the global economy in the short term by constructing the cities of our destruction.

Can cities shrink their water footprints by switching from remote groundwater acquisition to rainwater harvesting? UN-Habitat compared the existing spatial footprints

of London and Nairobi to that which would be required for them to be completely water self-sufficient. Based on the three most common building typologies in those cities, UN-Habitat took an average of the roof coverage in each and factored in annual rainfall and existing per capita water consumption to determine their respective rainwater footprints. Further, these were recalculated based on more aspirational rates of consumption. Data and mapping appear in the diagrams above.

Fig 30: Risk zone for flooding with a 5m sea-level rise
© UN-Habitat based on data from surgingseas.com (Climate Centre + SEDAC)

BANGLADESH   NETHERLANDS

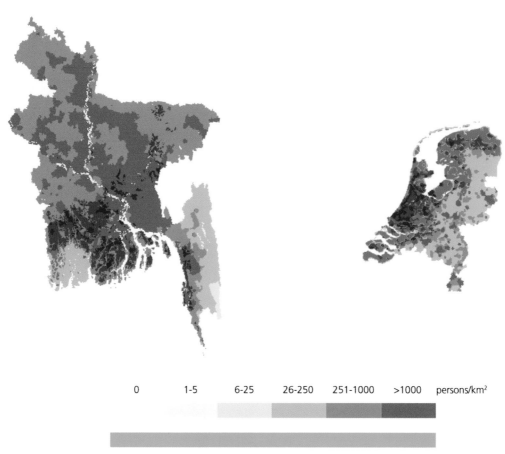

| 0 | 1-5 | 6-25 | 26-250 | 251-1000 | >1000 | persons/km² |

50 km

risk zone for flooding with a 5m sea-level rise

Time is running out fast—radical transformative innovation is needed to fend off disaster

Ovink's call is clear. Never has there been a more challenging time nor a greater urgency. While the Paris Agreement moves forward fragilely, suddenly without one major player, the world continues to move towards the edge. The world needs to consider radically more alternative routes to the future. Most of all, this means changing the way the world makes cities. Fewer than five years remain to change the world's current trajectory. If there is any hope of not exceeding a +2 Celsius degree world—let alone the +1.5 Celsius ambition of the COP21 Paris Agreement—then we need to generate very real change now. In other words, if the curves representing the effects of climate change mitigation and adaptation—CO2

emissions, renewable energy share, sea level rise, temperature rise, and so forth—are not reduced within the next five years, then the world will never ever reach the +2 Celsius degree goal.

The inherent slowness of climate change has generally yielded a slow approach and a focus on response rather than preparedness. However, the world can choose not to go slowly and incrementally, but rather to step up, leap frog and become transformative in its approach, collective actions and collaboration towards the development of cities, regions and nations.

One major hurdle is complexity—but addressing it effectively

first requires embracing it. This will create the necessary enabling environment for approaching climate change in a transformative manner. Specifically it will enable the arrangements for working in a multistakeholder, interscalar fashion at the interface of innovation and implementation, science and policy, and public and private institutions.

Rebuild by Design, initiated in New York following Hurricane Sandy, created alliances for change, mobilized the capacity of design to investigate and re-frame problems and yielded ultimately concrete projects. Bringing about cultural change requires strong coalitions. The programme has demonstrated how design, research and collab-

Fig 31: Flooding of settlements in Kalerwe, Kampala. The capital and largest city of Uganda is the 13th fastest growing city in the world, as well as one of the most thunderous places on Earth.
© UN-Habitat / Nicholas Kajoba

oration can go hand in hand with politics, policy development and investment strategies. Indeed the synergy between design and politics supports the critical processes of visualization, political dialogue and advocacy for reform.

People themselves will need to ensure adaptive, robust governance that is inclusive in both process and outcome. Design can support this by providing time to think, space for non-negotiated progress and a frame for decision making. The more people have a common connection based on a shared place the more feasible this is. It is not about a free ride for all, nor for back room plans; instead it is about governing by design, through an

inclusive, innovative and collaborative approach.

Harrison makes a similar appeal. Given the impact of climate change on weather patterns, rainfall and other forms of precipitation, cities should develop building typologies that can harvest and store as much water as possible ('water banks'). Such typologies must also be able to provide enough capacity to compensate for increasingly erratic time divisions between precipitation events. Efforts are already under way to demonstrate the overlooked potential of large-scale community based rainwater harvesting initiatives, based on a local, dispersed, decentralized and non-linear approach to infrastructural construction.

The question is open to what extent lack of (potable) water and/ or excess of water (sea level rise, flooding) will ultimately reshape the map of cities and global urbanization. Already local populations are contending with the difficult tradeoffs inherent in responding to acute crises ranging from local adaptation ('staying') or more drastic relocation strategies ('moving'), many of which will take decades to materialize.

If democracy is to survive it will have to resist internal populism and embrace external cooperation

The reach of human activity is all-encompassing, challenging traditional notions of liberal democracy

Dale Jamieson and Marcello Di Paola write about how no earthly place, form, process or system escapes the reach of human activity. At the beginning of the current epoch the earth had about six million people living as hunter-gatherers; today, there are more than seven billion people, expected to grow to nine billion by 2050. Many people today command resources that not even the nobility would have enjoyed a few centuries ago; and all of them have legitimate aspirations to decent standards of living. Between one-third and one-half of earth's land surface has already been transformed by human action; carbon dioxide in the atmosphere has increased by more than 30 per cent since the beginning of the industrial revolution; more nitrogen has been fixed by humans than all other terrestrial organisms combined; and more than half of all accessible surface freshwater has been human-appropriated.

The form of life that Homo Sapiens has come to live is resource-intensive, globalized, and production-and-consumption driven. Humanity is organized in highly complex systems bound together by oil and gas pipelines, electrical wires, air travel, highways, train tracks, fibre optic cables, and satellite connections. Technology enables the production levels that have allowed humanity to grow in size to today's unprecedented numbers. It enables shipping raw materials and goods across oceans and continents, and empowers people to move around in search of a better life, inspiration or simply a good time. It also enables 'action at a distance' that would once have seemed inconceivable.

But we are not in perfect mastery of nature. The conjunction of high population, consumption and technology has unprecedented implications. Small acts can reverberate far beyond their spatial and temporal locations in surprising and unwanted ways. Humanity is changing the climate as an inadvertent by-product of other activities, and this will have unforeseen consequences, many of which will be damaging to the very species that

Fig 32: Local dependence vs. global dependence over time
© Jerker Lokrantz / Azote, 2013

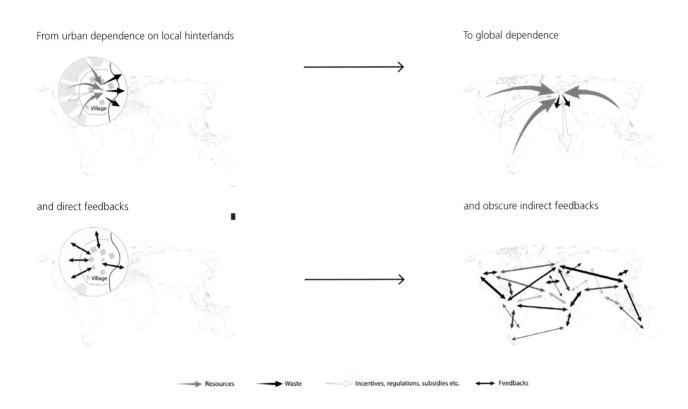

From urban dependence on local hinterlands

To global dependence

and direct feedbacks

and obscure indirect feedbacks

Resources · Waste · Incentives, regulations, subsidies etc. · Feedbacks

is bringing them about: beyond extreme weather events, humans can expect further epidemics, food and water shortages, political instability and mass migrations. The accumulation of apparently trivial, localized, individually innocuous acts can alter fundamental planetary systems in ways that have global consequences, which in turn are locally actualized.

There is widespread agreement in the scientific community that these human-driven processes may be leaving durable marks on the planet. Together we change the climate, erode the soil and alter hydrological cycles, thus harming and burdening humans and ecosystems in faraway places and times, and ultimately bringing trouble to the very places where we live. Life has always affected the earth, but the extent to which humanity today affects the planet (and thereby itself) is unprecedented. This challenges some of the underpinnings of liberal democracy, including the concepts of agency, responsibility, governance and legitimacy.

Fig 33: Disconnect between cause and effect

In a hypothetical world with clear lines of cause and effect (diagram on left), a given country's GHG emissions would put it at greater climate risk, which, in turn, would yield greater GDP loss. In the real world (diagram on right), many countries responsible for high emissions do not themselves experience correspondingly high levels of risk nor of loss, whereas many countries with low levels of emissions experience disproportionately high risk and loss.
© UN-Habitat

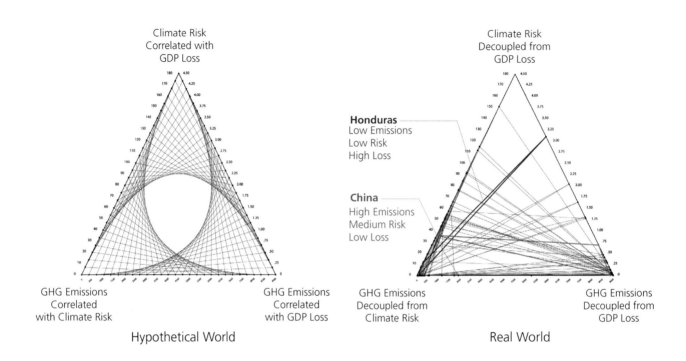

Hypothetical World

Real World

New agents, unclear responsibilities, veto players and legitimacy crises

Democracy is generally based on the notion that governments should act in the interests of all those who are governed. However, many democratic institutions arose at a time in which agents lived in close proximity, and whose decisions and actions had relatively direct impacts on each other. Around 1950, however, 'a structural shift' occurred 'from a world of discrete but inter-dependent national states to the world as a shared social space' (Held and McGrew, 2007: 2–3). Political decisions and actions taken locally now had planetary implications, impacting for better or worse the welfare and interests of people in all corners of the world. This represents an enormous asymmetry of power. The empire of the present

not only colonizes large areas of the planet but the global future as well. However, those on the periphery (including nature) cannot particip-ate, protest or retaliate.

New kinds of global agents have also emerged: multinational corporations, the International Monetary Fund (IMF), the World Trade Organization (WTO), financial networks and rating agencies, transnational social movements, private military companies, cross-border criminal cartels and others. Their decisions have significant impacts but lack accountability to individuals and governments. Ironically, the new global agent that many hope could coordinate a shared plan for the future—the United Nations—is

too accountable to governments, and thus too heavily constrained by competing national interests to play this role. Crises such as climate change have been brought about by and will have negative impacts on humans. Yet it is difficult to make specific claims about who is respons-ible for what. Agents of all kinds are implicated in the rise in global tem-peratures, which is both global and intergenerational. Its causal mech-anisms are also extremely complex. When no one in particular seems to be harming anyone in particular, no one seems to be responsible for the deaths and damages that occur. Uncertain of the culprit, no obituary will ever say of anyone that she or he was killed by climate change.

Fig 34: Influence of NRA as a veto player

© UN-Habitat

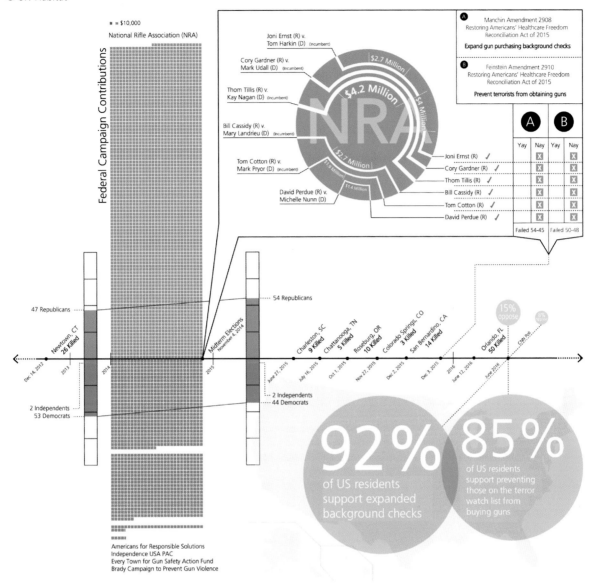

The current era is difficult to govern. With the emergence of China, Brazil and India, the world order is attempting to adjust to shifting power distributions. However, as the cooperation of these new giants becomes more valuable, the price for obtaining it rises. This is complicating negotiations, causing gridlock in international cooperation. Within countries, dysfunctional 'veto players'—which can include parliaments, political parties, powerful industries and others—also prevent changes to the status quo. This is attractive when the status quo is desirable (e.g. preserving important policies through periods in which they are unpopular). However, when the status quo is undesirable,

veto players block the flexibility needed for change. For every possible policy change there is always a 'do-nothing' alternative, all too easily fuelled by uncertainties about transition costs and final pay-offs. The imperatives of change are often hard to accept. As a result, the challenges of our era have thus far largely been met by inaction, squabbling and denial.

In many countries, confidence in government has never been lower. Populist movements are on the rise, advocating for change by popular demand that would circumvent entrenched veto players and institutional agents. Such movements are fired by vivid, visceral and even uncivil expressions of disagreement

that proliferate on the internet and intensify anger and impatience. And they represent substantive challenges to the legitimacy of liberal democratic institutions, which often either seem ineffective or corrupt. Citizens register a loss of jurisdiction over political life and even express difficulty in developing informed views about key issues. Much of what goes on in any given democratic country is, in fact, never consented to by its citizens. In the past, the governed could be expected to consent to policies that had beneficial consequences and were justifiable by the lights of public reason. The circumstances of today block all traditional sources of liberal democratic legitimacy.

Institutions of governance **will have to work at** *multiple scales* **in both space and time, incorporating the** *interests* **of the** *global* **with those of the** *local*, **and those of the** *future* **with those of the** *present.*

Dale Jamieson and Marcello Di Paola

States will have to muster the internal coherence to resist populism and the external coherence to be more cooperative

Innovation in both theory and practice is required if the core values of liberal democratic politics are to survive in this new epoch. The existing democratic deficit in liberal states will generally have to be reduced. All the same, and particularly in the case of climate change, states will have to muster both the internal coherence and strength to better resist populism, and the external coherence and strength to be more cooperative partners within the framework of supranational institutions. This seems to suggest, perhaps paradoxically, that political institutions will have to be more democratic in some respects and less democratic in others.

Governance today is cooperation-hungry at all levels, including intergenerationally. Institutions of governance will have to work at multiple scales in both space and time, incorporating the interests of the global with those of the local, and those of the future with those of the present. Currently, we heavily discount the interests of the future and the far. In any case, it is difficult to see how to adequately take into account the interests of the future and the far without unjustly subordinating the interests of the near and the present, especially given the centrality of the agency presupposition in liberal democratic theory. Democratic governments are supposed to be responsive to all those who are governed, but those

beyond their borders in space, time or citizenship are not governed but only affected.

Perhaps the best we can hope for is that we are entering a period of intense experimentation in both political theory and practice. Non-agents could find refuge in our politics through the introduction of institutions for the future, innovative global redistributive programmes, science courts, green courts, enlarged suffrage to children and advocates for animals and the rest of nature, and novel possibilities for participation. It remains to be seen if and how they will work, who will win and lose, who will be made responsible for what, and who will decide about

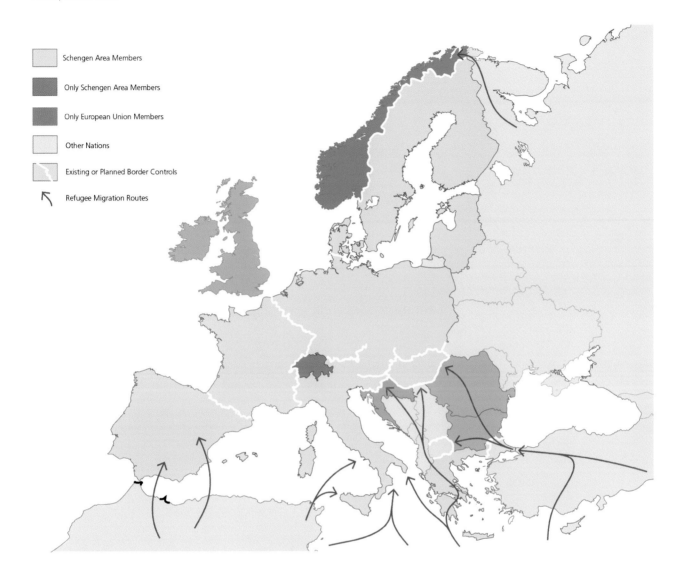

Fig 35: A theoretically border-free Europe with actual and planned borders
© UN-Habitat based on data from Business Insider, March 2016

Schengen Area Members

Only Schengen Area Members

Only European Union Members

Other Nations

Existing or Planned Border Controls

Refugee Migration Routes

all this. While we must begin to act now, we will not know the answers to many of these questions for a very long time. No single agent can solve the problems of our era.

Cooperation among political agents is necessary but it remains structurally elusive. Individuals have their daily preoccupations, politicians have their constituencies to protect, governments have national interests to promote, global agents have their own different agendas, and digital agents are a vast, enveloping force whose contributions are crucial yet unstable. The fact that the required cooperation also extends across generations complicates matters further. This shifting and only partially coherent

landscape of agency leaves us disoriented and sceptical about our capacity to manage our ecological entanglements. Indeed, the main obstacle to taking action on climate change may well be the deep sense of its inevitability and our inability to affect its course.

The irony is that after centuries of modernity and its contributions to human welfare and autonomy, we find ourselves with the widespread sense of a loss of agency. Together, we are remaking the planet and undermining the conditions of our own existence, though no individual or collective decision was ever made to do so.

A phenomenon like climate change creates the potential for ubiquitous tensions and trade-offs between the present and the future, and more generally between agents and non-agents – those who are governed, and those who are affected. Even if those benefits to non-agents were great and justifiable by public reason, they might not be consented to in democracies already accused of not being insufficiently responsive to their citizens. If consent is important, ignoring or heavily discounting the welfare and interests of non-agents may be a wrong that democracies cannot avoid committing.

WHO OWNS THE CITY?
SASKIA SASSEN

Cities have generally succeeded in enabling a variety of ownership regimes for their diverse material components. And they have done so across multiple historical periods and governing formats. This points to a remarkable capacity of cities to survive enormous, and often radical, transformations. In contrast, powerful formal actors—royal houses, government systems, the major enterprises of an epoch—have not. They are dead. But the cities themselves are still there: they have outlived far more powerful but closed systems. This marks a sharp difference between cities and other major entities, from rulers to private corporations.

Strong as these features of cities are, they are not indestructible. In this paper I focus on the massive increase in the buying of urban properties that is playing out today in a rapidly expanding number of cities. Of particular concern here are two features: one is the underutilization of those bought properties, and the other is the slippage in the capacity of existing urban legal regimes to govern, oversee, or regulate this explosion in acquisitions. While it is only a hundred or so cities that seem to be in play at this point, they signal a possibility of legal innovations that may alter long-existing traditions about who owns the city, notably, that no single entity owns the city. This multiplicity of ambiguous regimes that has ruled and enabled cities for centuries is today under direct threat from major corporate acquisitions and legal innovations.

Cities: complex but incomplete

A key marker of cities is that they are complex but incomplete systems that cannot be fully controlled. It is this mix of complexity and incompleteness that has given cities their long lives across enormously diverse historical periods. And a key consequence of this ambiguity is that cities have long been spaces where those without power have been able to make a history, a culture, an economy of sorts. The neighbourhoods—the spaces of modest, not rich or elite urban inhabitants, have outlived powerful regimes that have all come down.

These are also the features of cities that have enabled the powerless to make claims. Today the city remains

a far stronger enabler of such claim-making by those without power than are mines and plantations which once were such spaces but today are fully controlled and even militarized. Across the centuries it is also these features of cities that enabled the bazaar culture—where members of very diverse religions could trade with each other and constitute merchant traditions that cut across all kinds of differences. The bazaar was a space that enabled this. And when the workday was over, each different ethnic or religious group retreated to its community and engaged in its particular culture and religion. Out of this emerged the importance of trade and the civic, as we name it in western modernity—it was given other names in non-western geographies where these same features were evident. It is these centuries-old features of cities that continue to enable those without power. These are urban capabilities.

And it is these capabilities that are under threat today. They are literally being demolished in more and more of our great cities. It is this sense that what could outlive wars, power and time, is now being destroyed, devalued. This has certainly also happened in the past—and history has shown us that a city destroyed is a city ready to be rebuilt. Yet each epoch in time and space is shaped and re-shaped in specific ways.

My concern here is with our current period and its specifics. Against the larger historical survival of the urban, I examine sharp trends in a growing number of major cities that point to a disturbing, even if partial, de-urbanizing of those cities. Might these trends tell us a larger story? At its most extreme, are we witnessing the repositioning of the city as a valuable commodity—and perhaps even a financializing of that commodity?

Property regimes

Most buildings in a city tend to be privately owned. It has long been so in most countries. It continues to be so today, but with a difference. Much of the corporate buying of properties in major cities of the world has a weak utility function: buying not in order to use them, but rather just to own them. Many of these buildings are under used and functioning more as a storage space for capital.

This stands in sharp contrast with another accelerating trend in those same cities: the escalating price of modest housing which is now excluding more and more of the middle classes from home ownership. This has generated some major issues in a growing number of cities. One of these is that it is threatening the capacity of the working and middle classes to get housing, something that becomes quite problematic in the case of emergency staff, notably firefighters and nurses. Another is the proliferation of megaprojects where before there were streets, little parks, public offices that served residents needs, and more. The corporate buying of urban buildings which are then only partly used also stands in contrast to a third trend: the vast expansion of 'the periphery', an ambiguous zone of mostly low-rise, poor housing that is neither city nor quite slum.

The massive foreign and national corporate buying and under-using of urban buildings that took off after the 2008 crisis marks a new period. The juxtaposition of high prices and the underusing of those buildings departs from what was typical in past periods—most recently in the 1980s, when the global economy led to much foreign buying of valuable properties. The difference with that earlier period concerns both the lesser scale of buying compared to today's phase, and the stronger utility function of that earlier period—strong profits, getting a foothold in major financial centres, etc. A further difference is the juxtaposition of the underutilization of those properties with the extremely high demand for housing by the modest middle classes who have been priced out in a growing number of major cities. And then there are those extremely dense peripheries, on the one side, and those empty underused mansions.

This scale of corporate buying signals an emergent new phase in major cities. A hypothesis here is that at a time of somewhat generalized crisis along with a vast concentration of capital at the top of the system, the buying of buildings in major cities might be one of the better investments for the rich, though coming at a high price for cities. Another major question this raises is whether some of this buying of buildings is actually the buying of urban land. Here one key issue is whether the contracts being developed by today's corporate buyers begin to take over and neutralize older, often weakly formalized, regimes concerning who owns the land beneath the building. In many older cities the rules about land ownership go back to times when such contracts were likely to be shaped by custom. These types of questions are a key element for establishing what matters about this growing corporate investment and the contractual consequences it might entail for urban governance.

What is different in today's corporate buying of urban properties?

It is easy to explain the post-2008 investment surge as more of the same. After all, also the late 1980s saw rapid growth of national and foreign buying of office buildings and hotels, especially in New York and London. I already wrote about this in The Global City (1991, 2001, ch 7), notably, that a large share of buildings in the City of London were foreign owned at the height of that phase. Financial firms from countries as diverse as Japan and the Netherlands found they needed a strong foothold in London's City to access Continental European capital and markets.

There is, then, something familiar in this current post 2008 surge in acquisitions. But an examination of the current trends shows some significant differences and points to a whole new phase in the character and logics of foreign and national corporate acquisitions. Let me add that I do not see much of a difference in terms of the urban impact between national and foreign investment. The key fact here is that both are corporate and large scale: this is what is critical.

Six features stand out. One is the sharp scale-up in the buying of buildings, even in cities that have long been the object of such investments, notably New York and London. The Chinese have most recently emerged as major buyers in cities across the world. Today there are about a hundred cities worldwide that have become significant destinations for such acquisitions. Indeed the rates of growth are far higher in some

of these than they are in London and New York, even if the absolute numbers are still far higher in the top tier cities. For example, the foreign corporate buying of properties from 2013 to 2014 grew by 248% in Amsterdam/Randstadt, 180% in Madrid, and 475% in Nanjing. In contrast, the growth rate was relatively low for the major cities in each region: 68.5% for New York, 37.6% for London, and 160.8% for Beijing.

The second feature that stands out is the extent of new construction. In the older period of the 1980s-1990s it was often about acquiring buildings: notably high-end Harrods in London and Saks Fifth Avenue in New York, and trophy buildings such as Rockefeller Centre in New York. There were, however, also some massive new developments, notably in London and Tokyo. In the post-2008 period, much buying of buildings is to destroy them and to replace them with far taller and far more corporate and luxurious types of buildings—basically, luxury offices and luxury apartments.

The third feature is the spread of megaprojects with vast footprints. This inevitably kills much urban tissue: little streets and squares, density of street level shops and modest offices. Such megaprojects raise the density of the city, but they actually de-urbanize it. Thereby they bring to the fore the fact—easily overlooked in much commentary about cities—that density is not enough to have a city.

A fourth emergent feature, for now confined to a limited number of countries, is the foreclosing on modest properties owned by modest income households. This has reached catastrophic levels in the US, with the Federal Reserve data showing over 14 million households have lost their homes in a very short but brutal history of about seven years. One outcome is a significant amount of empty or under-occupied land. How this land might be used is unclear, but there it is.

A fifth feature is the development of a whole new market for high-end housing. This is an invented market, with minimum prices—practically speaking, it includes only properties of a minimum price of about US$ 20

million. This closed market functions in a limited number of cities. It represents yet another claim on urban land by those who are not necessarily deeply connected to the daily lives of those cities.

A sixth feature is the acquisition of whole blocks of underutilized or dead industrial land for site development. Here the prices paid by buyers can get very high. One example is the acquisition of a vast stretch of land in New York (Atlantic Yards) by one of the largest Chinese building companies for US$ 5 billion. Previously the land was occupied by a mix of modest factories and industrial services, modest neighbourhoods, and, more recently, artists' studios and venues as they were pushed out of lower Manhattan by large-scale developments of high-rise apartment buildings. This very urban mix of occupants in Atlantic Yards has been thrown out and will be replaced ultimately by fourteen formidable residential luxury towers.

Also here we see a sharp growth of density that actually has the effect of de-urbanizing that space. It will be a sort of de facto 'gated' space with lots of people. It will not be the dense mix of uses and diverse types of people we think of as urban. This type of development is taking off in many cities, mostly with virtual walls, but sometimes also with real walls. I would argue that with this type of development the virtual and the actual walls have similar impacts on the de-urbanizing of pieces of a city.

The basic facts

The latest estimate of the global value of real estate assets according to Savills is US$ 217 trillion; to clarify, this refers to all real estate that has been financialized so it can be bought and sold in diverse markets as an asset, without having to bother with the actual building. This includes all types of properties. It is important to recall that most property in the world is modest and has not been financialized. My focus in this paper is on large corporate buying of existing properties. These properties might be used as they are, renovated, let standing empty as a way of storing capital, or torn down in order to build a more valuable type of building that can deliver higher profits.

Taking just the two most recent years, corporate buying of existing properties reached over US$ 600 billion from mid-2013 to mid-2014 in the top 100 recipient cities, and over US$ 1 trillion from mid-2014 to mid-2015. These figures include only major acquisitions; in the case of New York, for instance, this means only properties with a minimum price of US$ 5 million dollars. Further, this list includes only the buying of property; it excludes large amounts spent on the buying of urban terrain for site development.

These top 100 cities as ranked by the value of national and foreign buying of property in 2013-2014 account for 10% of the world's population, but 30% of the world's GDP, and, even more extreme, 76% of property acquisitions that have entered the financial circuit. It is important to distinguish these financialized properties (a small minority of all properties in the world) from those that trade on more traditional real estate markets, many of which are now also global markets. The former exist in two very diverse circuits: one circuit is the familiar buying and selling of properties, and the other exists only in electronic space as a financial asset that can circulate in multiple markets and be bought and sold many times over.

Giving added weight to this pattern of acquisitions, in the current period growing numbers of developed countries have seen massive foreclosures on low and modest income households, especially in the US, several European countries, and some Asian countries. The US is where this particular type of abusive instrument was invented and has produced, according to the Federal Reserve, up to 14 million foreclosures that have led to owners losing their homes. Let me point out that 14 million homes can entail well over 30 million people. One result has been an abundance of unused houses in fairly central urban land, not an insignificant outcome at a time when urban land is of great interest to investors. This instrument can travel globally, so it has been sold in Europe where the foreclosures are also accumulating. By now Germany has over a million households under foreclosure; a lot in a country where most households rent rather than buy housing (see Sassen 2014, ch 3).

The instrument involved is perversely brilliant in that it allows investors to use these mortgages in order to build asset-backed securities. It persuades what are in fact mostly low-income households that they can buy a house, and asks them just to sign the contract, and, mostly, not to pay anything for years. All this financial instrument required in order to function was a signature, no money asked. The profits were to be made, and they were vast, by selling the financial instrument as an asset-backed security to the high-level investor world. How the newly emptied urban ground will be used is not certain. Corporate acquisitions and site development may well become the next step. The redeployment of urban land towards new uses has emerged as a major trend of the current period—and is, of course, part of a long history of urban rebuilding.

This proliferating urban gigantism has been strengthened and enabled by the privatizations and deregulations that took off in the 1990s across much of the world, and have continued since then with only a few interruptions (see Sassen 2008, chs 4 and 5, and 2014, ch 3). The overall effect has been a reduction in public buildings and an escalation in large corporate private ownership. This brings with it a thinning in the texture and scale of spaces previously accessible to the public—a space that was more than just public buildings. Where before there was a government office building handling the regulations and oversight of this or that public economic sector or addressing the complaints from the local neighbourhood, now there might be a corporate headquarters, a luxury apartment building or a mall.

Density alone does not a city make

We might ask what a city is if it cannot be simply identified by the density of its built environment. My answer is that density matters, but a city is a complex and incomplete system: in this mix lies the capacity of cities across histories and geographies to outlive far more powerful but fully formalized systems. London, Beijing, Cairo, New York, Johannesburg, Bangkok, to mention just a few, have all outlived multiple types of rulers and firms across the centuries.

In this combination of complexity and incompleteness also lies the possibility for those without power to be able to assert 'we are here', 'this is also our city'. Or, as the fighting poor in Latin American cities legendarily put it, 'estamos presentes': we are present; we are not asking for money, but just letting you know that we are present. To a large extent it is in cities where the powerless have left their imprint—cultural, economic, social—even if mostly in their neighbourhoods; eventually each one of these imprints can spread to a vaster urban zone as 'ethnic' food, music, therapies, and more. None of this can happen in an office park, no matter its density; in such privately controlled spaces low-wage workers can work but not make. Nor can they in increasingly militarized plantations and mines (where in the past workers could gain complexity in their powerlessness by the sheer concentration of their numbers). Today it is in cities where that possibility of gaining complexity in one's powerlessness and leaving a historic trace can happen—in our large, messy and somewhat anarchic cities because nothing can fully control such diversity of peoples and engagements.

When I ask myself where is today's frontier zone, my answer is: in our large cities. The frontier is a space where actors from different worlds have an encounter for which there are no established rules of engagement. In the old historic frontier this led to either negotiation with indigenous peoples or, mostly, to their persecution and oppression. The frontier space that is today's large, mixed city offers far more options. Those with power to some extent do not want to be bothered by the poor, whom they often abandon to their own devices. In some cities (for instance in the US and Brazil) there is extreme violence by police, and yet this can often become a public issue, which is something; perhaps a first step in longer trajectories of gaining rights. It is in cities where so many of the struggles for vindication have in the past and are today taking place. And in the long run, these struggles have partly succeeded. But this possibility of complexity in one's powerlessness; the capacity to make a history, a culture, and so much more; much of this is today threatened by the surge in large scale corporate redevelopment and privatizing of urban space.

2

THE SCIENCE OF URBANIZATION AND THE OPEN CITY

INTRODUCTION

Good urbanization, as outlined in the New Urban Agenda, requires a three decade time horizon, a focus on value creation, capture and sharing and a pact between all levels of government, which can no longer afford to be complacent. Governments must urgently guide urban configuration, particularly in fast-growing cities. This requires a systemic approach, that integrates municipal finance, urban planning and design and urban regulation to produce good urbanization.

In parallel, open-system thinking and designing allow cities to evolve and change. The over-specification of form and function in modernist urban planning has yielded brittle cities that are susceptible to decay. Urban time evolves slowly, so cities need to be designed on the basis of open-system thinking. This can be structured visually: porous walls and boundaries permit open passage between territories; incomplete form nurtures the possibility of action; and evolving narratives of development.

Accordingly, contemporary urbanism also provides an opportunity to reject the 'blank slate' vision of urban planning that has been so destructive. After all, the promise of 'something from nothing' usually hides a profit-fueled addiction to erasure. However, as we move beyond the destructive tabula rasa' urban planning, there is additional incentive to embrace an ethic of cohabitation.

Yet challenges remain. The Charter of Athens a manifesto for a func-

tional city drafted in 1933, has had an enduring impact and its consequences on the spatial state-of-art of cities can still be seen today. To overcome this, planning and design for their part should focus on metropolitan order and small-scale interventions that can adapt over time, allow appropriation and bridge social inequalities.

More concretely, UN-Habitat, working with New York University and the Lincoln Institute of Land Policy, has developed a global 'sample of cities', which shows that urban extent is increasing faster than population. This equates to unprecedented per capita rates of land consumption and a decrease in land use efficiency. Globally densities are declining and at the scale of the city-region this is yielding sprawl and segregation. However, there is growing practical guidance for governments related to laying out urban land and securing public space in advance of growth.

Within the city, formal and informal urban neighbourhoods are becoming increasingly fractured. In large part this is due to the reverse sequencing of informal neighbourhoods. Interscalar integration is required: external integrative networks wire segregated neighbourhoods into wider urban landscapes; social-logistical networks thicken circuits that support civic functioning; reopening ecological networks brings multiple benefits; and pinpointing interstitial interventions creates networks of smaller integrating open spaces. In the end,

government-led and self-led initiatives need to complement one another.

The concept of 'the commons' is another promising element, potentially bridging public and private, but it still eludes large-scale application in cities. Against the binary of public private, commons offer an essential 'third way'. Commons defy ownership but are not necessarily public However, if they are to be applied a a large scale in cities, they must find ways to balance access and sustainability. Negotiated urban planning may be key to extending their scope.

Nevertheless, local democracy often remains at odds with global sustainability interests. Yet cities themselves are not only the culprits behind and victims of the crises of global sustainability; they are increasingly seen as saviours of such crises. But this leads us to a type of catch-22: must we choose between planning without democracy and democracy without planning? At the very least, the scales of democracy and decision making are mismatched. Clearly cities cannot self-regulate without reference to extra-local settings. However, the path to a solution may lie in seeing them as interconnected archipelagos.

This section extracts from and synthesizes recent work by Serge Salat Marco Kamiya, Loeiz Bourdic, Richard Sennett, Amica Dall, Giles Smith Adam Kaasa, Ricky Burdett, Shlomo Angel, Anita Berrizbeitia, John Bingham-Hall, Jean-Louis Missika and Giannaolo Baiocchi.

Good urbanization requires a three decade time horizon, a focus on value creation, capture and sharing and a compact between all levels of government

Urbanization can function as a transformational driver of sustainable development, but not by default. Cities already face massive sustainability challenges in terms of infrastructure and housing deficits, food insecurity, lack of decent jobs and wasteful consumption patterns. Good urbanization does not happen by chance, but by design, readdressing the way cities are planned and financed and unleashing their transformative potential. This means having supportive rules and regulations, sound planning and design and a viable financial plan. UN-Habitat outlines these three interrelated fundamentals further, noting that they must be adjusted to the population dynamics and specific trends of each region.

Rapid urban growth requires governments to plan in advance, working with a three-decade time horizon. Long-term, integrated urban planning and design can optimize the spatial dimension of urban form. Without it, cities face the risk of low densities, disconnectivity, unbalanced public and private spaces, poorly articulated interfaces, lack of walkability, lengthy and expensive commuting patterns and exacerbated socioeconomic segregation.

Urbanization should be levered as a tool for development and value generation to maximize productivity and capture increased value for shared benefit. Without adequate financing, cities face the risks of increased inequality, lack of affordability, failing infrastructure and services and even bankruptcy. Local governments need fiscal health and creditworthiness. Building their capacity for municipal finance can promote the creation, sustainment and sharing of the value generated by urban development.

In cities, there must also be clarity and agreement on who does what, acknowledging the core responsibility of national and regional governments and aligning their duties at different levels. Urbanization is governed by the principle of the rule of law. Legal frameworks always underlie good governance, the rights and duties of the urban developer, acquisition and maintenance of public space and regulation of land use and development.

Fig 36: Favelas of Rio, Brazil, 2015
95% of inhabitants here are poor as compared to 40% for the city overall
© Paola Chapdelaine

No more business as usual: governments need to urgently guide urban configuration, particularly in fast-growing cities

Ignoring urban growth in the hope that it will not occur will simply allow it to take place unhindered and in a more costly and destructive way, yielding patterns that are difficult if not impossible to retrofit. Land on the urban fringe, cultivated for centuries and now converted to urban use, often still retains its old rural pattern, making integration into the city difficult. If an area is not properly laid out in advance of building it is likely to remain so for the foreseeable future. Many cities in developing countries urgently need a vast amount of properly planned, serviced and affordable land to accommodate their growing populations. To meet this goal, concerted public action must precede and guide the operations of the market.

Though urban population growth in developed countries is relatively low, urban areas are expected to double in extent by 2050 in a business-as-usual scenario, representing even higher per capita rates of land consumption. If cities in the developing world follow the trend of their developed world counterparts and continue to increase their per capita land consumption at 1% per annum, their land area will have tripled in the next three decades. At 2% per annum it will have more than quadrupled. Sub-Saharan Africa is even more extreme.

Even now, many low-density municipalities are facing bankruptcy because of the excessively high cost of maintaining long runs of trunk infrastructure for relatively sparse populations. And with residential densities in many of these cities far below the threshold required to make public transit viable, their residents must resort to long and costly commutes in private cars, to the detriment of their quality of life.

Contemporary urban expansion plans, if they exist, are usually rather short-sighted. Typically this means a 10-year planning horizon; very rarely a 20-year one. Assisting individual cities in preparing for their expansion requires the projection of both their populations and their urban extents some two-to-three decades in advance. This long time horizon allows cities to take advantage of the vacant and inexpensive lands on the urban periphery and manage potential speculation.

Fig 37: Estimating future urban expansion
© UN-Habitat / Shlomo Angel, NYU

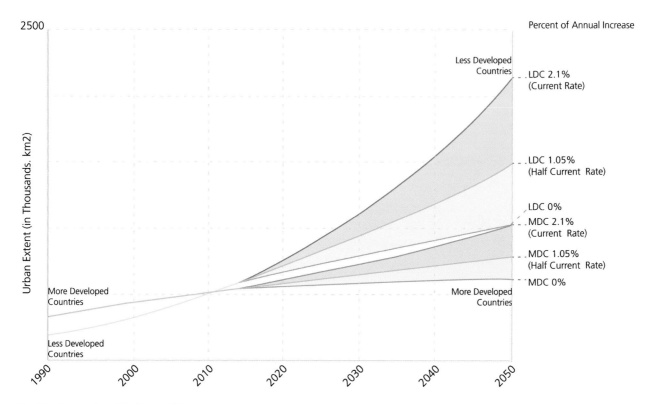

Fig 38: Growth of informality over time
© UN-Habitat / Shlomo Angel, NYU

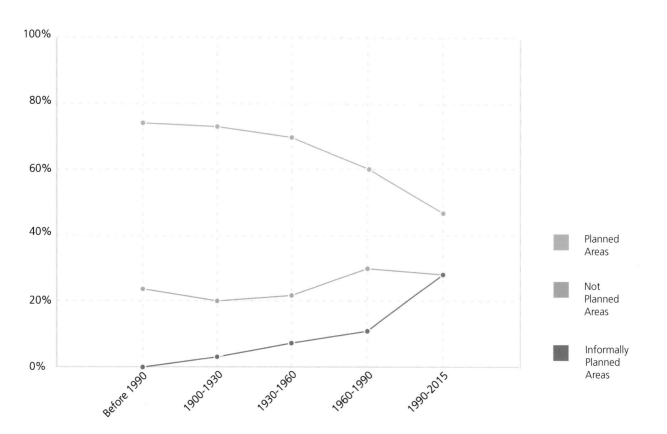

If an area is not properly laid out in advance of building it is likely to remain so for the foreseeable future. A minimum of public action must take place *before any private action materializes.*

Fig 39: The three fundamentals of good urbanization
© UN-Habitat

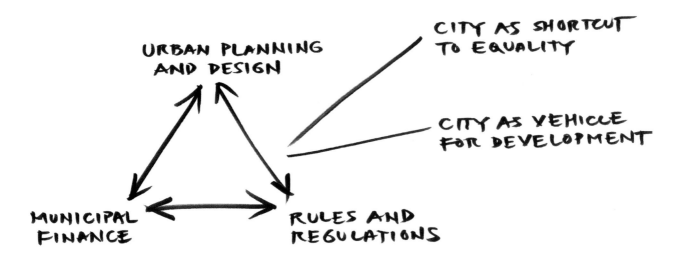

The systemic integration of municipal finance, urban planning and design and urban regulation will yield better urbanization

The major challenges facing cities and human settlements today are an outcome of the inadequate, ineffective urban legislation, design and financing. These challenges include unemployment, especially among youth; social and economic inequalities, often manifested in the emergence of slums and gated communities and proliferation of the informal sector; unsustainable energy consumption patterns; urban sprawl; and increasing emissions of greenhouse gases. Past approaches tended to address only the manifestations of the problems rather than the underlying systemic inadequacies that cause them. The market alone has failed to manage this urban growth and provide equitable cities.

National governments need to better understand the empirically positive correlation between urbanization and development. Serge Salat highlights how urbanization can be a powerful tool for transforming production capacities and income levels in developing countries. However, this requires a shift in the mindset of policymakers away from viewing urbanization as a problem towards viewing it as a solution.

There is growing evidence to demonstrate that well planned and designed urbanization can increase urban productivity and generate wealth ex novo. Its value can be captured, redistributed and re-invested to finance further productive urbanization, with benefits for all.

To achieve this, national and local governments need to adopt a systemic approach that is integrated rather than sectoral and transformative rather than fragmentary. This entails bundling the three fundamentals—urban legislation, urban planning and design, and urban finance—in a mutually-reinforcing way so as to maximize the value generated through urbanization while minimizing its costs. Well-planned city extensions, for instance, need municipal financing and sound rules and regulations to guide their implementation and growth. If combined with a regulatory framework that supports land-value capture and sharing, they can also increase urban productivity and revenue.

KENYA

41.6

MILLION PEOPLE

194

REGISTERED
URBAN PLANNERS

.47

URBAN PLANNERS
PER 100,000

UNITED KINGDOM

61.1

MILLION PEOPLE

23,000

REGISTERED
URBAN PLANNERS

37.6

URBAN PLANNERS
PER 100,000

Urban Planning and Design

According to Salat, integrated urban planning patterns are key to creating urban value. Efficient supply chains require an urban layout that minimizes the costs of transportation, collaboration, and knowledge sharing. As a result, improved connectivity and accessibility can also yield higher-level outcomes: increased GDP, enhanced job accessibility and decreased environmental pressure. Developing efficient city patterns requires articulating appropriate densities, highly variable FARs with fine granularity, and developing neighbourhoods according to transit-oriented development patterns that align intensity of land use with public transportation stations to lever their economic potential.

Another key attribute of good planning and design is mixed-use neighbourhoods, which are characterized by the presence of multiple uses in buildings and/or spaces. The notion of mixed uses is not new but it still struggles to replace the land-use zoning approach as promoted by the Charter of Athens, resulting in monofunctional areas. As city dwellers in the 20th century had to commute increasingly between different single-function locations to be able to undertake all required activities, they became increasingly more car dependent, exacerbating traffic congestion and accelerating urban sprawl.

Mixed-use neighbourhoods tend to attract people from different socioeconomic backgrounds, regions, and countries, fostering a place's internal capacity to create new industries, activities, and livelihoods for their residents. Mixed uses also have social mixity benefits. They help create neighbourhoods conducive to inclusive growth whereby low-income residents are incorporated into the economic fabric of a city, providing further economic mobility and income gains.

National and subnational governments define the planning and design tools that can be used at the city level. Only they can ensure that local governments can access the necessary capacities to use and implement the tools and define how communities, private sector and public institutions can co-produce good urbanization through participatory mechanisms.

Fig 42: Planned city extension in Wuzhou, China
© UN-Habitat

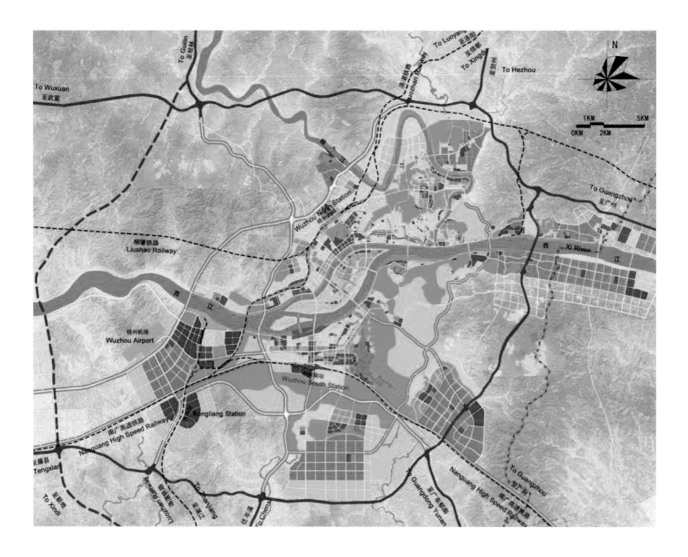

Fig 43: Planned city extension in Rubavu, Rwanda
© UN-Habitat

Property tax, as an efficient source of local revenues, represents less than 3-4% of local revenues in most developing countries compared with 40-50% in cities in Australia, Canada France, UK, and US.

Municipal Finance

Financing good urbanization, implementing planned city extensions with all the required services and infrastructure, requires sound municipal finance.

Urban revenue can be generated primarily through taxes, public assets (for instance, public land and other publicly owned property) and central government transfers to municipal authorities. The more economically developed the city, the less it tends to depend on transfers. In cities such as New York, Stockholm, Seattle and Tokyo, locally based revenues are over USD$ 3,000 per capita each year. However, in many cities in the developing world, locally generated urban yearly revenue ranges from USD$ 100 to USD$ 500 per hab-

itant and up to less than USD$ 50 in smaller cities in Africa and South Asia.

Facing deficits, local authorities, if in a position to do so, usually turn to external revenue sources such as bonds or funding from international financial markets. There is nothing inherently wrong with this but bonds require creditworthiness, which can be expensive and complex to obtain and require repayment in the future. Moreover, there is insufficient acknowledgement and understanding of how good urbanization can generate and capture urban revenue as an endogenous source of finance. Generally speaking, its three priority sources are land assets, productive

capacities, and financial management capacity.

By monitoring and updating public and private land assets, municipal governments can establish a foundation for land-value sharing. In turn, this enables all interested parties (for instance, residents and local governments) to apply urban planning tools to renew and expand cities, revitalize neighbourhoods and increase property values. Cities that apply these tools are able to generate more revenue from property taxes and 'betterment levies', and to direct those resources toward improving housing for residents and compensating proprietors with income. Thus begins a virtuous cycle of city renewal and expansion.

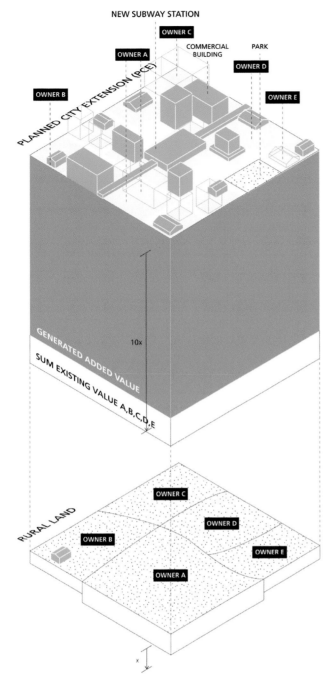

As illustrated above, improving and expanding the layout of cities enhances the productive capacity and mobility of people and goods, allowing urban areas to generate more income from the private sector. On the one hand, cities with improper transport systems cannot connect people to jobs, and firms are unable to compete and generate sufficient income. These municipalities tend to lose revenue, hampering their ability to provide public goods. On the other hand, cities that offer a good environment in which to live and an efficient urban layout in which to produce, attract people and firms and create sustainable sources of income.

Though it is often under-rated, improving financial management from the top to the bottom can have significant benefits. Understanding account-ing principles, receiving training on capital investment plans and setting up basic electronic govern-ment systems may have immediate results. Local governments require national governments to decide on transfer and redistribution mech-anisms and create the enabling framework for the necessary muni-cipal finance.

Fig 45: Contrasting settlement patterns and their respective performance measures
© UN-Habitat based on data from Alain Bertaud and Harry W. Richardson (1990)

ATLANTA

BARCELONA

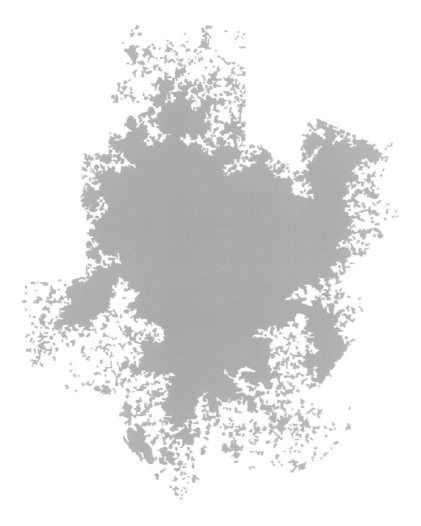

Population: 2.5 million
Built-up area: 4,280 km²
Density: 5.84 p/ha

Population: 2.8 million
Built-up area: 162 km²
Density: 172.84 p/ha

ATLANTA   BARCELONA

CO2 emissions per capita from passenger transport

7.4 tons/ha 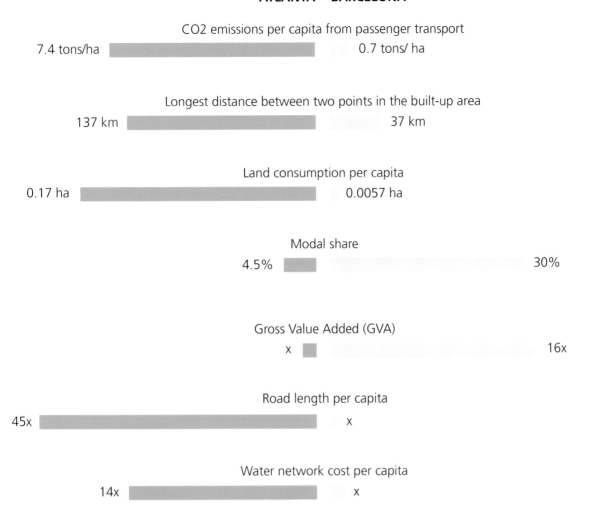 0.7 tons/ ha

Longest distance between two points in the built-up area

137 km   37 km

Land consumption per capita

0.17 ha   0.0057 ha

Modal share

4.5%   30%

Gross Value Added (GVA)

x   16x

Road length per capita

45x   x

Water network cost per capita

14x   x

Percentage of population within proximity of public transit

r = 800 m   r = 600 m

4%   60%

Legal Frameworks

A sound urban legal framework should protect the public interest while encouraging private investments and allow functional and spatial transformation over time. In contrast, a lack of rules and regulations make it hard or impossible to produce sustainable urbanization. Without them, governments cannot secure sufficient land for streets, public space and rights of way, whether through conversion or expropriation. Land rights and security of tenure define how resources are owned and used. Fit-for-purpose land administration is a necessary innovation to acknowledge and govern the diversity of both formal legal, informal and customary systems, reflecting a continuum of land rights. This

calls, also, for accountable institutions that can design, improve and enforce laws adaptable to the urban reality and the ever-changing context, allowing cities to grow over time.

If the legal framework is the basis for the proper functioning of the market, its absence can lead to market failures; these in turn can prevent transactions from yielding an efficient outcome. Weak legal frameworks affect land, housing, and financial markets. Consequently, public intervention is necessary to fix markets.

For land markets to function properly, governments must be able to implement planning policies

providing affordable access to commercial and residential properties with appropriate densities and mixed land uses. Public authorities must be able to act responsively to readjust land and have access to suitable areas for economic purposes. This demands several prerequisites: recorded tenure rights, implemented planning, absence of illegal and improper use of land, and a mechanism for land valuation and to raise income from land taxation.

Providing a legal framework does not happen overnight; it should occur in parallel with increasing technical capacity. Secondly, national governments and their legislative arms must create the

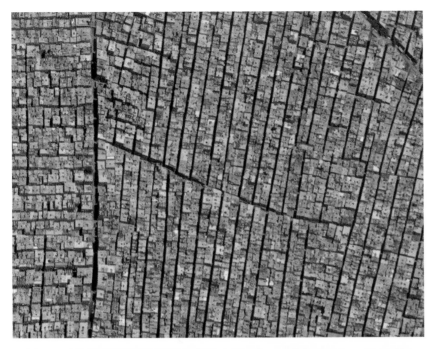

Fig 48: Inadequate land for streets and arterial roads—narrow streets on the fringe of Cairo, Egypt
© Bing Maps (Microsoft Product Screenshot reprinted with permission from Microsoft Corporation)

Fig 49: Barriers to densification—large minimum lot sizes in suburban Cleveland, Ohio, USA
© Bing Maps (Microsoft Product Screenshot reprinted with permission from Microsoft Corporation)

necessary legal framework. To the extent possible, such frameworks should provide subsidiarity by delegating the tailoring of these framework to local governments. Third, it thus follows that legal frameworks should be easily adaptable because context, environment and socioeconomic conditions are location-specific variables.

Open-system thinking and designing allow cities to evolve and change

Over-specifying form and function yields brittle cities susceptible to decay

Richard Sennett writes that cities are failing due to government policy, persistent social ills, and economic forces beyond local control. The city is not its own master. Sennett argues that we need to imagine just what a clean, safe, efficient, dynamic, stimulating, just city would look like, concretely, because we need those images to confront critically our masters with what they should be doing. However, our critical imagination of the city is weak. One reason is that although urbanists have access to more resources than in the past, they do not use them very creatively. Another is the over-determination both of the city's visual forms and its social functions. The technologies which make exper-

imentation possible have been subordinated to a regime of power which wants to impose order and control. What's missing in modern urbanism is a sense of time—not time looking backward nostalgically but forward-looking time; the city understood as process, its imagery changing through use; an urban imagination formed by anticipation, friendly to surprise.

Le Corbusier's 'Plan Voisin' in the mid 1920s proposed replacing a large swath of Paris with uniform buildings (the use of which would be coordinated by a single master plan) thereby eliminating public life on the ground plane of the street. In other words, it would have destroyed the unregulated

social elements of the city which produce change over time. This dystopia became reality in various ways, such as segregated housing neighbourhoods for the poor and monofunctional suburban neighbourhoods for the middle classes. The proliferation of zoning regulations in the 20th century is unprecedented in the history of urban design and it has deterred local innovation and growth, freezing the city in time.

The result of this over-determination is the Brittle City. Modern urban environments decay much more quickly than urban fabric inherited from the past. As the functions change, buildings are now destroyed rather than adapted

The closed system betrays the 20th century bureaucrat's horror of disorder. *But its antidote is not the free market or private enterprise. The real contrast is* a different kind of open social system.

Richard Sennett

for reuse; indeed, the over-specification of form and function increases susceptiblity to decay without necessarily stimulating urban growth. 'Growth' in an urban environment is more complicated than replacing what existed before. It requires a dialogue between past and present—evolution rather than erasure. The bonds of community cannot be conjured up in an instant, with a stroke of the planner's pen; they require time to develop. Segregating functions, homogenizing population and preemptive zoning and regulation all fail to provide communities the time in space needed for growth. The Brittle City is a symptom. It represents a view of society itself as a closed system with two essential attributes:

equilibrium and integration.

The closed system ruled by equilibrium supposes something like a bottom line in which income and expenses balance. In state planning, information feedback loops and internal markets are meant to insure that programmes do not 'over-commit' or 'suck resources into a black hole'—such is the language of recent reforms of the health service, familiar again to urban planners in the ways infrastructure resources for transport get allocated. The limits on doing any one thing exceedingly well are set by the fear of neglecting other tasks. In a closed system, a little bit of everything happens all at once.

Second, in a closed system, each part has a place in an overall design, with anything contestatory or disorienting to be rejected. This puts an obvious bar on experiment. In fact, modern city planning has tried to forestall threats by accumulating a mountain of rules defining the historical, architectural, economic, and social context. The closed system betrays the 20th Century bureaucrat's horror of disorder. But its antidote is not the free market or private enterprise (which, while they often speak the language of freedom, have only manipulated closed bureaucratic systems for private gain by the elite). The real contrast is a different kind of open social system.

If *density* **and** *diversity* **give life,** **the life they breed is** *disorderly.*

Jane Jacobs

Urban time evolves slowly, but it can be structured visually

Sennett credits the idea of an open city to Jane Jacobs in the course of arguing against the urban vision of Le Corbusier. She tried to understand what results when places become both dense and diverse, as in packed streets or squares, their functions both public and private; out of such conditions, she believed, arose the unexpected encounter, the chance discovery, the innovation.

Jacobs sought to define particular strategies for urban development, once a city was freed of the constraints of either equilibrium or integration. These included encouraging quirky, jerry-built adaptations or additions to existing buildings and uses of public spaces that did not fit neatly together (such as putting an AIDS hospice square in the middle of a shopping street). In her view, big capitalism and powerful developers tended to favour homogeneity: determinate, predictable, and balanced in form. The role of the radical planner therefore was to champion dissonance. She famously declared 'if density and diversity give life, the life they breed is disorderly'. The open city feels like Naples; the closed city feels like Frankfurt. Jacobs believed that in an open city, as in the natural world, social and visual forms mutate through chance variation; people can best absorb, participate, and adapt to change if it happens step-by-lived-step. This is evolutionary urban time—the slow time needed for an urban culture to take root, then to foster, then to absorb chance and change. It is why Naples, Cairo, or New York's Lower East Side, though resource-poor, still 'work' in the sense that people care deeply about where they live. People live into these places, like nesting. Time breeds that attachment to place.

In Sennett's own thinking, he has wondered what kinds of visual forms might promote this experience of time. Can these attachments be designed by architects? Which designs might abet social relationships which endure just because they can evolve and mutate? The visual structuring of evolutionary time is a systematic

Fig 50: Design for movement through streets
© Richard Sennett

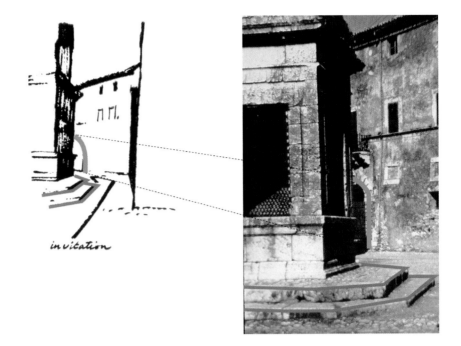

invitation

wings

property of the open city. To make this statement more concrete, he describes three systematic elements of an open city: (1) passage territories, (2) incomplete form, and (3) development narratives.

key-hole

Fig 51: Cell membrane representing porous walls and boundaries
© UN-Habitat

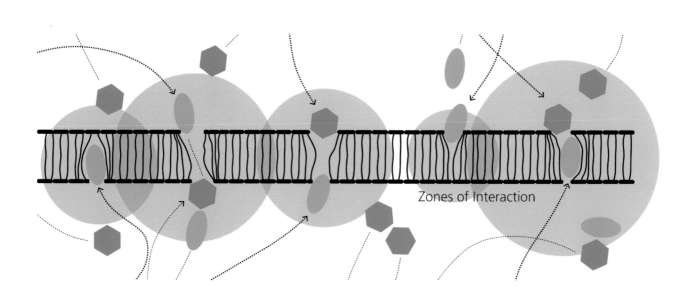

Zones of Interaction

Porous walls and boundaries permit open passage between territories

We know the city as a whole by passing through its different territories. However, planners and architects have much difficulty designing this experience of passage. Part of this lies in how they use walls. Historically, walls have literally closed in cities. Until the invention of artillery, people sheltered behind walls when attacked; the gates in walls also served to regulate commerce coming into cities, often being the place where taxes were collected. Though they shut closed, they also served as sites for unregulated development in the city; houses were built on both sides of medieval town walls; informal markets selling black-market or untaxed goods sprung up nestled against them;

the zone of the wall was where heretics, foreign exiles, and other misfits tended to gravitate, again far from the controls of the centre. These walls functioned much like cell membranes, both porous and resistant. That dual function of the membrane is an important principle for visualizing more modern living urban forms.

Whenever we construct a barrier, we have equally to make the barrier porous; the distinction between inside and outside has to be breachable, if not ambiguous. The usual contemporary use of plate-glass for walls doesn't do this; true, on the ground plane you see what's inside the building, but you can't touch, smell, or hear anything

within; the plates are usually rigidly fixed so that there is only one, regulated, entrance. The result is dead space on both sides of the wall. In contrast, the idea of a cellular wall, which is both resistant and porous, can be extended from single buildings to the zones at which the different communities of a city meet.

Planners and architects also need to pay more attention to boundaries. The boundary is an edge where things end; the border is an edge where different groups interact. In natural ecologies, borders—such as the shoreline of a lake—are the places where organisms become more interactive, due to the meeting of different physical condi-

Fig 52: Line of visitors at the bottom of the Eiffel Tower, Paris, France, 2014
© Emmeline Heymes / In Situ - Sciences Po

tions and species. Not surprisingly, it is also at the borderline where the work of natural selection is the most intense. Whereas the boundary is a guarded territory that establishes closure, the border functions more like a medieval wall, as a liminal space. In the realm of human culture, territories consist similarly of boundaries and borders. In cities, there is a contrast between gated communities and complex, open streets but the distinction cuts deeper in urban planning. We usually look for and try to strengthen community life at its centre; the edge condition is seen to be more inert. Indeed modern planning practices, such as sealing the edges of communities with highways, create rigid boundaries lacking any porosity. This in turn usually diminishes the exchange between different racial, ethnic, and class communities.

By privileging the centre we weaken the complex interactions necessary to join up the different groups of the city. In contrast, locating new resources at the edges between different racial and economic groups can open the gates between them. Borders can serve as tense—rather than friendly—sites of exchange. This evokes some of the predatory quality of border conditions in natural ecologies. However, taking that risk, which planners are now doing under more explosive conditions in Beirut and in Nicosia, is the only way in which we create conditions for a socially-sustained collective life in cities; ultimately, isolation is not a true guarantor of civil order. The porous wall and the edge as border create liminal space at the limits of control, limits which permit the appearance of things, acts, and persons unforeseen, yet focused and sited. Sociologically and urbanistically, these sites concentrate differences on the horizon, at the periphery—differences that stand out since one is aware one is crossing from one territory into another.

How can the discipline of design, which is situated in the concrete and particular, create spaces that contain *the possibility of action?*

Amica Dall and Giles Smith

Incomplete form nurtures the possibility of action

Incomplete form is Sennett's second systematic property of the open city. Amica Dall and Giles Smith explore this concept further. They maintain that the freedom to occupy, use and understand public space in different, new and conflicting ways is the freedom to re-imagine contest and change both our public life and, through this, many of the most formative aspects of our private lives. Usually we imagine freedom as a negative quality; the absence of constraint. Freedom is only really present in the mind of the actor at the moment it is contested, or understood to be at risk. It can only meaningfully be said to exist if it can be acted on: freedom is contained in possibility of action, and expressed in action itself. How can the discipline of design, which is situated in the concrete and particular, create spaces that contain the possibility of action?

Freedom, like play, has indeterminate outcomes. Designers have to accept the uncertainty and multiplicity of behaviours they are seeking to support and produce space in which a multiplicity of things can happen; behaviours whose form and meaning they cannot know, imagine or predict. Dall and Smith argue that formal public spaces, in their aspiration towards neutrality, generally offer a resistance-less environment. They are designed to be very easy to move through, down to details that can actually prevent anyone spending too much time in them; the implicit assumption being that in public space resistance is not a good thing. Yet the harder an environment tries to remove resistance, the more it actually makes forms of resistance harder to identify or experience in a tactile hands-on fashion. In an aspiration to flexibility, those spaces actually prevent anyone acting on them in a sustained or meaningful way.

Openness can be created through an excess of meaning and possibility rather than through the removal of obstruction. Most people can read their environment sensitively. On the other hand, they are not very skilled at translating that feeling into language or talking

about it in a critical way, but that has no connection to how powerfully the space acts on them. Too many designers expect to resign responsibility at a certain point, imagining that the outcome of their work will be a finished, complete space. However, this shuts down the creation of meaning at a very early point in the lifespan of a space. Instead, they need to design as if for play—to create opportunities for impulsive, mysterious behaviour; the creation of deliberate complexity, wherein different meanings coexist in tension with each other. This encourages conflict, and conflict is an integral part of creating genuine public life.

Rather than a mere gap that allows people to move around, public space must foster the negotiation of demand. If individuals and groups cannot actively express how their interests might be different from those of others, then collectively it becomes extremely difficult to debate and structure relations amongst each other. Uncertainty is a necessary condition of life in the world. However, the capacity to embrace doubt, and act clearly in doubt has largely evaded architectural production. Designers have both responsibility and agency in the creation and maintenance of the freedom to occupy, use and understand public space. Freedom does not need to be enacted through physical change—public space acts as powerfully at the level of embedded meaning as it does at the level of formal resistance. Designed interventions can interrupt, contest and make visible the ideas embedded in a space, and open up, rather than close down meaning. New public spaces should be designed to actively produce this kind of multiplicity and tension.

Fig 55: Triveni Sangam: celestial-terrestrial microcosm (2005-6) of Ganga and Yamuna Rivers in Allahabad, India

Combining photography and cartography, this drawing maps the choreography of urban settlement, agriculture, and festivals in relationship to the periodicity of the southwest monsoon. The tones of violet correspond to points of time within a single revolution of the Earth about the sun. The panoramas, on the next page, provide perspectival snapshots of the changes taking place at the Triveni Sangam and correspond to the tones of violet.
© Anthony Acciavatti

Narratives of development must be allowed to evolve

For Sennett, the work of urban planners and designers must shape narratives of urban development by focusing on the stages in which a project unfolds. This is the third characteristic of the open city. All good narrative has the property of exploring the unforeseen; of admitting conflict and dissonance. This relates to the Darwinian conception of growth as a continual struggle between equilibrium and disequilibrium. An environment rigid in form and static in programme is doomed in time, but biodiversity gives the natural world the resources to provision change. That ecological vision makes equal sense for human settlements, but it is not the vision that guided 20th century state planning. Neither state capitalism nor socialism

embraced growth in the Darwinian sense, in environments that permitted interaction amongst organisms with different functions and powers.

When the city operates as an open system, incorporating principles of porosity of territory, narrative indeterminacy and incomplete form, it becomes democratic not in a legal sense, but as physical experience. In the past, thinking about democracy focused on issues of formal governance; today, it focuses on citizenship and issues of participation. Participation has everything to do with the physical city and its design.

Throughout the 19th and 20th centuries, champions of democratic practices have identified democratic

space with small, local communities and face-to-face relationships. Today's big and ethnically diverse city houses people belonging to many different communities. For cities becoming global in scale, the problem of citizen participation is how people can feel connected to others whom they cannot know. Democratic space means a creating a forum for these strangers to interact. The Millennium Bridge in London has generated growth unrelated to its own purposes, stimulated informal mixing among people and prompted an ease among strangers. This is democratic space. Bridging the divide between inside and outside and inviting engagement and identification are all for urban design to achieve.

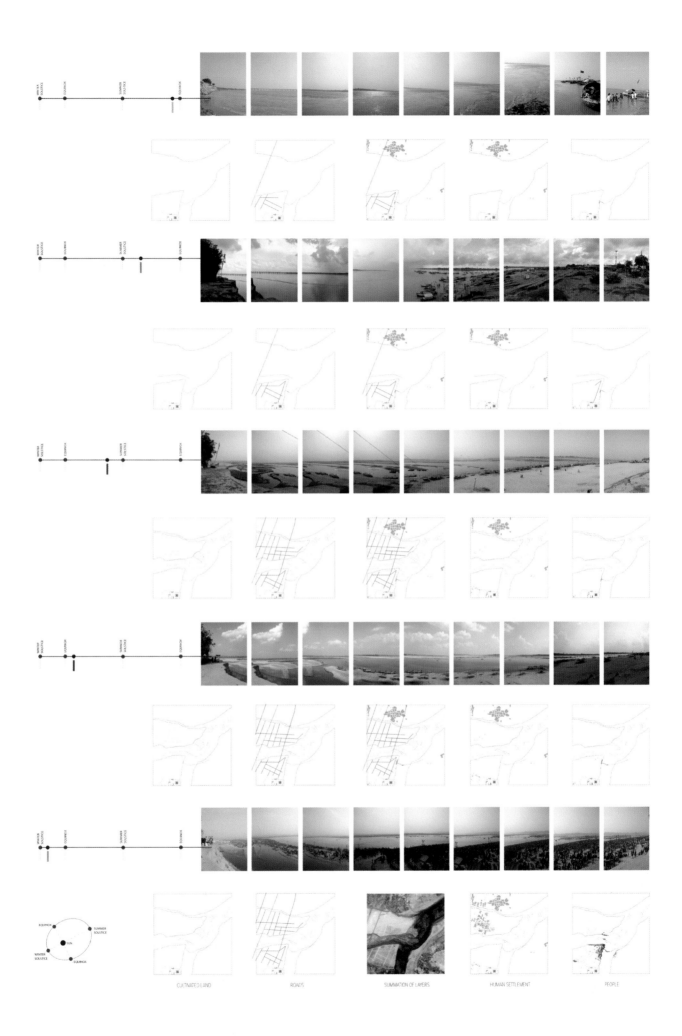

CULTIVATED LAND   ROADS   SUMMATION OF LAYERS   HUMAN SETTLEMENT   PEOPLE

2.3

Contemporary urbanism provides the opportunity to set aside the blank slate for an ethic of cohabitation

The 'blank slate' vision of urban planning has been destructive

Le Corbusier, lead-author of the original CIAM Charter of Athens in 1933, was famously troubled by the way in which the mess of real life infringed upon his architecture. As result, he took to photographic editing and montage to better represent the way he thought his architecture should be seen. He would take the negatives of the photographs of his architecture and erase the surrounding images of nature, urban life, other buildings, people, the sky, the sun, the ground. What were left were photographic representations of his buildings completely isolated, floating in white, empty space. With this method, Le Corbusier soon came to believe that the photograph could better represent his ideas about

architecture than could the built object from which the photograph was taken. For him, the process of architecture was the illusion of control. If the reality of context was the obstacle to its realization, and erasure was a possible solution to the problem in photographic editing, then perhaps erasure needed to happen in real life.

Adam Kaasa writes that as with all technologies, urban planning promises freedom and transformation as much as destruction and violence. Most famously, the sociologist Zygmunt Bauman made clear how mundane technologies of efficiency, often discussed in terms like 'progress', were crucial technologies of the holocaust. Equally,

urban planning is intimately linked to the histories of the technologies of war; from aerial photography that allowed the mapping and dissection of land into actionable property, to the technologies of demolition emerging from new developments in explosives and bombs. The destruction from bombings during the Spanish Civil War was at times intentionally targeted to specific urban areas with the idea already formed about what the reconstruction of the site would be. War was used as an urban planning tool. The modernist 20th century clearly linked war, the technologies of city building and the fantasy of the tabula rasa.

To create architecture is *to put in order functions and objects.*

Le Corbusier

There is no logic that can be superimposed on the city; *people make it, and it is to them,* *not buildings, that we must fit our plans.*

Jane Jacobs

Fig 57: Map of displacement of leaseholders at Heygate Estate, Southwark, London
© UN-Habitat based on data from Southwark Council

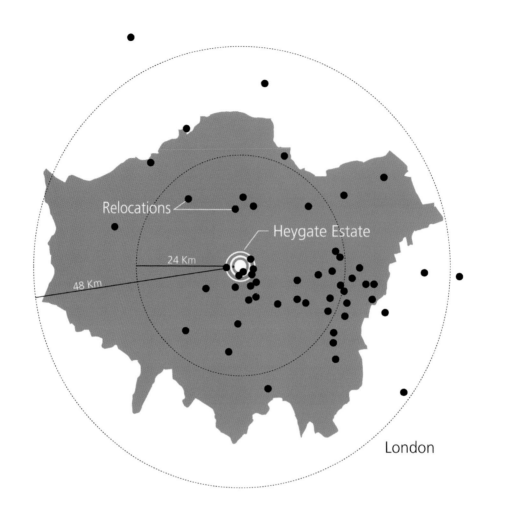

The promise of 'something from nothing' usually hides a profit-fueled addiction to erasure

Every act of planned urban erasure is met with a promise of what is to come. Kaasa likens this to the 'future perfect'. Using visual technologies, an image of a site or development can be produced to such a compelling quality, that it is as if it already existed, in a perfect state, in the near-future. This is what is carefully sold to a polity in order to legitimate what is necessary in the present: the blank slate. It is, most often, a false promise, one which assures that all the present conditions that mark the erasure as necessary will be resolved once the erasure takes place.

Tabula rasa urbanism argues that the resolution of a present anxiety or decline, or political issue can only, and only ever, emerge from

a fresh start; that destruction is a necessary precursor to creation. However, this also masks the violence of erasure and displacement.

In the 1950s in Mexico City, architect Mario Pani proposed a modernist housing complex for 100,000 people called Nonoalco Tlatelolco, after the Mesoamerican settlement on that site that had previously been erased by the Spanish. Pani wanted to solve the 'problem' of the tugurio, or slum, by being given a huge plot and being allowed to raze and evict the owners and tenants. In short, he wanted to erase the people to which he promised the future. Le Corbusier proposed the same for Paris for his Plan Voisin; post-war

Britain was full of half-bombed damaged city areas; and from Pruitt-Igoe in St Louis onwards, erasure has been the primary mode of dealing with post-war modernist social housing units in many parts of the world, themselves built on the idea of tabula rasa modernist urbanism. Most recently, the Heygate Estate in London, which contained affordable housing for 5,000 families, was demolished. Many modest retrofits had been proposed with the backing of many residents. But even the less-preferable promise of complete rebuilding and rehousing on site was soon forgotten to profit, and the developers used spreadsheets of 'viability assessments' to blackmail and threaten local councils. In the

Fig 58: (Above) *Invisible Angels*, Heygate Estate, London, 2009
Invisible Angels is a photographic series made after the majority of residents were evicted or relocated from the Heygate Estate. The site was subject to controversy for various reasons including high levels of poverty and future redevelopment plans, which presented a conflict of interest for the council. Running concurrently with the Heygate demolition plans, the UK press was increasingly portraying young groups of men standing on urban streets as threatening gangs. The undertones of racist stereotyping revealed problems within society and press more than necessary truths for any individual young men targeted.
© K. Yoland

Fig 59: (Left) Heygate estate demolition
© Surprise Truck, CC BY 2.0

place of the post-war temple to affordable, publicly-owned housing, a new urban form for the violently rich is currently being constructed.

Erasure always presents itself as necessary and benevolent. To create the Olympics, for example, it has become commonplace to first create a blank slate in the city from which to build new and expensive infrastructure. For the Rio de Janeiro Olympic Games in 2016, an estimated 77,000 people were displaced to construct the image of a blank slate Olympic arena district and athletes village in Barra Tijuca, along with other infrastructure projects (including a community of some 3,000 people with deeds to their properties, only twenty

families of which were rehoused on site). The London Olympics of 2012 spawned a similar erasure but not before an architect and sociologist had mapped the entire site to show a piece of a city that was thriving but unprofitable to—and ultimately wilfully destroyed by—the dominant political class.

The Olympics enable a state of exception whereby processes already occurring in the city are centralized, enhanced and sped up to violently disastrous effect. They promote the undemocratic development of urban land, land brought into public domain, terraformed with public monies, and sold off to develop for the profit of sovereign international funds and global retail giants, as

well as the securing of housing as an investment rather than a place to live. The products of urban erasure are then sold back to those who paid for them as gifts—gifts to a wholly different population than those who were erased from the site to begin with. Tabula rasa urbanism might be good for certain businesses, and for shoring up an accumulation of capital, but it cannot be argued for as the only alternative for urban development, change, or growth. The idea of 'nothing', or of 'from scratch', or of 'starting fresh', of an origin with nothing and no-one in it, outside of geography, history, politics, climate, people, is not only unethical, it is impossible. The tabula rasa, the blank slate is not just fantasy, if enacted it is necessarily violent.

Fig 60: Boulevard Diderot, Paris, France
Confrontation between protesters and the police on 1 May 2016 during the annual inter-union
march, which also gave rise to a protest against the government's recent law on labour.
© Baptiste Genevée Grisolia

Cities need to embrace a new ethic of cohabitation

We do not get to—nor should we desire to—choose with whom to cohabit the earth. This suggests that a new urban ethic should be at the core of our efforts to build more just cities. An urban ethic of cohabitation speaks to segregation, to the unequal distribution of public and private mobility in the city, to gated communities of fear, to the gendered built environment, to urban manifestations of apartheid and genocide, and to the persistence of coloniality, to name a few. Modern technologies of urban planning, of security and militarization of cities, of urban governance, surveillance and control allow for just the opposite of cohabitation. The history of the city in the twentieth century was about tabula rasa rupture—a

literal metaphor of physical erasure and utopian rebuild (and occasionally dystopian social reordering). An ethics of cohabitation is a condition of our political life, and therefore a profound and necessary choice.

Adam Kaasa therefore asks how we might build a city that is not about control over space, but rather, is about living in a complex and diverse social and physical world. This mode of design thinking requires a rigorous interrogation of what is presently there on a site of possible intervention. It asks what geographic, topological contexts are present? What histories are presently being made? Who is there? What are their narratives, their obstacles, their dreams and

their creative outputs? All too often in the 20th century, the urban planning profession has been as much about proposing a problem to be solved as about proposing the solution. Planning and architecture have always been deeply embedded in the political processes that determines what will be a problem to solve.

Kaasa's examination of 20th-century architectural drawings, maps, visualisations of statistical data and photographs in Mexico determined that not only are they propositional, but that they often work to negotiate or translate the propositional into a fact. Once turned into a fact they could be deployed to legitimate radical urban change—sometimes for the better, but not always. In

Fig 61: Community consultation with inhabitants of Bordeaux, France, to discuss urban development scenarios in the Bastide-Brazza neighbourhood
© DGaA-Bordeaux Métropole

Fig 62: Kilifi, Kenya, 2016
Village residents committee from Majengo going through the new maps after successful participatory design and mapping exercise under the Participatory Slum Upgrading Programme of UN-Habitat
© UN-Habitat / Julius Mwelu

Mexico City, it was decided that the urban problem was housing, particularly localized in slums around the historic core. The solution was to build large modernist superblocks based on aesthetic cues from CIAM's functional city—based on a diagnosis whose ideological core was perfectly consistent with that found in the Charter of Athens, drafted in 1933. In contrast, an ethic of cohabitation requires a significant shift in emphasis from looking for solutions to recalibrating what we think of as an urban problem (and confirming that the problem has not been inadvertently formulated within the construct of tabula rasa urbanism). Collectively we need to use tools of the social, physical and behavioural sciences,

as well as, and perhaps even more so, the capacity of the humanities, and the visual and performing arts to sit with and think athwart complexity, rather than flatten its diverse, obtuse and difficult angles and perspectives.

Kaasa suggests that the problems we identify are as much a product of tabula rasa thinking as are the solutions we find fit for purpose. In other words, the tabula rasa solution becomes a self-fulfilling prophecy. If tabula rasa had been taken off the table from the beginning, a dramatically different vision of an Olympic games in London might have taken place—one whose cohabitation constraint might have questioned the demands of the IOC Olympic

authorities. An ethics of cohabitation demands that we question the very assumptions guiding urban planning. Cohabitation interrupts the speed of urban development, whereas erasure, demolishing and creating large swathes of tabula rasa urban development operates at the speed of capital. The myth that money can be made from nothing within our financialized world forgets the incalculable network of social, educational, political, cultural, historical and relational infrastructure that contributed to a start-up's creation. Something is never from nothing. The sooner we understand cohabitation as an intimate and planetary ethic, the better chance we will have of building the humble cities of the future.

2.4

Planning and design should operate at both metropolitan and neighbourhood scales and provide adaptable interventions that bridge social inequalities

We need to create resilient urban form

Ricky Burdett points out that designers, developers, investors and policymakers are faced with increasingly difficult choices regarding how to intervene within changing urban landscapes. How to maintain the structure of the city when it undergoes profound transformations? Who is the city for? How to reconcile public and private interests? Who pays and who gains? The city planners of London, Paris, Barcelona, Hamburg and New York are grappling with the same questions as the urban leaders of African, Latin American and Asian cities, even though the levels of deprivation and requirements for social infrastructure are of a different order of magnitude.

While scholars, planners and architects continue to debate the connections between democracy and urban form, most would agree that time and appropriation are critical to the creation of a sense of collective identity. As Rahul Mehrotra has also argued, the temporal dimension is critical to understanding the dynamics of everyday social life in many cities of the developing world. For example, the multiple and temporary uses of public spaces in Mumbai requires a far more open and non-deterministic environment than one that is specifically tied to a single functional use—the fundamental precept of the Charter's espousal of the 'functional city'. It is virtually impossible to create an 'instant city' that also

has the vital overlaying complexities of urban life that Richard Sennett defines in his defence of the 'open' city. Nevertheless its opposite, the 'brittle' urbanism that he critiques as resistant to social and temporal change, is all too well embodied by the recently-constructed realities of New York's Battery Park City, London's Canary Wharf and Paris' La Defense.

Yet other less formal but nonetheless 'planned' ordering systems seem to have stood the test of time, adapting to economic and political cycles in ways that have enriched the urban grain, creating greater density and complexity in the everyday urban experience. The 'figure-ground' map describes

Fig 63: Sunday morning in the chawls at Dadar, India
© Chirodeep Chaudhuri

the democratic spatial structure of the city whose form has accumulated over time (under everything but democratic regimes). The iconography of the map reveals the layering of time and negotiation that marks a broadly organic process of urban change.

New York and Barcelona provide models of urban resilience. The 200-year old Manhattan grid, a brutally honest piece of real estate subdivision carved out of earth and rock, has served the city well as New York grew from a small trading post to major port and manufacturing hub, and then on to become one of the world's top financial centres. The city of New York has densified, rethought its zoning, adapted to economic restructuring, become more mixed in parts, more homogeneous in others. Warehouses have turned into lofts, factories into workplaces and railways have become walkways, but the grid has remained constant. The combination of building typologies and continuous porosity has allowed (but not necessarily caused) the city to adapt to extremes of economic and social transition, establishing an endemic connection to the democratic process of change in North American culture and society over the last two hundred years, a lesson that seems not to have been learnt by the current generation of 'city fathers' of expanding city regions. Building on the New York experience, the 19th century Catalan engineer Ildefonso Cerdà not only bequeathed the term 'urbanism' but also created a spatial infrastructure of urban expansion which saw Barcelona through a period of extreme growth, violent repression by a fascist dictatorship and political rebirth after the death of General Franco in 1975. Both New York and Barcelona reveal, in their own macro geometric order, a degree of resilience: an urban form that has adapted to the process of gradual accretion and democratic change without the need for 'telescopic urbanism' or brutal application of the Charter of Athens. In effect these cities have been retrofitted over time.

Fig 64: London Olympics: effects on social equity?
© LSE Cities (2013)

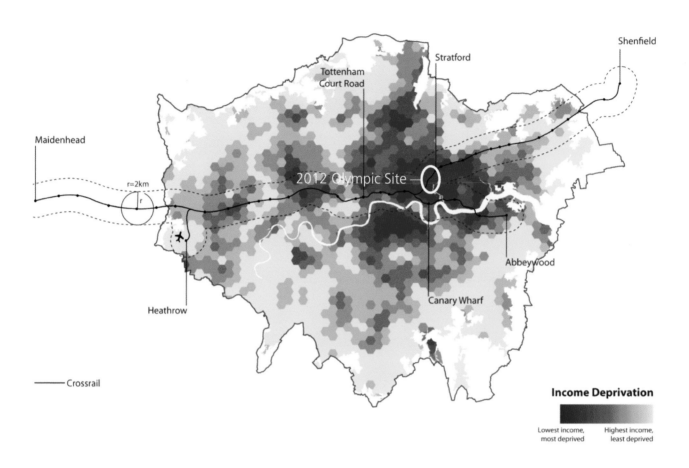

The sum of small-scale interventions can be transformative

At the micro scale of the backstreets of Istanbul, São Paulo and Mumbai there is evidence of creative ingenuity which both fosters identity and promotes a form of inclusion amongst the most excluded. It is this emerging architecture of contingency rather than representation, which Burdett suggests has a greater impact on the average urbanite than any metropolitan urban policy or government plan.

Despite Cape Town being a relatively wealthy city, its black population still lives in largely segregated ghettoes in substandard conditions. As Edgar Pieterse has put it, 'Cape Town is a highly differentiated and malleable city, always filled with almost endless promise, but also continuously undermined by a variety of constraints and pressures.' An exemplary project was the judiciously named Violence Prevention Through Urban Upgrading in Cape Town's 'former' township of Khayelitsha. This 'urban acupuncture' project involves some strong and confident architectural interventions—well-designed, modern, multi-storey beacon community buildings that stand out in a flat single-storey sprawling landscape, clear pedestrian routes that link the main residential areas to immensely popular rail stations, as well as play areas overlooked by homes and public buildings where children enjoy the outdoors unsupervised (a rarity in this violent neighbourhood).

Together these interventions create a composite urban whole that literally transforms the sense of identity and well-being of the entire community, proving that careful attention to the quality of public spaces and mobility corridors, especially in the harshest environments, can dramatically change the experience and horizons of a neighbourhood. Most importantly, it is an initiative that both captures the 'cityness' of Khayelitsha by building on its spatial DNA and recognizing that its success will be determined by its adaptation over time. A model example, in many ways, of a process of intervention through accretion rather than rupture that allows its constituents to forge new identities around the public spaces and institutions of the project.

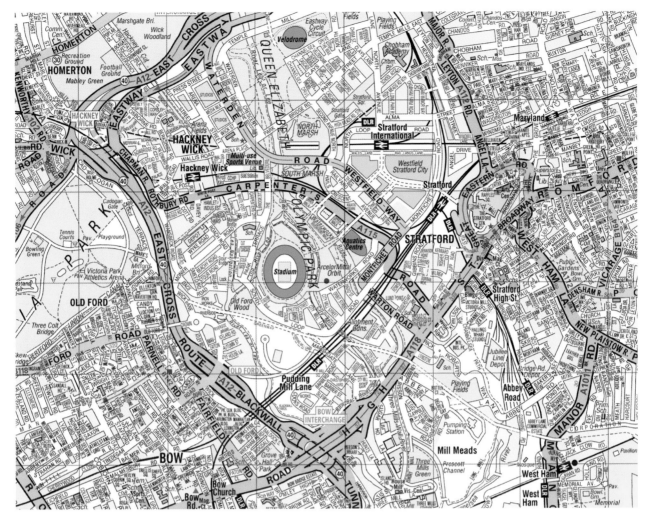

Fig 65: Imaginary post-Olympics London A-Z map
In 2010 Allies and Morrison prepared an imaginary A-Z map showing how the Olympic Park and neighbouring areas might look in the future. This A-Z image was used by Boris Johnson to help illustrate the public launch of the legacy masterplan.
© Allies and Morrison Architects, CC by 2.0

The potential of hybrid urban strategies

Building on its 'Londoness' rather than opting for some novel telescopic intervention or Charter-like typology, the 2012 Olympics planning approach is a thinly concealed attempt at curing one of the city's most enduring spatial inequalities: the deep imbalance between London's relatively wealthy western half and more deprived eastern fringes where the Games were located.

Burdett argues that the city's inherent spatial flexibility has played an important role in developing the relatively delicate intervention that may over a long period of time, perhaps 20 or 30 years, lead to a more durable impact on its urban metabolism. In this respect it is a hybrid example of urban innovation, where equal attention has been given to the overall spatial framework and its potential to adapt and absorb change at the smaller scale over time.

The Olympics project in London was conceived with the intention of leaving behind a real 'piece of city', that connects the new with the old, and which over time will bring about sustained level of social improvement to existing and new communities. Housing, office buildings and hotels have been erected where temporary facilities and sponsors' pavilions stood during the summer of 2012. This is a slow process that will take up to 30 years to complete, but this recognizes the limitations of the market take-up and the need to allow time to create community and identity in an area where there was none previously.

With over 35 new bridges, footpaths and links, the urban design of the Olympic Legacy plan is a topological distortion of London's spatial structure which has at least the potential to stitch this formerly disconnected site back into the intricate web of East London. The flexible urban armature already demonstrates resilience by allowing smaller-scale initiatives, temporary structures and local activities to inform how the overall picture will evolve.

A process of intervention through accretion rather than rupture allows its constituents to forge new identities around the public spaces and institutions of the project.

Ricky Burdett

Towards a more open, malleable and incremental urbanism that recognizes the role of design and space in making cities more equitable

Burdett argues that both small-scale interventions and metropolitan order play their part in structuring social cohesion and engendering a sense of urban democracy. They provide opportunities for people in cities to make the most of their circumstances, either by making small improvements whose impact exceed their size in terms of quality of collective life or through flexible and resilient open spatial networks that optimize the democratic potential of their urban residents.

Both forms of urban intervention afford a degree of adaptability that is intrinsic to the process of societal change. They understand the importance of incompleteness and recognize the role of time in making cities feel urban. Neither were envisaged nor encouraged by the rigid spatial instruments promoted by the Charter of Athens over 80 years ago. The lessons from small-scale acupuncture projects are that they have the potential to foster – rather than negate – capacity building and social cohesion. The lessons from flexible large-scale metropolitan plans are that a malleable urban framework lends itself to a process of gradual adaptation and accretion, which allows change without causing rupture of the city's fragile spatial and social urban fabric. 80 years on from the certainties of the Charter of Athens, it is the role of urban planning and design professions to re-frame the contemporary debate about cities, accepting indeterminacy and embracing incompleteness.

Fig 66: Joan Clos at the Urban Age 10 Global Debates, London, 2015
© Catarina Heeckt

THE OPEN CITY
RICHARD SENNETT

The Closed System and the Brittle City

The cities everyone wants to live in should be clean and safe, possess efficient public services, be supported by a dynamic economy, provide cultural stimulation, and also do their best to heal society's divisions of race, class, and ethnicity. These are not the cities we live in.

Cities fail on all these counts due to government policy, irreparable social ills, and economic forces beyond local control. The city is not its own master. Still, something has gone wrong, radically wrong, in our conception of what a city itself should be. We need to imagine just what a clean, safe, efficient, dynamic, stimulating, just city would look like concretely—we need those images to confront critically our masters with what they should be doing—and just this critical imagination of the city is weak.

This weakness is a particularly modern problem: the art of designing cities declined drastically in the middle of the 20th century. In saying this, I am propounding a paradox, for today's planner has an arsenal of technological tools—from lighting to bridging and tunneling to materials for buildings—which urbanists even a hundred years ago could not begin to imagine: we have more resources to use than in the past, but resources we don't use very creatively.

This paradox can be traced to one big fault—the over-determination both of the city's visual forms and its social functions. The technologies which make possible experiment have been subordinated to a regime of power which wants order and control. Urbanists, globally, anticipated the 'control freakery' of current planning law by a good half century; in the grip of rigid images, precise delineations, the urban imagination lost vitality. In particular what's missing in modern urbanism is a sense of time—not time looking backward nostalgically but forward-looking time—the city understood as process, its imagery changing through use, an urban imagination formed by anticipation, friendly to surprise.

A portent of the freezing of the imagination of cities appeared in Le Corbusier's 'Plan Voisin' in the mid 1920s for Paris. The architect conceived of replacing a large swath of the historic centre of Paris with uniform, X-shaped buildings; public life on the ground plane of the street would be eliminated; the use of all buildings would be coordinated by a single master plan. Not only is Corbusier's architecture a kind of industrial manufacture of buildings. He has tried in the 'Plan Voisin' to destroy just those social elements of the city which produce change in time, by eliminating unregulated life on the ground plane; people live and work, in isolation, higher up.

This dystopia became reality in various ways. The Plan's building-type shaped public housing from Chicago to Moscow—housing estates which came to resemble warehouses for the poor. Corbusier's intended destruction of vibrant street life was realized in suburban growth for the middles classes, with the replacement of high streets by monofunction shopping malls, by gated communities, by schools and hospitals built as isolated campuses. The proliferation of zoning regulations in the 20th century is unprecedented in the history of urban design, and this proliferation of rules and bureaucratic regulations has disabled local innovation and growth, freezing the city in time.

The result of over-determination is what could be called the Brittle City. Modern urban environments decay much more quickly than urban fabric inherited from the past. As uses change, buildings are now destroyed rather than adapted; indeed, the over-specification of form and function makes the modern urban environment peculiarly susceptible to decay. The average life-span of new public housing in Britain is now forty years; the average life-span of new skyscrapers in New York is thirty-five years.

It might seem that the Brittle City would in fact stimulate urban growth, the new now more rapidly sweeping away the old, but again the facts argue against this view. In the United States, people flee decaying suburbs rather than re-invest in them; in Britain and on the Continent, as in America, "renewing" the inner city most often means displacing the people who have lived there before. 'Growth' in an urban environment is a more complicated phenomenon than simple replacement of what existed before; growth requires a dialogue between past and present, it is a matter of evolution rather than erasure.

This principle is as true socially as it is architecturally. The bonds of community cannot be conjured up in an instant, with a stroke of the planner's pen; they too require time to develop. Today's ways of building cities—segregating functions, homogenizing population, pre-empting through zoning and regulation the meaning of place—fail to provide communities the time in space needed for growth.

The Brittle City is a symptom. It represents a view of society itself as a closed system. The closed system is a conception which dogged state socialism throughout the 20th Century as much as it shaped bureaucratic capitalism. This view of society has two essential attributes: equilibrium and integration.

The closed system ruled by equilibrium derives from a pre-Keynesian idea of how markets work. It supposes something like a bottom line in which income and expenses balance. In state planning, information feed-back loops and internal markets are meant to insure that programs do not 'over-commit,' do not 'suck resources into a black hole'—such is the language of recent reforms of the health service, familiar again to urban planners in the ways infrastructure resources for transport get allocated. The limits on doing any one thing really well are set by the fear of neglecting other tasks. In a closed system, a little bit of everything happens all at once.

Second, a closed system is meant to integrate. Ideally, every part of the system has a place in an overall design; the consequence of that ideal is to reject—to vomit out—experiences which stick out because they are contestatory or disorienting; things that 'don't fit' are diminished in value. The emphasis on integration puts an obvious bar on experiment; as the inventor of the computer icon, John Seely Brown, once remarked, every technological advance poses at the moment of its birth a threat of disruption and disfunction to a larger system. The same threatening exceptions occur in the urban environment, threats which modern city planning has tried to forestall by accumulating a mountain of rules defining historical, architectural, economic, and social context—context being a polite but potent word for repression; ensuring that nothing sticks out, offends, or challenges.

As I say, the sins of equilibrium and integration bedevil coherence, planners of education as much as planners of cities, planning sins which crossed the line between state capitalism or state socialism. The closed system betrays the 20th century bureaucrat's horror of disorder.

The social contrast to the closed system is not the free market, nor is the alternative to the Brittle City a place ruled by developers. That opposition is in fact not what it seems. The cunning of neo-liberalism in general, and of Thatcherism in particular, was to speak the language of freedom whilst manipulating closed bureaucratic systems for private gain by an elite. Equally, in my experience as a planner, those developers in London, as in New York, who complain most loudly about zoning restrictions, are all too adept in using these rules at the expense of communities.

The contrast to the closed system lies in a different kind of social system—not in brute private enterprise—a social system which is open rather than closed. The characteristics of such an open system and its realization in an open city are what I wish to explore here.

The Open System

The idea of an open city is not my own: credit for it belongs to the great urbanist Jane Jacobs in the course of arguing against the urban vision of Le Corbusier. She tried to understand what results when places become both dense and diverse, as in packed streets or squares, their functions both public and private; out of such conditions comes the unexpected encounter, the chance discovery, the innovation. Hers is a view reflected in the bon mot of William Empson that 'the arts result from over-crowding.'

Jacobs sought to definite particular strategies for urban development, once a city is freed of the constraints of either equilibrium or integration. These include encouraging quirky, jerry-built adaptations or additions to existing buildings; encouraging uses of public spaces which don't fit neatly together, such as putting an AIDS hospice square in the middle of a shopping street. In her view, big capitalism and powerful developers tend to favor homogeneity: determinate, predictable, and balanced in form; the role of the radical planner therefore is to champion dissonance. Her famous declaration goes, 'if density and diversity give life, the life they breed is disorderly.' The open city feels like Naples and the closed city feels like Frankfurt.

For a long time, I dwelt in my own work happily in Jacobs' shadow—both her enmity to the closed system [though the formal concept is mine not hers] and her advocacy of complexity, diversity, and dissonance. Recently, in re-reading her work, I've detected glints of something lurking beneath this stark contrast.

If Jane Jacobs is the urban anarchist she is often said to be, then she is an anarchist of a peculiar sort, her spiritual ties are closer to Edmund Burke than to Emma Goldmann. She believes that in an open city, as in the natural world, social and visual forms mutate through chance variation; people can best absorb, participate, and adapt to change if it happens step-by-lived-step. This is evolutionary urban time, the slow time needed for an urban culture to take root, then to foster, then to absorb chance and change. It is why Naples, Cairo, or New York's lower East Side, though resource-poor, still "work" in the sense people care deeply about where they live. People live into these places, like nesting. Time breeds that attachment to place.

In my own thinking, I've wondered what kinds of visual forms might promote this experience of time. Can these attachments be designed by architects? Which designs might abet social relationships which endure just because they can evolve and mutate? The visual structuring of evolutionary time is a systematic property of the open city. To make this statement more concrete, I'd like to describe three systematic elements of an open city: (1) passage territories, (2) incomplete form, and (3) development narratives.

Passage territories

I'd like to describe in some detail the experience of passing through different territories of the city, both because that act of passage is how we know the city as a whole, and also because planners and architects have such difficulties designing the experience of passage from place to place. I'll start with walls, which seem to be structures inhibiting passage, and then explore some of the ways edges of urban territory function like walls.

Walls
The wall would seem an unlikely choice; it is an urban construction which literally closes in a city. Until the invention of artillery, people sheltered behind walls when attacked; the gates in walls also served to regulate commerce coming into cities, often being the place in which taxes were collected. Massive medieval walls such as those surviving in Aix-en-Provence or in Rome furnish a perhaps misleading general picture; ancient Greek walls were lower and thinner. But we also mis-imagine how those medieval walls in themselves functioned.

Though they shut closed, they also served as sites for unregulated development in the city; houses were built on both sides of medieval town walls; informal markets selling black-market or untaxed goods nestled against them; the zone of the wall was where heretics, foreign exiles, and other misfits tended to gravitate, again far from the controls of the centre. They were spaces which would have attracted the anarchic Jane Jacobs. But they were also sites which might have suited her organic temperament. These walls functioned much like cell membranes, both porous and resistant. That dual function of the membrane is, I believe, an important principle for visualising more modern living urban forms. Whenever we construct a barrier, we have equally to make the barrier porous; the distinction between inside and outside has to be breachable, if not ambiguous.

The usual contemporary use of plate-glass for walls doesn't do this; true, on the ground plane you see what's inside the building, but you can't touch, smell, or hear anything within; the plates are usually rigidly fixed so that there is only one, regulated, entrance within. The result is that nothing much develops on either side of these transparent walls; as in Mies van der Rohe's Seagram Building in New York or Norman Foster's new London City Hall, you have dead space on both sides of the wall; life in the building does accumulate here. By contrast, the 19th century architect Louis Sullivan used much more primitive forms of plate glass more flexibly, as invitations to gather, to enter a building or to dwell at its edge; his plate glass panels function as porous walls. This contrast in plate glass design brings out one current failure of imagination in using a modern material so that it has a sociable effect.

The idea of a cellular wall, which is both resistant and porous, can be extended from single buildings to the zones at which meet the different communities of a city.

Borders
Ecologists like Steven Gould draw our attention to an important distinction in the natural world, that between boundaries and borders. The boundary is an edge where things end; the border is an edge where different groups interact. In natural ecologies, borders are the places where organisms become more interactive, due to the meeting of different species or physical conditions. For instance, the place where the shoreline of a lake meets solid land is an active zone of exchange; here is where organisms find and feed off other organisms. The same is true of

temperature layers within a lake: where layer meets layer defines the zone of the most intense biological activity. Not surprisingly, it is also at the borderline where the work of natural selection is the most intense, whereas the boundary is a guarded territory, as established by prides of lions or packs of wolves. The boundary establishes closure, whereas the border functions more like a medieval wall. The border is a liminal space.

In the realm of human culture, territories consist similarly of boundaries and borders—in cities, most simply, there is a contrast between gated communities and complex, open streets. But the distinction cuts deeper in urban planning.

When we imagine where the life of a community is to be found, we usually look for it in the centre of a community; when we want to strengthen community life, we try to intensify life at the centre. The edge condition is seen to be more inert, and indeed modern planning practices, such as sealing the edges of communities with highways, create rigid boundaries, lacking any porosity. But neglect of the edge condition—boundary-thinking, if you like—means that exchange between different racial, ethnic, or class communities is diminished. By privileging the centre we can thus weaken the complex interactions necessary to join up the different human groups the city contains.

Let me give as an example a failure of my own in my planning practice. Some years ago I was involved in plans for creating a market to serve the Hispanic community of Spanish Harlem in New York. This community, one of the poorest in the city, lies above 96th Street on Manhattan's upper east side. Just below 96th Street, in an abrupt shift, lies one of the richest communities in the world, running from 96th down to 59th Street, comparable to Mayfair in London or the 7th Arrondissement in Paris. 96th Street itself could function either as a boundary or a border. We planners chose to locate La Marqueta in the centre of Spanish Harlem twenty blocks away, in the very centre of the community, and to

regard 96th Street as a dead edge, where nothing much happens. We chose wrongly. Had we located the market on that street, we might have encouraged activity which brought the rich and the poor into some daily commercial contact. Wiser planners have since learned from our mistake, and on the West Side of Manhattan sought to locate new community resources at the edges between communities, in order, as it were, to open the gates between different racial and economic communities. Our imagination of the importance of the centre proved isolating, their understanding of the value of the edge and border has proved integrating.

I don't mean to paint a Panglossian picture of such ventures in planning: opening up borders means people of different strengths are exposed to competition. Borders can serve as tense rather than friendly sites of exchange—evoking some of the predatory quality of border conditions in natural ecologies. But taking that risk, which planners are now doing under more explosive conditions in Beirut and in Nicosia, is the only way, I believe, in which we create conditions for a socially-sustained collective life in cities; ultimately isolation is not a true guarantor of civil order.

The porous wall and the edge as border create essential physical elements for an open system in cities. Both porous walls and borders create liminal space; that is, space at the limits of control, limits which permit the appearance of things, acts, and persons unforeseen, yet focused and sited. The biological psychologist Lionel Festinger once characterized such liminal spaces as defining the importance of "peripheral vision;" sociologically and urbanistically, these sites operate differently than those places which concentrate differences in a centre; on the horizon, at the periphery, at the border, differences stand out since one is aware one is crossing out of one territory into another.

Incomplete form

This discussion of walls and borders leads logically to a second systematic characteristic of the open city: incomplete form. Incompleteness may seem the enemy of structure, but this is not the case. The designer needs to create physical forms of a particular sort, "incomplete" in a special way. When we design a street, for instance, so that buildings are set back from a street wall, the space left open in front is not truly public space; instead the building has been withdrawn from the street. We know the practical consequences; people walking on a street tend to avoid these recessed spaces. It's better planning if the building is brought forward, into the context of other buildings; though the building will become part of the urban fabric, some of its volumetric elements will now be incompletely disclosed. There is incompleteness in the perception of what the object is.

Incompleteness of form extends to the very context of buildings themselves. In classical Rome, Hadrian's Pantheon co-existed with the less distinguished buildings which surrounded it in the urban fabric, though Hadrian's architects conceived the Pantheon as a self-referential object. We find the same co-existence in many other architectural monuments: St. Paul's in London, Rockefeller Centre in New York, the Maison Arabe in Paris—all great works of architecture which stimulate building around themselves. It's the fact of that stimulation, rather than the fact the buildings are of lesser quality, which counts in urban terms: the existence of one building is sited in such a way that it encourages the growth of other buildings around it. And now the buildings acquire their specifically urban value by their relationship to each other; they become in time incomplete forms if considered alone, in themselves.

Incomplete form is most of all a kind of creative credo. In the plastic arts. it is conveyed in sculpture purposely left unfinished; in poetry it is conveyed in, to use Wallace Steven's phrase, the 'engineering of the fragment.' The architect Peter Eisenman has sought to evoke something of the same credo in the term 'light architecture,' meaning an architecture planned so that it can be added to, or more importantly, revised internally in the course

of time as the needs of habitation change. This credo opposes the simple idea of replacement of form which characterizes the Brittle City, but it is a demanding opposition.

Narratives of development

Our work aims first of all to shape the narratives of urban development. By that, we mean that we focus on the stages in which a particular project unfolds. Specifically, we try to understand what elements should happen first, and what then are the consequences of this initial move. Rather than a lock-step march toward achieving a single end, we look at the different and conflicting possibilities which each stage of the design process should open up; keeping these possibilities intact, leaving conflict elements in play, opens up the design system.

We claim no originality for this approach. If a novelist were to announce at the beginning of a story, here's what will happen, what the characters will become, and what the story means, we would immediately close the book. All good narrative has the property of exploring the unforeseen, of discovery; the novelist's art is to shape the process of that exploration. The urban designer's art is akin.

In sum, we can define an open system as one in which growth admits conflict and dissonance. This definition is at the heart of Darwin's understanding of evolution; rather than the survival of the fittest [or the most beautiful], he emphasized the process of growth as a continual struggle between equilibrium and disequilibrium; an environment rigid in form, static in programme, is doomed in time; bio-diversity instead gives the natural world the resources to provision change.

That ecological vision makes equal sense of human settlements, but it is not the vision which guided 20th century state planning. Neither state capitalism nor state socialism embraced growth in the sense Darwin understood it in the natural world, in environments which permitted interaction amongst organisms with different functions, endowed with different powers.

I'd like to conclude not with a statement of regret over the decline of planning, but by making a connection between the systematics of the open city to the politics we all espouse—the politics of democracy. In what sense could the spaces I've described contribute to the practice of democracy?

Democratic space

When the city operates as an open system—incorporating principles of porosity of territory, narrative indeterminacy and incomplete form—it becomes democratic not in a legal sense, but as physical experience.

In the past, thinking about democracy focused on issues of formal governance; today, it focuses on citizenship and issues of participation. Participation is an issue which has everything to do with the physical city and its design. For example, in the ancient polis, the Athenians put the semi-circular theatre to political use; this architectural form provided good acoustics and a clear view and of speakers in debates, more, it made possible the perception of other people's responses during debates.

In modern times, we have no similar model of democratic space—certainly no clear imagination of an urban democratic space. John Locke defined democracy in terms of a body of laws which could be practiced anywhere. Democracy in the eyes of Thomas Jefferson was inimical to life in cities; he thought the spaces it required could be no larger than a village. His view has persisted. Throughout the 19th and 20th centuries, champions of democratic practices have identified them with small, local communities and face-to-face relationships.

Today's city which is big, filled with migrants and ethnic diversities is a city in which people belong to many different kinds of community at the same time—through their work, families, consumption habits and leisure pursuits. For cities like London and New York becoming global in scale, the problem of citizen participation is how people can feel connected to others whom, necessarily, they cannot know. Democratic space means a creating a forum for these strangers to interact.

In London, a good example of how this can occur is the creation of a corridor connection between St. Paul's Cathedral and the Tate Modern Gallery, spanned by the new Millennium Bridge. Though highly defined, the corridor is not a closed form; along both banks of the Thames it is prompting the regeneration of lateral buildings unrelated to its own purposes and design. And almost immediately upon opening, within its confines this corridor has stimulated informal mixings and connections among people walking the span, prompted an ease among strangers which is the foundation for a truly modern sense of 'us.' This is democratic space.

The problem of participation cities face today is how to create, in less ceremonial spaces, some of the same sense of relatedness among strangers. It is a problem in the design of public spaces in hospitals, in the making of urban schools, in big office complexes, in the renewal of high streets, and most particularly in the places where the work of government gets done. How can such places be opened up? How can the divide between inside and outside be bridged? How can design generate new growth? How can visual form invite engagement and identification? In principle good urban design can answer these questions.

ON REDISTRIBUTION POLICIES AND THEIR IMPACT ON GOOD URBANIZATION

JOAN CLOS

When addressing the problem of urbanization, we tend to focus on the role of the local authority because of its direct responsibility for urban planning and management and its visible impact on the daily life of citizens. In modern society, however, The State has been playing an increasingly important role in defining urban outcomes. Three in particular merit our attention.

First, The State defines the governance framework that sets the rules of the game for urbanization. This is because The State has the sovereignty to delimit the degree of power of local governments as well as to stipulate their financial envelopes. Second, The State develops the policies of redistribution related to public welfare services such as health, education,

unemployment, retirement, pensions, affordable housing and minimum wage. And third, the modern state is responsible for safety and security policies and has the legitimacy to use public force if considered necessary.

In some countries it delegates part of this function to local authorities. However, the substantive power remains with The State, and this allows it to delegate execution to local authorities without losing sovereignty or responsibility. As a consequence of its roles and functions, the modern State affects the everyday quality of life of its citizens; the state itself becomes a crucial determinant of urban quality of life. The final quality of urbanization is, therefore, a joint outcome of local and central government performance,

particularly related to the delivery of effective services.

The impact of central governments on cities is particularly evident in national policies of redistribution. Redistribution can be said to constitute a set of tools, advanced by the modern state during the 19th and 20th centuries, whose purpose was to distribute opportunities and resources more equitably and fairly. It cannot be overemphasized that the quality of life of urban citizens, especially those in the middle and lower classes, depends very much on the provisions of the modern welfare state. The transfer of resources to poor families is a key attribute of governments that are sufficiently capacitated to promote equality through the welfare state model. This has been

Fig 67: Public social expenditure as a percentage of GDP
© UN-Habitat based on data from OECD

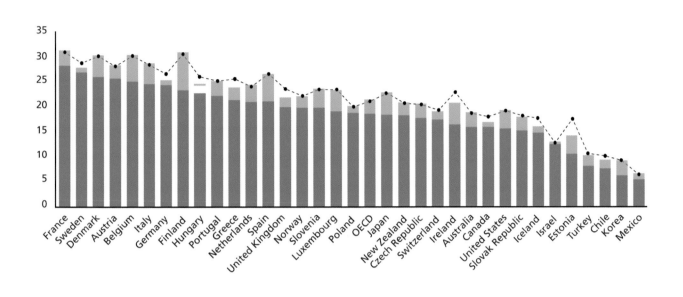

2007 Peak Level

--•-- Peak Level after 2007

2014 Peak Level

the case in many developed countries and some developing countries after the Second World War, which was the most successful period of the welfare state worldwide.

However, since the crisis of the welfare state at the end of the 1970s, we have seen a reduction in the size of the welfare state in many countries. And since the crisis of 2008, austerity policies have further challenged welfare transfers to poor families, including the urban poor. Only the countries that took decisive action to overcome the crisis of 2008 have seen a net positive outcome. For example, in the United States, the introduction of The Patient Protection and Affordable Care Act ('Obamacare'), coupled with economic growth and

increased employment, increased the wellbeing of a sizeable proportion of citizens. In most places, however, austerity policies are on the rise and this is severely challenging the state's ability to simultaneously maintain the welfare state and limit unemployment, especially youth unemployment, despite the concomitant increase of total social expenditure. Such issues are further exacerbated wherever migration rates have increased, particularly in cities and poor communities. In certain contexts this can produce explosive sociopolitical problems. The graphic above illustrates the concomitant increase in expenditure in the welfare state after the 2008 crisis, which is related mainly to automatic correctors such as unemployment coverage.

The outcome of urbanization, including its impact on the prosperity of citizens, is heavily determined by the presence or absence of redistributive mechanisms. Broadly speaking, successful cities are equitable cities and equitable cities almost always require not only a competent local government, but also an efficient welfare state. Together, they are able to provide the safety nets that guarantee improved wellbeing. This underscores the critical role of The State in ensuring the positive outcome of urbanization. Interscalar cooperation of this sort is also key in responding to shocks. Where there is no functioning welfare state, rapid urbanization correlates strongly with high levels of inequality. Typically this takes the form of a very small, wealthy

Fig 68: Social expenditure as a percentage of GDP and of total general government expenditure
© UN-Habitat based on data from OECD

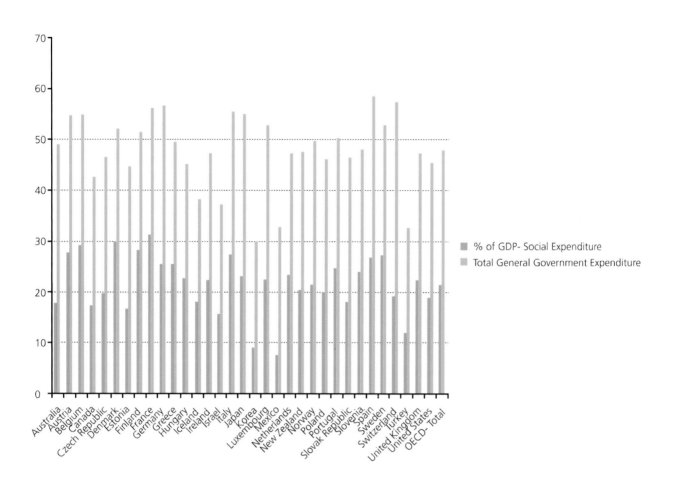

% of GDP- Social Expenditure
Total General Government Expenditure

upper class, a small middle class and a large proportion of poor people.

If we look at expenditure per capita, European countries such as Denmark, Finland, France, and Sweden spend 30-35% of their GDP on welfare state services while other countries such as Indonesia spend barely around 2%. And in most countries in the developed world, redistribution-related expenditures constitute a substantial part of the national economy. They also provide a significant service by guaranteeing private demand in the overall macroeconomic equilibrium. In countries in the developing world, relatively low 'welfare state' expenditures make it impossible to do this.

In Nordic countries, which have the longest tradition of employing a welfare state model, a significant share of public sector expenditure is at the local level. This is the result of a division of labour between the central and local government by which the former devolves the management of a large share of welfare-type services to the latter. In such countries the total share of public expenditures by local authorities tends to be much higher since, apart from their traditional municipal functions such as urban planning they undertake a complementary function as co-managers of the welfare state. In contrast, other OECD countries (as well as developing countries) still rely heavily on the central government for the management of welfare services, even when they are scarce.

Another important issue is the role of local authorities in public investment. In many countries local authorities manage as much as 60% of total public investment, making them important public investment actors. Though the volume of an individual city's investment is relatively low, the sheer number of local governments makes them, in aggregate, significant for national economies; more than half of total public investment in many countries. Unfortunately, where local governments are not supported by a well-functioning welfare state, they face the dilemma of choosing where to spend; i.e. between the pressing social needs of the population and more strategic long term public investments. In cities where resources are very limited, this is dire.

Fig 69: Subnational share of national public investment (2012)
© UN-Habitat based on data from OECD

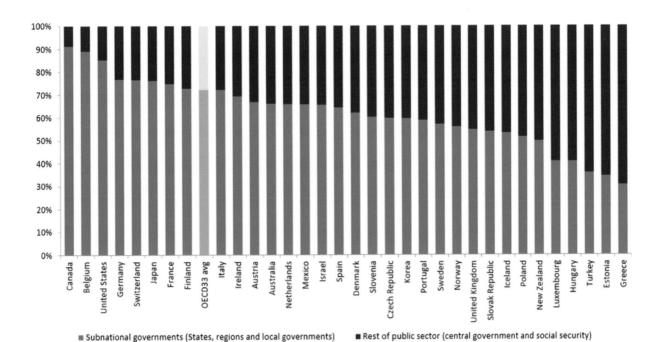

■ Subnational governments (States, regions and local governments)   ■ Rest of public sector (central government and social security)

The interrelation between central and local governments is complex, challenging the provision of equitable welfare, good urban development. This complexity tends to generate a 'catch-22' that requires strong political effort to address. It is not easy to overcome the inherent conflicts of interest. Priorities need to be set, but they will not necessarily be technical ones because neither sound information nor predictable outcomes are readily available. Nonetheless, urbanization has the capacity to generate endogenous development and create value out of rules, regulations and good design (all of which are relatively cheap). Managing speculative urbanization requires addressing politically complex issues such as land administration, private property rights and taxation.

State redistribution policies anchor sustainable urbanization because humans are sensitive to fairness and thus tolerate only a certain level of inequality. And inequalities are very visible in cities where people live in compact settings. Local and central governments need to work hand in hand to ensure redistribution and generate the positive outcomes of urbanization. The importance of the central government, which was not highlighted in the outcomes of Habitat I and II, is clear now. In virtually every example of good urbanization over the last 20 years one can clearly see the commitment of national governments over a long-term time horizon. National governments, including parliaments, also need to strengthen local governments and ensure strong policies of redistri-

bution. Without both, the outcome of urbanization will never be optimal.

Morocco has implemented a public housing policy with a nationwide tax on cement, which has generated funds for public housing. In Ethiopia, the government has implemented an exemplary national policy on affordable housing. Singapore has long provided high-quality public housing focused on ethnic integration, which has been critical to its development. China has developed a national policy addressing industrialization and urbanization in tandem. And the Brazilian state of São Paulo has introduced a building rights tax, which funds slum upgrading. These examples show that where there is a will there is a way to couple local and national policies.

UN-Habitat Sample of Cities shows that contemporary patterns of urbanization can reap greater benefits

UN-Habitat's sample of cities: need for an urban-specific evidence base

In 2000, the world had 4,231 cities with populations of at least 100,000. Urban statisticians frequently refer to this as the 'Universe of Cities'. To complement it, UN-Habitat has adopted a Global Sample of Cities, comprising 200 cities that represent 5%—and are scientifically representative of—the Universe of Cities. The Sample is distributed over eight world regions with similar urbanization patterns, to facilitate monitoring and reporting.

Without studying each and every city in the world, the Sample of Cities facilitates the tracking and understanding of what is happening in the world's cities using new statistical tools and techniques. It also helps detect global and regional urbanization patterns in the Universe of Cities.

Monitoring the progress of urbanization must necessarily focus on cities as units of analysis. For this reason, the Sample defines cities as dense, contiguous built-up areas, including the open spaces in and around them. The resulting areas may contain and cut across numerous municipal jurisdictions. In contrast, cities defined by their municipal boundaries are often inappropriate for monitoring urban expansion because they do not correspond to the built-up area of the urban agglomerations associated with them.

The Sample of Cities provides a platform for collecting data and reporting on global trends. Data collected for all cities of the sample can be generalized to produce global and regional estimates. The Sample will be available through open source data to advance efforts to connect data and information to decision-making.

The Sample also facilitates the monitoring of urban-specific metrics that can help to understand emerging global challenges and their regional differentiation. The ones that require the biggest political commitments and policy shifts are outlined in the following pages.

Fig 70: The administrative boundary and urban extent in Beijing and Buenos Aires, 2015
© UN-Habitat / Shlomo Angel, NYU

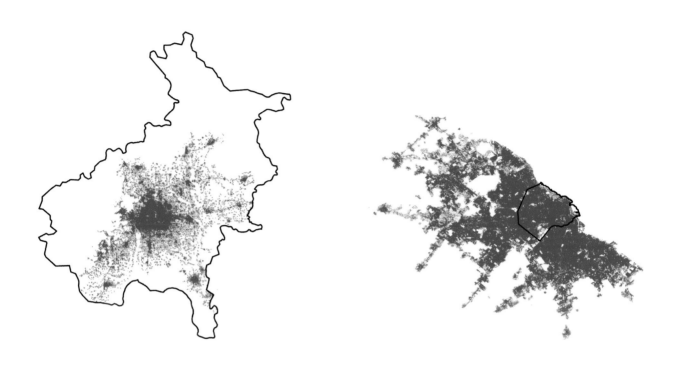

Cities defined by their municipal boundaries are often inappropriate for monitoring the urban expansion *because they may not correspond to the built-up area of the urban agglomerations associated with them.*

Shlomo Angel

Fig 71: Urban extent of Bogotá, Colombia (2015)

Using freely-available Landsat imagery, Shlomo Angel classified land into built-up space (urban, suburban and rural built-up space), open space (fringe, captured and rural open space), and water areas. In this manner a city's built-up areas and open spaces can be 'clustered' into a unified urban extent.

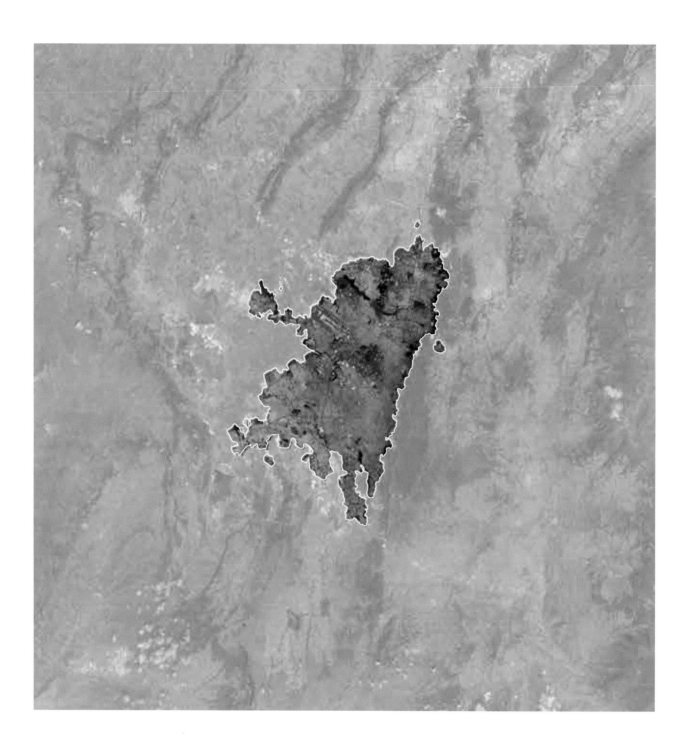

Fig 72: Urban extent of Wuhan, China (2015)

© UN-Habitat / Shlomo Angel, NYU

Using freely-available Landsat imagery, Shlomo Angel classified land into built-up space (urban, suburban and rural built-up space), open space (fringe, captured and rural open space), and water areas. In this manner a city's built-up areas and open spaces can be 'clustered' into a unified urban extent.

Fig 73: Urban expansion 1990 - 2015
© UN-Habitat / Shlomo Angel, NYU

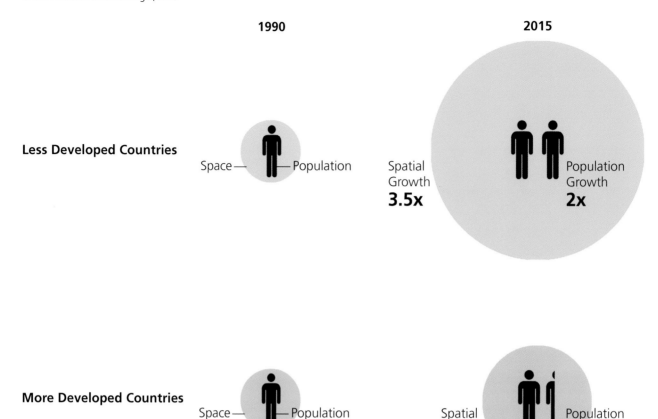

Urban extent is increasing faster than population, leading to unprecedented per capita rates of land consumption and a decrease in land use efficiency

Whereas cities generally have very limited scope for guiding population growth, the conversion of land to urban use is very much within the realm of influence of urban policy. Shlomo Angel has analyzed how fast the land occupied by cities is expanding in comparison to the growth of their populations. Angel defined each of the 200 Sample cities by the extent of their contiguous built-up area. Then he analyzed their satellite imagery over a 25-year period to understand the urban expansion patterns specific to each city.

Between 1990 and 2015, the population of cities in less developed countries doubled, while their urban extents increased by a factor of 3.5. This means that, spatially, they expanded nearly 60% faster than their populations. In more developed countries the population of cities increased by a factor of 1.2, while their urban extents increased by a factor of 1.8, representing a rate of spatial expansion 67% faster than the population rate. In all regions of the world, then, urban land use was roughly one-third less efficient in 2015 than it was in 1990.

Many of the advantages typically associated with cities—proximity of the factors of production, increased specialization, shorter daily commuting times and the viability of multiple modes of transportation—arise from density and agglomeration. Cities are incrementally forfeiting many of these advantages as they develop along increasingly dispersed patterns. The strong correlation between urban sprawl and GHG emissions is striking, and its implications for climate change are particularly worrisome.

Angel also concluded that most of the residential fabric in the expanding areas of cities was unplanned and disorderly, especially in less developed countries, and had often taken place in defiance of municipal plans and regulations. Indeed, in these areas the share of residential fabric laid out before occupation was lower than in the pre-1990 urban areas in all regions of the world.

Fig 74: Comparison of urban expansion
© UN-Habitat / Shlomo Angel, NYU

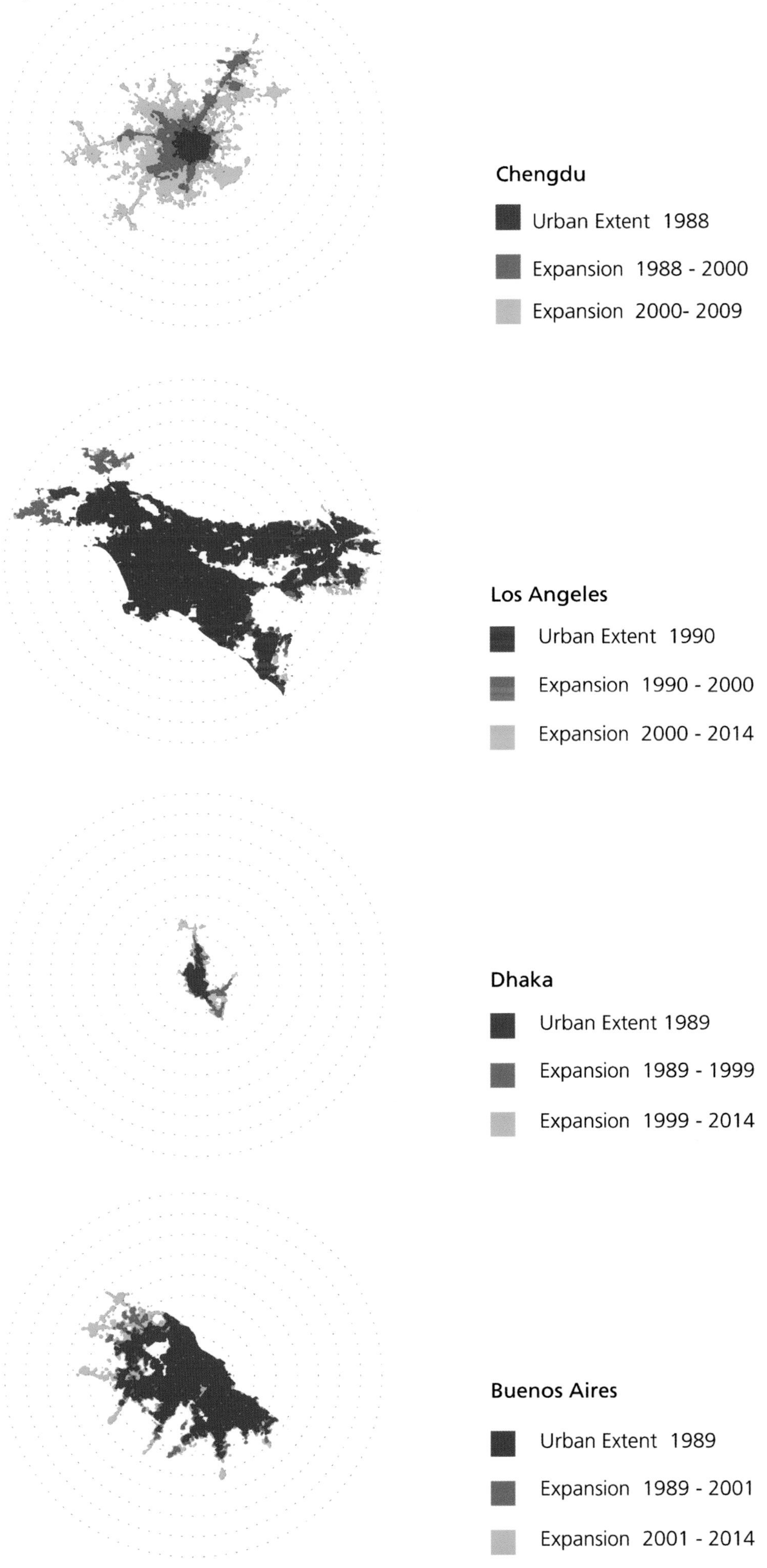

Chengdu

■ Urban Extent 1988

■ Expansion 1988 - 2000

■ Expansion 2000- 2009

Los Angeles

■ Urban Extent 1990

■ Expansion 1990 - 2000

■ Expansion 2000 - 2014

Dhaka

■ Urban Extent 1989

■ Expansion 1989 - 1999

■ Expansion 1999 - 2014

Buenos Aires

■ Urban Extent 1989

■ Expansion 1989 - 2001

■ Expansion 2001 - 2014

**Fig 75: Cartogram showing per capita urban land
consumption rates,
aggregated from the Sample of Cities**
© UN-Habitat based on data from UN DESA

Land-Rich Developed Countries

Latin America & the Caribbean

Europe & Japan

Western Asia & North Africa

Sub-Saharan Africa

Southeast Asia

East Asia & the Pacific

South & Central Asia

Fig 76: Lagos and Paris comparison
© Angel et al., 2011

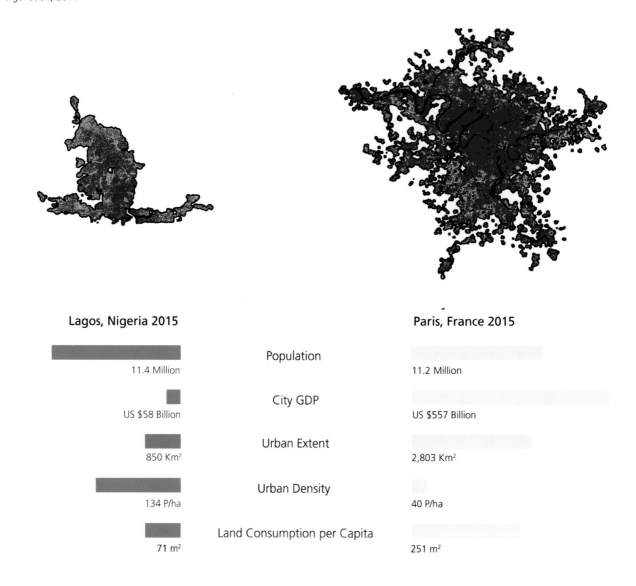

Lagos, Nigeria 2015		Paris, France 2015
11.4 Million	Population	11.2 Million
US $58 Billion	City GDP	US $557 Billion
850 Km²	Urban Extent	2,803 Km²
134 P/ha	Urban Density	40 P/ha
71 m²	Land Consumption per Capita	251 m²

Whereas cities have very limited scope for guiding population growth, the conversion of land to urban use is very much within the realm of influence of urban policy.

Fig 77: Built-up densities in
25 representative cities, 1800-2000
© Angel et al., 2011

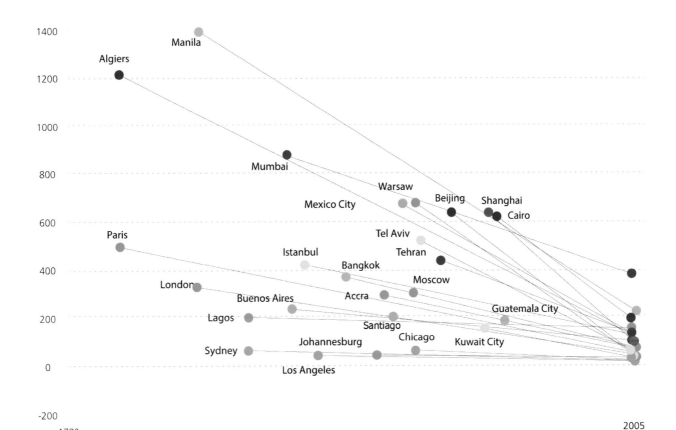

Built-up area densities in 25 representative cities, 1800-2000
Source: Angel et al.. 2011

East Asia and the Pacific

Western Asia

Latin America and the Caribbean

Southeast Asia

Northern America

Europe and Japan

South and Central Asia

Sub Saharan Africa

Land-Rich Developed Countries

Fig 78: Average density of urban extent

© UN-Habitat / Shlomo Angel, NYU

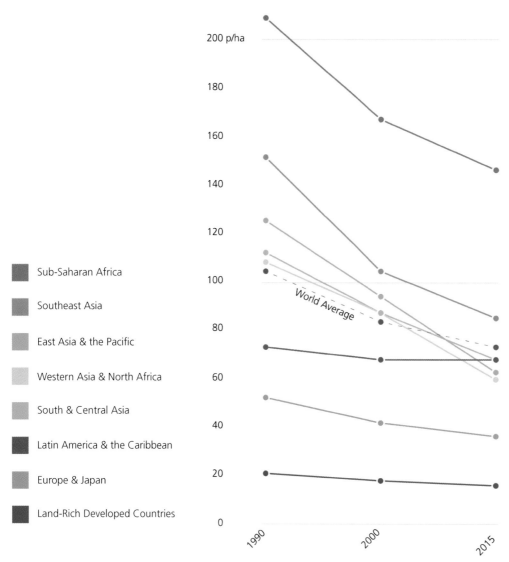

Legend:
- Sub-Saharan Africa
- Southeast Asia
- East Asia & the Pacific
- Western Asia & North Africa
- South & Central Asia
- Latin America & the Caribbean
- Europe & Japan
- Land-Rich Developed Countries

Urban densities are declining worldwide, though defining universally appropriate densities remains problematic

Average urban density represents the inverse of per capita land consumption, or the total city population divided by its built-up area. Angel found that average built-up area densities were significantly different among three world regions: in 1990, average built-up area densities in Europe and Japan were one half of those in developing countries; in land-rich developed countries they were only one-sixth.

New growth is declining precipitously in density, risking losing many of the advantages described previously, in particular the advantages of economies of agglomeration and value creation. At the same time, it is also failing to provide the open space that lower densities,

in theory, are conducive to. Urban densities in less-developed countries declined at an average annual rate of 2.1% between 1990 and 2015 (as opposed to 1.5% in more developed countries).

Certainly one size does not fit all. Defining locally-appropriate densities is contingent on a number of factors, including amounts of open space and public transport infrastructure as well as cultural perceptions of (and tolerance for) crowding. And high density does not necessarily equal quality, as illustrated by most of the informal settlements in the developing world. Simple quantifications of overall urban density tell us little about the quality of urban space

generated. However, high-resolution satellite imagery has helped detect other attributes key to qualifying density.

First, the distribution, connectivity and accessibility of arterial roads have an impact on productivity and socio-economic inclusivity. Angel found that the paucity of arterial roads in the expansion areas of cities is failing to connect them effectively to metropolitan labour markets. The share of the built-up area within walking distance of wide (18+ meters) arterial roads has also declined over time. Second, the area dedicated to and distance between streets and the block sizes have an impact on connectivity and spatial integration. Most expansion

Fig 79: Mismatch of people and job density Johannesburg, SA

© UN-Habitat based on data from Urban Morphologie Institute/
Spatial Development Framework 2040

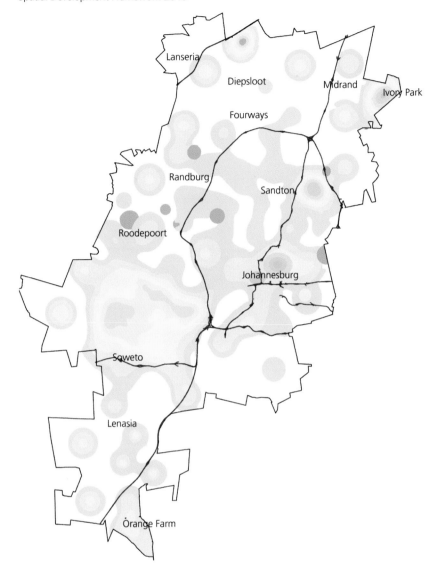

Residential density in 2010

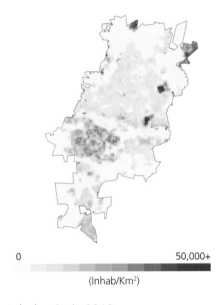

0   50,000+

(Inhab/Km²)

Job density in 2010

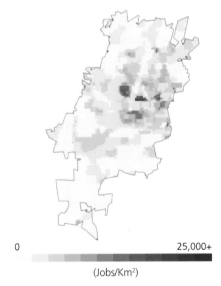

0   25,000+

(Jobs/Km²)

areas do not allocate enough land to local streets in conjunction with allowing block sizes to grow, segregating neighbourhoods, minimizing redundancy in route selection, reducing walkability and hampering the use of non-motorized transport. And third, the organization, location and integration of housing, although hard to measure, correlates strongly with factors such as affordability, non-car based mobility and access to labour markets.

The need to ensure more affordable housing further compounds the determination of appropriate densities. While the Sample of Cities contains a wide variation in housing sector performance, a preliminary analysis of the survey data indicated that in 2015 housing was largely unaffordable. There is a global housing affordability crisis that the formal, private housing market alone has failed to confront.

Angel argues that for housing in fast urbanizing regions to be adequate, ample and affordable, land on the urban periphery must remain in plentiful supply. Housing affordability should also encompass considerations about the location of the housing built, the per capita cost to providing access to basic services and infrastructure, the viability of public transport and access to jobs. Other qualifications include the collateral costs of various types of commute: public transport is much more environmentally friendly, frees up personal time and comes at a lower overall cost to the individual user and society. Transport by private vehicles contributes to a greater extent to CO_2 emissions, consumes personal time and is more costly to the individual and society in the long term. More detailed evidence and practical guidance are needed that can help shape and support the necessary public action to define appropriate densities throughout urban areas while ensuring economies of agglomeration, affordable housing and minimal cost to society. Without an empirical basis for their decisions, however, urban policy makers are far more likely to be guided by market preferences.

More detailed
evidence and practical guidance
are needed to help shape and
support the necessary public action
to define appropriate densities.

Fig 81: Median house price to income ratio differences under occupant affordability and median affordability across geographic regions
© UN-Habitat / Shlomo Angel, NYU

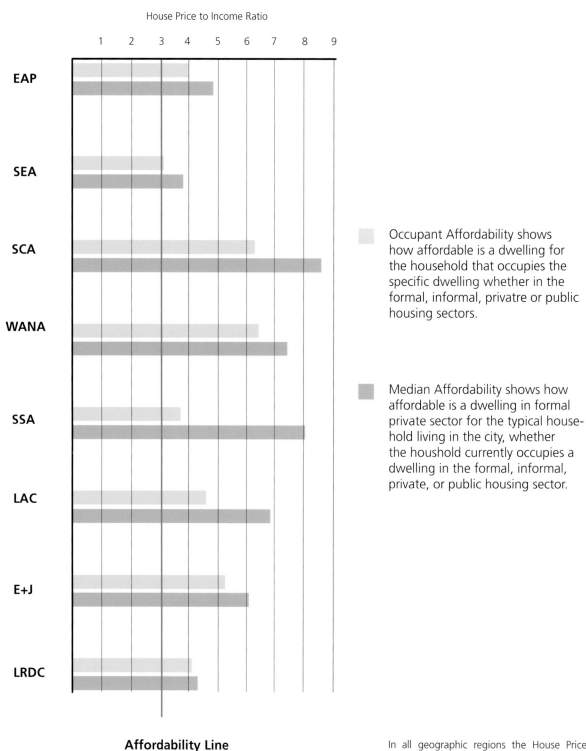

House Price to Income Ratio

Occupant Affordability shows how affordable is a dwelling for the household that occupies the specific dwelling whether in the formal, informal, privatre or public housing sectors.

Median Affordability shows how affordable is a dwelling in formal private sector for the typical household living in the city, whether the houshold currently occupies a dwelling in the formal, informal, private, or public housing sector.

Affordability Line

In all geographic regions the House Price to Income Ratio by Median Affordability standards is higher than the House Price to Income by Occupant Affordability standards. The differences are exacerbated in areas where the informal sector and public housing sector constitute higher shares of the housing stock

Fig 82: Median rent affordability and occupant rent affordability shown as share of household income contribution to rent by geographic region

© UN-Habitat / Shlomo Angel, NYU

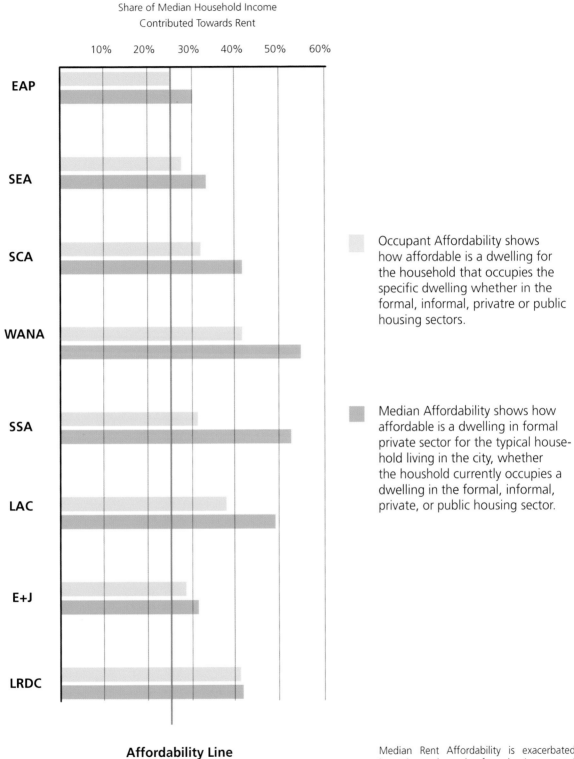

Occupant Affordability shows how affordable is a dwelling for the household that occupies the specific dwelling whether in the formal, informal, privatre or public housing sectors.

Median Affordability shows how affordable is a dwelling in formal private sector for the typical household living in the city, whether the houshold currently occupies a dwelling in the formal, informal, private, or public housing sector.

Median Rent Affordability is exacerbated in regions where the formal private rental market is too expensive for the median household. In these cases, households rent in the more affordable informal and public housing sectors.

Integrative networks combine government- and self-led approaches and expand the right to the city

The reverse sequencing of informal neighbourhoods requires integration at multiple scales of the urban landscape

Urban landscapes are a collection of interconnected systems that determine the quality of urban life. They extend beyond perceived boundaries, forming a shared commons that undergirds even the most disparate parts of the contemporary metropolis. Although constituting extreme conditions of economic power and cultural representation. Anita Berrizbeitia is of the opinion that the informal and the formal city share a geographical region, an ecology, a hydrological structure and, to varying extents, services such as water, energy, transportation, and other infrastructures. However, zooming in, fissures that fragment and divide the city, quickly become apparent: they are the result of the manner in which the same territory has been differently intervened. Urban landscapes are multifunctional. Socially, they constitute public space for recreation and interchange; aesthetically, they ameliorate harsh environmental conditions; ecologically, they perform as metabolic agents that processes energy and produce waste; and structurally, they serve as frameworks for capitalist development.

The term 'informal city' refers to a reversal in the sequence of building the modern city, rather than to its physical form or the techniques used for its construction. Dwelling units, self-built by their occupants rather than by developers, precede the construction of infrastructure, which, in the formal city, requires significant investment, coordination, planning, and specialized construction technologies, usually by public-private partnerships that operate within established frameworks of planning policy or master planning within municipal, state, or federal governments. As a result, although densely built, informal cities do not have the services that the formal city enjoys: there are few, if any, paved roads, no garbage collection, sewer systems, water supply, or public spaces. The environmental conditions are precarious at best; they are unhealthy and dangerous in the majority of cases.

Although informal or self-built

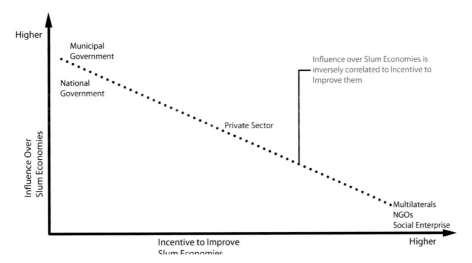

Fig 84: Influence over slum economies

© UN-Habitat based on data from The Rockefeller Foundation

cities emerged slowly more than a century ago, they reached exponential growth during this last stage of globalization, and in many instances today constitute at least 25%, and in some case as much as 50%, of the inhabitants of the city, forming the most significant urban expansion in its entire history. They also represent a significant part of the economy in the form of real-estate transactions, street-wide cottage industries, home-based micro-businesses, and manufacturing enterprises that make everything from food to clothing to machinery. The next stage in the evolution of the contemporary city must be, then, an urbanism of integration, where the landscape is one system in

the larger collection of urban networks that facilitates and mediates relations between the informal sector and the formal city and its economy.

While the planned districts of the contemporary city have many such networks, informal cities have predominantly one type, pedestrian streets, and a series of often severely compromised drainage ways in the form of polluted creeks. Integration with the rest of the city must, therefore, occur through the insertion of new networks that connect at different scales from the personal to the neighbourhood scale, and from the local to the territorial. External integrative networks, social-logistical networks,

ecological networks, and interstitial networks are each intended to accomplish a different type of connectivity.

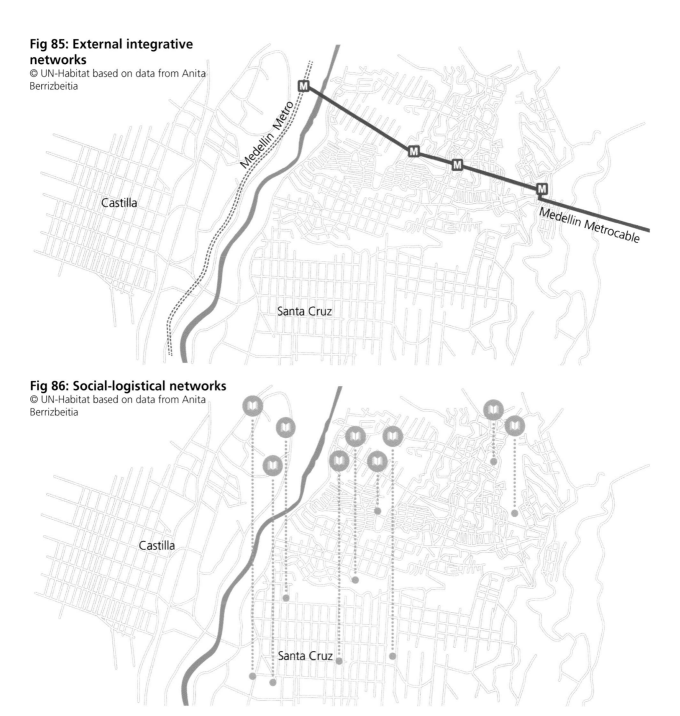

Fig 85: External integrative networks
© UN-Habitat based on data from Anita Berrizbeitia

Castilla

Medellin Metro

Santa Cruz

Medellin Metrocable

Fig 86: Social-logistical networks
© UN-Habitat based on data from Anita Berrizbeitia

Castilla

Santa Cruz

External integrative networks connect the self-built cities to those networks that organize the planned city, such as public transportation, sanitation, energy, and water systems. These integrative infrastructures are fundamental to further integration because they facilitate and mediate relations across the spectrum of development in the city. One example is an urban corridor comprised of multimodal and non-motorized transit routes that connect public spaces and facilities and integrate peripheral neighbourhoods into the urban dynamic.

Other such networks incorporate electricity, drainage and sewer systems, ideally incorporating the interests of local residents into their programming as part of a multi-scalar and multi-pronged approach to the renovation of the self-built city. The result is a 'thick solution' in which service infrastructure is overlapped with public space and public buildings across different scales.

For external integrative networks to perform well they have to be wired into their respective territory. Therefore a series of inventories need to be made in advance of their design and implementation. The objective of these inventories is to uncover the inherent 'intelligence' of the place, including where systems are located and why, what they connect and who they serve, how they enhance flows of movement, labour, and materials, and the greater function they have in the region as a whole.

Although linking self-built cities to large-scale infrastructure is critical to integration, internal neighbourhood-scale networks can provide an armature of programme, identity, and city support to the otherwise homogeneous fabric of self-built cities. Social-logistical networks facilitate the everyday routine of the residents of the community by connecting a variety of community organizations and facilities to foster community ties, social resiliency, and promote a wide range of associative civic functions. They can give identity and structure to a

new backbone of pedestrian streets that build on existing corridors of transportation or of shopping districts (where people already are) as starting points for the introduction of a larger and more robust network that will coalesce established social practices into an identifiable linear internal core. These social-logistical networks should be visually and spatially distinct, and easily recognizable by the residents that participate in its activities. Ideally they should also be developed through a process that tied community, private sector, and municipal and state governments.

Social-logistical networks connect people to community assets through the principle of broad availability and accessibility (i.e. many assets and within easy reach). As is the case with external integrative networks, an inventory and analysis of neighbourhood assets needs to take place to maximize the effects of internal connectivity. Neighbourhood assets include plazas, schools, churches, daycare centres, playgrounds, community centres, markets, pharmacies, and other everyday-life resources as well as community organizations, neighbourhood associations, and other institutions. Local networks can also be 'thickened' by creating open space clusters such that their proximity increases their impact, visibility, and the regenerative capacity of the social and physical fabric of the place. Finally, they should also connect to the larger transportation networks to facilitate and increase public uses of the space. Interventions that build on systems already in place, whether physical, institutional, economic or social, build a resilient network that is grounded in the everyday life of the citizens that support it.

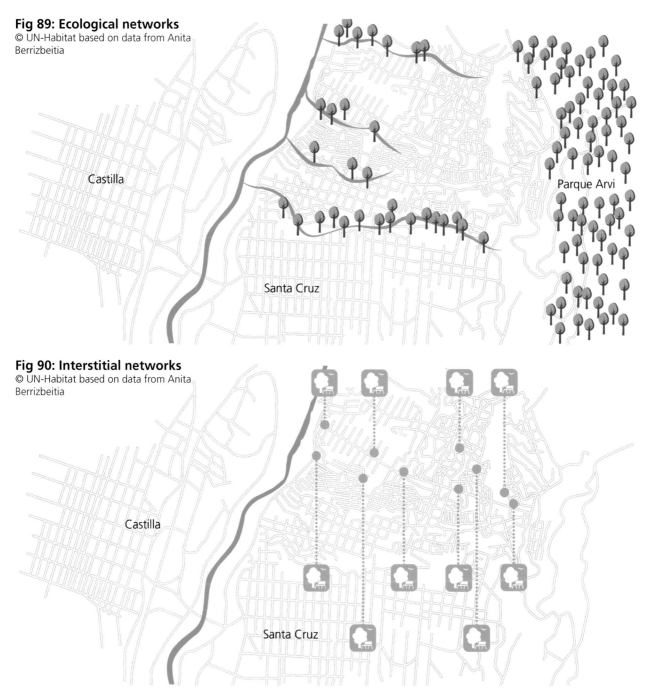

Fig 89: Ecological networks
© UN-Habitat based on data from Anita Berrizbeitia

Castilla

Santa Cruz

Parque Arvi

Fig 90: Interstitial networks
© UN-Habitat based on data from Anita Berrizbeitia

Castilla

Santa Cruz

Ecological networks contribute to the environmental quality and stability. To remain resilient and self-sustaining, these systems need to be interconnected and open-ended. In well-planned cities, urban ecological systems include corridors (e.g. rivers, streams and other drainage ways, streets, parkways and boulevards, rights-of-way, and easements) that connect islands of habitat (e.g. parks, forests, vegetable plots, gardens, arboreta, and patches of urban wild) that have recreational, environmental, and climatic functions. Together they can re-integrate larger ecological networks shared by the planned and self-built cities that have been severed or fragmented in the collision between the two.

Ecological systems also provide important services to the city, such as the mitigation of urban heat island effects, flood control, water and soil cleansing and mitigation of unpredictable risk. Self-built cities often emerge on land that is deemed either undevelopable or too expensive to develop given market conditions, such as very steep hills or deep ravines. Since the land is typically cleared of all vegetation, self-built cities are at very high risk of landslides and flooding. Any ecological network that is inserted into self-built cities must address these risks.

Given the space constraints in self-built neighbourhoods and the impossibility of redundancy in their

infrastructural networks, each piece in the ecological system needs to perform several functions. For instance, pedestrian streets—the predominant corridor type in self-built cities—can also provide ecological functions, such as ventilation and drainage. Patches of left over urban wilds can be expanded for enhanced ecological function. The planting of trees, can, over time, form an extensive green canopy over the neighbourhoods, providing shade, soil stabilization and food. Roofs can accommodate cisterns that collect storm water and reduce runoff and the risk of erosion. To take advantage of these interventions many very densely-built neighbourhoods will need to increase their proportion of open

120

space, and this will require the strategic removal of houses and construction of relocation housing.

Lastly, and related to the previous case, is the insertion of a constellation of small open spaces that together form an interstitial network in the city. In traditional rehabilitation projects in self-built cities, these are typically referred to as urban acupuncture because they are self-contained, precise, spatial interventions. Although these types of spaces do not work for every community, they present an opportunity for the saturation of the environment with small, easily accessible, and diverse recreational and social possibilities. For example, a series of small playgrounds and public spaces scattered throughout can provide identity to neighbourhoods through the installation of murals and public art, urban furniture, play and exercise equipment, the creation of programming, and the management of risk through limited hours of access, and neighbourhood-based surveillance.

Such localized interventions can become seed projects for larger urban renovations. In addition, the resulting constellation of public spaces gives locus to an already well-established social and political organization, facilitating coordination strategies between individual households, and the diffusion of information.

Fig 93: Slum redevelopment in Manaus, Brazil
This plan incorporates all four types of integrative networks.
© Bing Maps (Microsoft Product Screenshot reprinted with permission from Microsoft Corporation)

New Housing and Interstitial Land

New Housing on Landfill

Parks and Urban Facilities on Landfill

External integrative networks wire segregated neighbourhoods into wider urban landscapes

Participatory design processes are standard practice in self-built cities, and they reaffirm the value of community engagement and pride of place. However, equally important in the conceptualization of the urban landscape of the self-built city is the interface between space and institutional and community networks. External integrative networks of public infrastructure are dependent on government funding, and cannot be implemented independently. However, the other three networks are fine-scaled, localized, infrastructural interventions that do not depend exclusively on external, publicly funded, labour. Self-built city residents can be primary agents of change. If, in addition to their houses, they improve their streets and open spaces for economic return (both directly through income generation and indirectly through service improvement), the economic impact will be significant.

Planning for the interface between space and people must allocate tasks according to sources of funding and labour. There is already precedent for this in self-built cities. Examples of such entrepreneurial activities include trash collection, sorting, recycling and management in the trash sheds, water collection and distribution, cleaning and maintenance of drainage ways, erosion control planting and maintenance and street cleaning. These types of participatory design mechanisms also provide a critical, direct connection between the needs of communities and wider planning strategies.

Public spaces and landscapes in the planned city exist in the long run because they are supported by established public and private institutional frameworks and privately funded institutions. In self-built cities, community groups will increasingly have to instigate and support the practices necessary for a 'culture of landscape'; practices that took centuries to emerge in cities in the developed world. Nevertheless, the public landscapes of self-built cities will still require institutional support and legal frameworks if their emerging integrated public spaces are to remain representative of all.

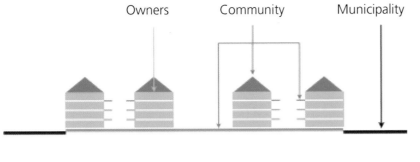

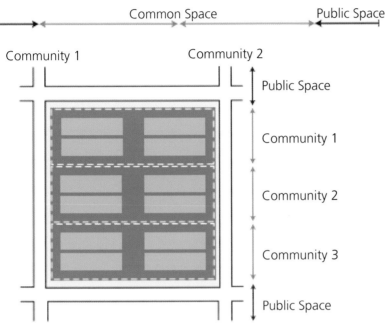

Fig 94: Article 182: Brazilian Urban Policy

Article 182 establishes the principles of the social function and creates instruments for the state to tax or force the utilization of properties that are not inhabited and therefore do not fulfil the social function.

Inserting networks in self-built cities will inevitably entail the lamination of programme and infrastructure (e.g. bundling the primary drainage, water collection and storage functions, with public space and housing). 'Thick solutions' not only avoid the problem of single-function infrastructures that plague the formal city, they become highly efficient in conjoining the social, the ecological, and the urbanistic.

As with their underlying challenges, self-built cities' intervention strategies must be multi-scalar, from the individual to the systemic, and encompass a broad range of physical, temporal, as well as organizational strategies. The challenge is to avoid applying to these sites the extreme abstract rationality and functionalism of normative Western practices in favour of a more direct and unmediated urbanism, one where the logics of daily life, of establishing webs of relations between neighbours and of enabling flows of labour and goods are more effective tools against the forces of social and economic marginalization and spatial fragmentation. Incremental, micro or fine-grained strategies, although in opposition to the large-scale infrastructural projects of the modern city, must nevertheless be grounded or embedded within the logic of larger ecological structure of the place. As such, the individual and the environment are tied to a logic that bypasses standardized modes of planning.

Multi-layered ecological and infrastructural systems, hinged on local labour and participation, can begin with micro-scale interventions but accrue to disseminate large-scale effects. The self-built city of the future is integrated, inside and outside, through a web that is dependent on partnership and coexistence. In this vision, landscape is not the empty, cleared space of migrant colonization, nor the last layer of a consolidated neighbourhood, but the foundational matrix that will support the social and economic advance of its community as it restructures the environmental integrity of the place, and its linkages to its greater metropolitan context.

Commons can compensate for public/private deficiencies if they achieve sufficiently large-scale application in cities

Against the binary of public/ private, commons offer an essential 'third way'

John Bingham-Hall writes about the increasing privatization of urban space as a controversial accompaniment to the real estate boom in many inner cities in recent years. Many new 'public' spaces are owned and managed by private development companies, with restrictive by-laws limiting the range of activity they can play host to, rather than local authorities with public mandates to allow gathering, protest and so on. This was most starkly demonstrated during the Occupy movement, when it became clear that private owners such as the Corporation of London and Canary Wharf Group had rights to evict protesters from streets and squares that by their nature as open spaces in the city

might have been assumed to be in public hands. If cities are to remain viable places for people to develop the strong associational and social life fundamental to healthy human existence, they must incorporate a range of public spaces and 'third' places in which urban citizens can come together.

Certainly, privately-owned businesses such as cafés, pubs and nightclubs can support public social life and street buzz. However, a purely consumption-based approach to public space leaves little room for people to come together over productive activities—producing, growing, decision-making—around which can form much stronger bonds

and communities, and thus urban societies. Not only does the commercial public realm lack in ways to support strong forms of public togetherness, it also excludes many whose financial circumstances do not allow them to partake in the activities it offers. Those without the means to pay for entertainment are also separated from the means to use urban space and attempts to claim a space in the new public domain are often branded as anti-social behaviour and legislated out by the culture of by-laws that exists to preserve the best possible commercial environment.

This leads to a dangerous segregation in cities. With changes to local authority funding, the investment

Fig 95: New York City Police Department guards an empty Zucotti Park
© David Shankbone, CC by 2.0

Fig 96: Flint protesters resist their treatment during the city's water crisis outside of the Michigan State Capitol before the state speech on 19 Jan. 2016
© The Detroit News / David Guralnick

that comes with private development is now essential to the maintenance of the urban streetscape, favouring a business-led model. However, the tensions and disaffection emerging from the inequality of access this creates are a growing problem, evidenced by increasing unrest in cities across the world. This poses a huge challenge for urban governments, as well as developers whose interests are harmed by this conflict, to find more diverse models to apply to the operation and design of urban space, allowing for forms of gathering and working together in public that lie outside of the market logic. Urban society will be revitalized by the provision of space for people to produce their own food, energy, culture, democracy and learning in strong organizational and associational ways. There already exist many examples of grassroots projects supporting this kind of collective participation in and ownership of urban space, often under the banner of 'urban commons'.

Fig 97: Shufat School (2014)
Designed by Sandi Hilal, Alessandro Petti, Livia Minoja for the UNRWA Infrastructure and Camp Improvement Program, the design of the school is inspired by the pedagogical approach cultivated by Hilal and Petti in Campus in Camps (www.campusin-camps.ps). The Shufat School embodies an 'architecture in exile'. Through its spatial and programmatic configuration this architecture in exile attempts to actively engage the new 'urban environment' created by almost seventy years of forced exile. Perhaps this is a fragment of a city yet to come.
© Anna Sara / Campus in Camps

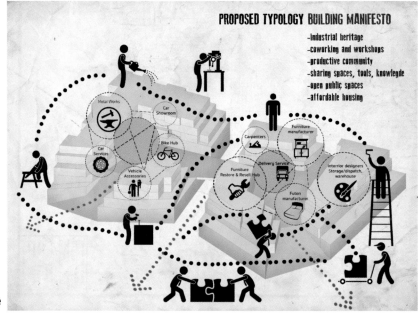

Fig 98: The industrial valley, Tottenham
The project is a proposition to tackle the problem of land shortage, increasing land values, gentrification and privatization of public space. By vertical arrangement of city activities into a single urban block it would support close collaboration between them.
© Katarzyna Skrucha, Tatjana Geta

Commons defy ownership but are not necessarily public

Commons have traditionally been uncultivated fields around a town or village allowing the 'commoners' of that community the right to sustain themselves by grazing animals and collecting wood and wild food. Elinor Ostrom was awarded the Nobel Prize for Economics for showing that natural resources like forests and fisheries are highly effectively managed by commons-like organizations that allow a self-managed community of users equal access, without private ownership or state control. Common, then, is not the same as public. Public denotes an asset owned by a local or national authority on behalf of all the citizens of that jurisdiction, whether or not they make use of it. 'Common',

on the other hand, suggests a community of commoners that actively utilize and upkeep whatever it is that is being commoned. Some governments define common land as under specific ownership (often private) but with a 'right to roam' granted to anyone who wishes to do so. Some village greens also have the 'rights of common'—such as grazing livestock—and associations of commoners have formed to encourage the enactment of these rights. These are isolated and rural in nature though, and there are very few instances in which ordinary citizens can work collectively to make use of urban land or spaces for productive means that go beyond the recreational.

Scholars have started to look at how commoning might be practiced or applied conceptually to realms beyond the natural world. One example is the Creative Commons movement, which aims to make it easier for individuals to share writing, images, music and art for non-profit purposes, creating a common pool of creative resources that is enriched the more it is used and produced by its participants.

In cities, the presence of others confers value in ways that cannot be quantified. Safety, street buzz and neighbourliness are all things that have been conceptualized as commons: intangible assets that cannot be owned yet can be both produced and enjoyed collectively

by the city's users and inhabitants. The city also contains natural resources that are neither publicly nor privately owned, but common to all its inhabitants (clean air, for example). Although the state can intervene in its management, no organizational body can confer or deny access to it.

In fact, the city as a whole has been thought of as a common. Its individuals, institutions, buildings, cultures, laws and services may be owned or controlled in a specific way, but the city's overall growth derives from the synthesis of these many parts, with no singular ownership, and is therefore something we have 'in common' rather than co-own.

Urban sociologist David Harvey describes clearly how things we think of as public are not always common:

'Public spaces and public goods in the city have always been a matter of state power and public administration, and such spaces and goods do not necessarily a commons make. Throughout the history of urbanization, the provision of public spaces and public goods (such as sanitation, public health, education, and the like) by either public or private means has been crucial for capitalist development... While these public spaces and public goods contribute mightily to the qualities of the commons, it takes political action on the part of

citizens and the people to appropriate them or to make them so.'

As debates about the extent of state responsibility and the degree to which private enterprise can build cities becomes increasingly acute, Bingham-Hall maintains that the commons offers a third way between the sometimes simplistic and ideological counterpoint between 'public'—which does not always mean accessible to all—and 'private'—which does not always mean closed off to all—in the city. The question, then, is whether new urban commons can be designed into the city and what form these would take.

Common suggests a community of commoners that actively utilize and upkeep *whatever it is that is being commoned by them.*

John Bingham-Hall

Commons need to balance access and sustainability if they are to scale up

What we traditionally conceive of as 'the public' is in retreat: public services are at the mercy of austerity policies, public housing is being sold off and public space is increasingly no such thing. In a relentlessly neo-liberal climate, the commons seems to offer an alternative to the battle between public and private. The idea of land or services that are commonly owned and managed speaks to a 21st-century sensibility of participative citizenship and peer-to-peer production. In theory, at least, the commons is full of radical potential.

Can commoning be scaled up to influence the workings of a metropolis—able to tackle questions of housing, energy use, food distribution and clean air? In other words, can the city be re-imagined as commons, or is commoning the realm of tiny acts of autarchy and resistance?

Allowing common space for housing, food production, environmental management and culture (which are almost entirely marketed in some cities) would be a powerful catalyst for associational life in urban communities, not only in terms of resource production but also the indirect building of community identity. As it stands, public space design is almost entirely focused on aesthetics and makes reference to its local community symbolically, through public art for example. Togetherness is supposed to emerge from the sharing of streets and

squares. This kind of simple co-presence, however, only brings people alongside one another and not into direct contact. By providing urban space in which people can collectively apply energy and time with a tangible return, the range of spaces away from home and work could be hugely diversified beyond the consumption-based model of the urban public. Bingham-Hall cautions that for this approach to gain traction, developers, public bodies and the activists and organizations undertaking projects, will need to address some serious questions.

Commons very often rely on a self-managed organizational structure, requiring a core, stable group of commoners. When they are

Fig 101: Parckfarm, Brussels, 2015
People gathering around the common table also allowing activities of Urban Gardening
© Lieven De Cauter

Fig 102: Vauban Sustainable Urban District (Eco District) Freiburg, Germany
The participatory process of the District's construction to place between 1993 and 2006, enabling a high degree of coordination between future residents and the local government
© Daniel Schoenen

working with physical resources like land, rather than online networks, the number of people who can sustainably become active members of this structure must be limited. Unlike a truly public space, into which every citizen has unfettered access and which does not rely on their direct effort for its upkeep, commons may sometimes need to become somewhat closed groupings. The balance between access and sustainability will be a key issue for urban commons. This issue is particularly acute in the context of global cities, where communities are constantly in flux, with changing populations through constant in- and out-migration. For the benefits of commoning to be distributed widely, organizations undertaking

commoning must find ways to resist the tendency to become entrenched within and exclusive to the stable elements of communities, which are often the more privileged.

Bingham-Hall asks whether commons can ever realistically achieve a level of reach beyond the very local. For people to work directly together through self-management, scale is a natural limiting factor. The social reach of any given project in urban space might be limited to walking distance from its location, for example. For city-wide undertakings overarching organizational structures inevitably emerge, which start to look like corporations or public bodies. So this scale may only be achieved through a systemic

restructuring that applies commoning to our urban infrastructures en masse. For this to happen, commoners need to find a much more cohesive language for defining their way of working, the value it creates and the organizational systems they use. Only in doing this will they build a movement convincing and mainstream enough to influence governmental thinking on the scale that the Green movement has since the 1960s. If they can, the future city might have the chance of rearranging itself around models of public life that involve cooperative action and benefit rather than one in which the necessities of urban survival are distanced from consumers by markets, corporations and public bodies.

Fig 103: Al-Fawaar Square, near Hebron, Palestine. 2008-2014
© Luca Capuano

Negotiated urban planning is key to extending the scope of the commons

Jean-Louis Missika reminds us that cities are continually competing for talent, firms and investments, but that these do not guarantee clean air, nice public spaces and a good social mix. They require strong municipal involvement and an investment in the 'commons'. Above all, cities should require social housing in all private housing projects, ensuring a social mix in all neighbourhoods and give back to pedestrians spaces dominated by cars. No area of the city should be reserved for a certain part of the population. Nor can urban process be exclusive to elected representatives and real estate developers. We need negotiated urban planning, which can be achieved through four types of strategies.

The first targets private urban projects. Missika notes that public administrative buildings are often the least open ones, while private projects sometimes create de facto public spaces. In its 'Reinventing Paris' competition of 2014, the city transferred land plots no longer strategic for municipal ownership to the proposers of the most innovative projects. The city had encouraged developers to team up with start-ups, architects, artists and final users to define programmes that fit current metropolitan uses, systematize the reuse of existing materials and find innovative financial and legal arrangements. The commons emerged in all projects. Collective spaces—guest rooms, kitchens and teleworking spaces—prevailed over individual spaces in

housing and office projects, and often provided free services and leisure for the neighbourhood and beyond.

Second, urban intervals are necessary to accommodate activities that do not fit into classical real estate programmes. These include emergency shelters, working units for those who cannot pay traditional office rents and spaces for gathering and event organizing. Temporary spaces offer different uses than permanent ones, with cheaper rents, and the fact of having an end date creates a special atmosphere. However, encouraging them is never a simple decision for a local authority, because of the risk of occupants refusing to leave or increased disorder in an area. But temporary occupation offers the addi-

Fig 104: Al-Fawaar Square, near Hebron, Palestine. 2008-2014
Built as a house without a roof, the square in Fawaar refugee camp embodies the women's right to the public.
Conceived paradoxically as an enclosed space protected by four walls and through the direct participation from the
refugee community the square is the only public space in the camp.
© Luca Capuano

tional benefit of urban prefiguration. The observation of the way people occupy space is a great inspiration for the design of its future and permanent configuration. Ultimately local authorities have the responsibility to ensure that no space gets wasted while it could be useful for some citizens.

Third, no common should be hijacked by one part of the population at the expense of the majority of citizens. One example is the management of riverbanks: in many cities, riverbanks were designed as urban highways at a time when urban planning prioritized the most space to cars. But as the river is a space of respiration and promenade, there has been a growing recognition that this should be given back to pedestrians. Paris accom-

modated a lively debate in advance of closing its left riverbanks to cars, but once implemented it was broadly accepted. Plans to close the right riverbank to cars (in progress at time of writing) have once again generated strong debate with some motorists asserting that they cannot bear to yield more street space. However, the city maintains that nothing should prevent it from giving that common back to a majority of Parisians.

Finally, indetermination is key. Public authorities cannot entirely plan the uses of a space, which must be co-designed by citizens. Place de la République, a square at the centre of Paris, had been mostly dedicated to cars. In transforming it for a broader range of uses the city chose a design

that resisted predefining a specific programme. Its design was a bet on the future, because the city did not yet know if people would be willing to occupy a vast empty space. But the resulting République square became an assembly point for all Parisians; a space for everyday activities, tributes and civic movements. Immediately after the terrorists attacks in 2014-15, Parisians gathered at République square, representing its popular conception as an urban common open to all people and uses. Collaborative methods are full of promises, but we are only at the beginning of 'commoning' and must remain watchful of the risks of appropriation. In that sense local governments will have to function both as watchdogs and managers of citizen expectations.

Planning without democracy or democracy without planning? How cities might have it both ways

Local democracy is often at odds with global sustainability efforts

There is no doubt that climate change is one of the pressing issues of our time, an existential threat on a planetary scale, and that it is surrounded by uncertainties. Ironically, the most vexing uncertainty is not scientific, but social and political: one of the greatest unknowns is whether we will have the collective capacity to act simultaneously in time to prevent the worst scenarios. Gianpaolo Baiocchi argues that we know more or less what to do: reduce emissions, and there is general agreement on the catastrophic consequences of failing to do so. We do not know how to do it: which emissions, what mechanisms, and at whose cost. But the biggest question is whether we will be able to mobilize our governance structures at the various levels— global, national, sub-national—to enforce the necessary reduction targets.

How to govern global problems in a world of nation-states, or even more generally, how to manage the commons in a world of self-interests? Some of that discussion turns on the role of the *demos*— the popular will—in this thorny set of questions. One of the central issues is one of scales: democracy is lived, experienced, and practiced locally and in the short-term, while problems sometimes need to be governed nationally or transnationally and over longer time-scales. The worry, the argument goes, is that the local demos will sometimes—or perhaps most of the time—opt for an obstructive approach (often described as 'not in my backyard', or NIMBYism) when larger problems will require that things actually go in someone's backyard.

Richard Sennett gives the very poignant example of post-Hurricane Sandy reconstruction in the US. '[T]hose who lived along the coast wanted to rebuild the places they had lived in,' and this 'was translated into expenses that local communities were willing to pay in order to erect storm walls and barriers.' Yet, 'scientific opinion,' was that 'this strategy is not sustainable, and has argued that some communities should be broken up, others abandoned, others recon-

Fig 105: Uncontrolled urban growth in the Amazon Rainforest, Parauapebas, Brazil
© UN-Habitat based on data from Google Earth

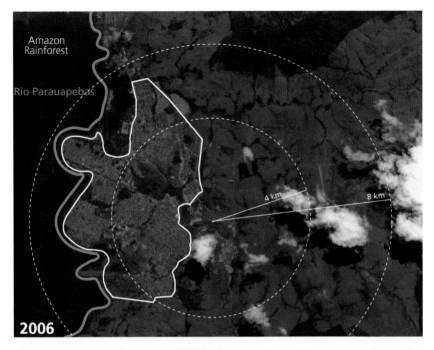

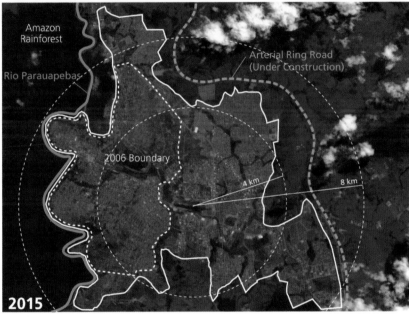

figured drastically.' This is a clear example of a contrast between 'self-determination,' and 'the need to work with natural forces beyond the control of debates and votes in a particular city.' '[H]ow to practice governance under these conditions'? Political terms like 'autonomy,' 'local control,' and place-based rights have become 'closed political fantasies' in a world that calls for open-systems thinking. One of the proposed solutions is to partially or fully insulate important decision-making from the reach of the demos altogether. The so-called 'eco-authoritarian' thinkers of the 1970s made the argument that some 'aspects of democratic rule would have to be sacrificed in order to achieve

sustainable future outcomes' (Held 2011:1). Some scholars have called modern democracy an impediment to dealing with climate change: '[e]ven the best democracies agree that when a major war approaches, democracy must be put on hold for the time being [...] climate change may be an issue as severe as a war. It may be necessary to put democracy on hold for a while.

Others have pointed to the limits of our institutions. We are faced, Jameson writes, 'with the largest collective action problem that humanity has ever faced.' 'Evolution,' he goes on, 'did not design us to deal with such problems, and we have not designed political institutions that are con-

ducive to solving them'. The other side of this coin altogether is not so much the limits of institutions but democracy's potential in addressing climate change. Given that climate change is less a technical issue than an inter-relational one, there is an opportunity to rethink the way we imagine the demos as a protagonist—certainly not the only one—and the possibilities it affords before the challenges we face. Once we separate democracy from governance, or at least stop reducing the former into the latter, we can more fully explore what an expanded democratic imagination might do.

Fig 106: City as the saviour
©LSE / Green Economy Report

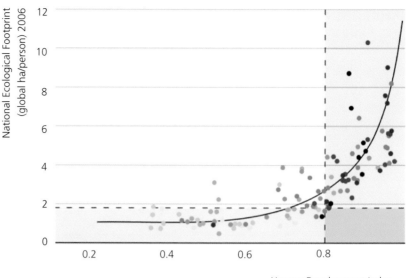

| <20% | 30-40% | 50-60% | 70-80% | >90% |
| 20-30% | 40-50% | 60-70% | 80-90% | |

Fig 107: City as the culprit
©LSE / Green Economy Report

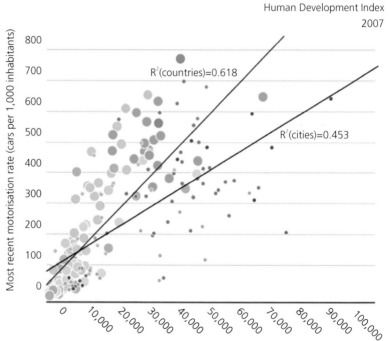

Cities are simultaneously the culprit, victim and saviour

Cities are today seen as both a key site of production of emissions, a strategic site for intervention in the form of ecological planning, as well as a kind of key actor in the form of city alliances for climate action. In other words, as simultaneously the culprit, victim, and saviour. There is general consensus that cities matter a lot for climate change. This concern is evidenced in the stand-alone Sustainable Development Goal adopted in 2015 (SDG 11), the immense scholarly and practitioner interest in the last decade in forms of sustainable urbanism, and innumerable reports on cities, sustainability, and climate change. Yes, the question remains: what role is there for urban democracy in the face of climate change?

Not only are cities today home to an unprecedented parcel of the global population, this parcel is only expected to grow, and grow quickly over the next few years.

Cities will experience much of the vulnerability to climate change. Currently it is estimated that one billion people live in informal urban settlements, and this number is expected to grow, as much of the urban population growth over the next fifteen years is to take place in Africa and Asia. These challenges are compounded by the fact that much of the growth will be in what currently are secondary cities that do not have the infrastructure or centrality of so-called primate cities in Global South contexts. In

addition, many of these cities are near oceans or rivers. The urban poor are, of course, most at risk by virtue of the nature of informal settlements and their lack of a social safety net. Today, one billion people live in informal settlements where basic infrastructure deficiencies make them especially vulnerable to natural disasters. This number is expected to increase by another billion and a half over the next fifteen years.

However, part of the urgency is also with the central role of cities in producing emissions. As populations grow in cities, so does their footprint. As LSE Cities recently argued, a group of just 468 cities will contribute "60% of global

Fig 108: City as the victim
©UN-Habitat based on data from Washington Post, Reuters, Weather Underground

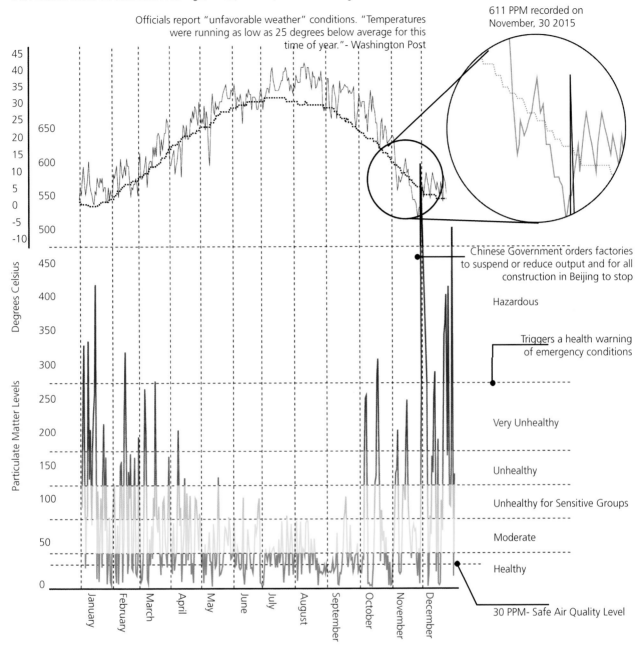

Officials report "unfavorable weather" conditions. "Temperatures were running as low as 25 degrees below average for this time of year."- Washington Post

611 PPM recorded on November, 30 2015

Chinese Government orders factories to suspend or reduce output and for all construction in Beijing to stop

Hazardous

Triggers a health warning of emergency conditions

Very Unhealthy

Unhealthy

Unhealthy for Sensitive Groups

Moderate

Healthy

30 PPM- Safe Air Quality Level

Degrees Celsius

Particulate Matter Levels

January February March April May June July August September October November December

GDP growth and over half of global energy-related emissions growth" over the next decade and a half. This also means, though, that cities have the potential to reduce emissions by capitalizing on economies of scale (e.g. densifying) and investing in basic services infrastructure. There is agreement that significant changes will have to take place in cities, both in terms of mitigation and adaptation. This coincides with the question of cities as agents, or perhaps, as site of agency. On one hand there is significant optimism for city-based action. If international arenas are thought to be too difficult to move beyond deadlock, and national states too entrenched in their patterns, proponents point to sub-national or local govern-

ments with enthusiasm. There is today also a sense that, as one report put it, 'local governments can act more quickly and efficiently than the central state and that they are essential for ensuring that national plans reach the local level.' Much recent research has thus pointed to leadership of particular local cities in taking action, especially the so-called 'early adopters,' including Mexico City, Durban, Cape Town, Curitiba, Singapore, Ho Chi Minh City, Quito, and others. Some scholars have argued that city governments can pressure the international community to act, while others see them as an alternative altogether to international or national policy. In addition, there are many examples of city-to-city

networks as a type of local protagonism that can help transcend levels, institutions, and interests. Today, for example, there is C40 Climate Leadership Group, ICLEI-Local Cities for Sustainability, 100 Resilient Cities and United Cities and Local Governments.

> # *Democracy is not consensus. Democracy is a conflict that is well managed. It's about how you manage that conflict—sometimes for the minority, sometimes for the majority. But it has to happen.*
>
> Jaime Lerner

Must we choose between planning without democracy and democracy without planning?

Despite the enthusiasm, though, there is also a thorny set of questions around governance. Local governments are increasingly being asked to assume a key role in coordinating environmental interventions, despite often lacking capacity or jurisdictional authority. As a recent report summarizes it, 'urban governance is a key issue in the quest for sustainable cities. Apart from general limitations in capacity and resources, important issues are how to develop clear arrangements of cooperation between governments at city, regional and national scales; the involvement of citizens in processes of change; maintaining the political momentum for sustainable development beyond the electoral cycle;

and oversight with private-sector involvement and public–private partnerships'.

Two normative proposals have impact on the question of urban democracy. Giddens argues for a 'return of planning,' as well as a new kind of relationship between the state, business and civil society. A central limit of this proposal is that, in some instances, it ultimately limits democratic decision-making in favour of expert planners. On the other hand, some scholars have for some time been working on democratizing expertise – finding ways to imagine and conceptualize forums and settings where democracy and expertise are articulated. However, a key problem with deliberative

proposals is that while they may indeed create spaces for deliberation, the outputs of deliberation do not have binding power.

The proposals of Giddens and of the deliberative democrats have parallel problems. A crucial limitation of Giddens' planning is that it relies on experts and circumscribes the reach of demos, the problem with deliberative democrats is that it creates inclusive spaces without linking them to decision-making or longer term views. Is our choice one between planning without democracy and democracy without planning?

Yet participatory democracy at the local level may well be a viable and

Fig 110: Urban renewal project in Turkey, 2006
Law 5366 also known as the "Urban Renewal Act" which passed in 2005 has endured criticism for its potential to induce gentrification patterns.

desirable way to manage urban affairs. Participatory democracy is most meaningful when it is inclusive and deliberative but also when it is sovereign. In this vision of the democratic city, participation is linked to decision-making, and the chain of popular sovereignty is protected from both undue bureaucratic interference or elite interests. Of course, deciding on the location of a playground, the allocation of municipal infrastructure budgets, or whether to raise municipal wages or increase the number of running buses, are decisions a world away from the technical, political, and jurisdictional complexity than the kinds of decisions we are faced with. And the stakes, we might add, are of course, infinitely lower.

Even if we have not figured out the precise institutional arrangements to enact such an experiment, this does not mean that we should dismiss it.

Fig 111: Governing city populations
©LSE Cities (2014)

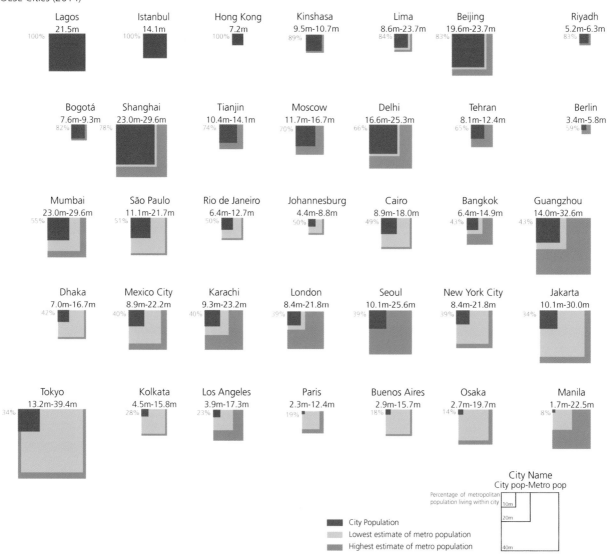

The scales of democracy and decision-making are mismatched

The concerns that Sennett articulates about closed fictions of local autonomy in an interconnected world are absolutely pivotal to the rethinking here. However, open-systems theorizing calls for a much broader imagination of what democracy might come to mean. We need to radically expand the reach of the demos, not only because it is normatively desirable, but because it is necessary. This goes some way towards addressing what Ulrich Beck has called a tabooed question, 'where is the everyday support from below, the backing of everyday people of different classes, different nations, different political ideologies, different countries, which are affected differently supposed to come from?" (Beck 2010).

A first set of arguments for the need of extending the reach of the demos has to do with correcting the current power asymmetries between actors that has prevented more decisive change in the first place. One of the centrepieces of the arguments for the deliberative approach is that more inclusive and consensual arrangements—such as corporatism, where trade unions have a seat at the table—outperform other arrangements in terms of providing and enforcing environmental regulations. More critical analysts of democracy have pointed to the fact that an increasing number of decisions, because of their technical demands or their global scope, are insulated from the democratic decision-making.

Whether we are speaking of the specifics of global trade policy, the global property rights of water, environmental regulation, or the management of complex financial instruments, there are an increasing number of manifold important decisions that take place in juridical or expert settings completely beyond the reach of the demos. In those more privileged settings the powerful interests can express themselves. The growing power of corporate interests, and the concomitant emptying out of the power of democratic institutions to hold them accountable, is a growing post-democratic condition. We are living in a context of profound mismatch between scales of democracy and scales of

138

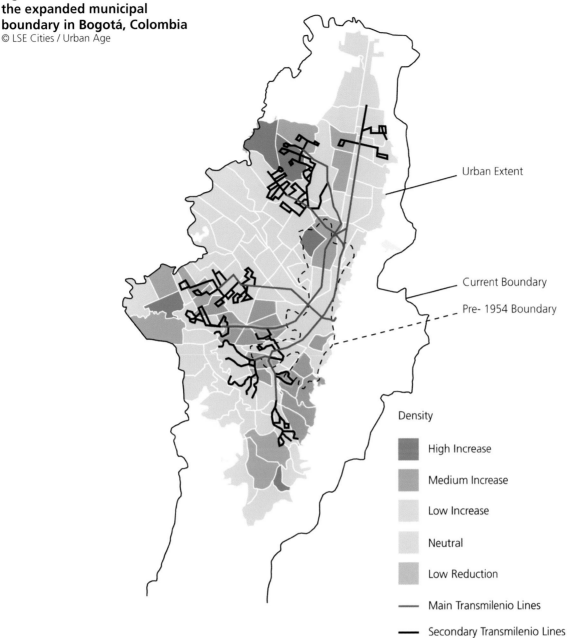

Fig 112: Dense transit corridors in relation with the expanded municipal boundary in Bogotá, Colombia
© LSE Cities / Urban Age

Urban Extent

Current Boundary

Pre- 1954 Boundary

Density

High Increase

Medium Increase

Low Increase

Neutral

Low Reduction

Main Transmilenio Lines

Secondary Transmilenio Lines

decision-making, and where the capacity of actors to interfere at various scales varies widely.

Scholars have long documented the out-sized corporate influence on environmental policy, particularly in the US. '[T]he network connections between the power elite, policy planning network, and the state' not only provide elites 'with disproportionate access to the [executive and legislative branches of government], they also provide (…) disproportionate influence over US foreign and domestic policy' (Downey 2015: 60). It is 'merchants of doubt' and not an uneducated population, that often account for the lack of environmental regulation on climate change in

countries such as the US (Oreskes and Conway 2010). And while at global summits, corporations have a less direct role in negotiations, they still play significant roles in influencing national governments. A more robust and expansive democratic imagination would be one that should be able to hold elite and business interests in check and regulate markets in favour of disfavoured populations.

A second argument about the necessity of more expansive conception of democracy has to do with power of democracy to create solidarity and legitimacy, and relatedly, to unleash powers of creativity and creative-problem solving. If a more robust democracy is able to hold

interests from those above in check, then one that taps into people's capacities to think creatively about the world around them might go some way to the 'getting support from below' that Beck, above, worries about. Climate change will no doubt require belt-tightening, changed consumption patterns, and willingness to rethink how we live and work in cities. It is hard to imagine how those choices would be legitimate to populations unless they were intimately involved in cooperative problem-solving and in making decisions about how, exactly to carry those out. The many examples of local leadership on environmental issues, in fact, prove that there exists a local capacity to go beyond narrower conceptions of self-interest.

CONTEMPORARY URBANISM
RICKY BURDETT

Cities today are being made and re-made at a faster pace and at a larger scale than ever before. Yet, the way they are planned and designed is lodged in an ideological and spatial model that is, at best, 80 years out-of-date. Despite the increasing complexity and specificity of the global urban condition, many of the 94 recommendations of the 1933 Charter of Athens[1] still determine the generic forms and physical organization of 21st century city. These design choices matter because urban form affects the way cities respond to social and environmental challenges.

Regularly spaced high-rise towers, separated by dead space and wide roads into rigid functional zones define the instant cities of Songdo in South Korea, Gurgaon in India or the new urban realities of Kigali and Luanda. Similar typologies mark the dormitory towns on the edges of Istanbul or the centrally planned metropolitan uber-region of Jing-Jin-Ji (120 million people around Beijing) and the economic hubs of the Yangtze and Pearl River deltas in China. These landscapes are familiar, even commonplace in different geographies of the urbanizing world.

As cities expand and reconfigure themselves, 'urban space' has increasingly become the territory of negotiation and confrontation between public and private interests; between politicians, planners, architects and real estate agents; and between banks, financial institutions, speculators, developers and landowners. Yet, the physical solutions remain stubbornly uniform—despite the diversity of architectural styles and commissioning bodies—reflecting a close affinity between the realpolitik of urbanization and the vested interests of the key actors involved in shaping urban planning regimes. The Charter's spatial recommendations have played an instrumental role in the dynamics of these transactions in many cities across the globe since its publication in the aftermath of World War II.[2]

A glance at different hotspots of urbanization confirms that the original recommendations and the implied ideologies of the Charter of Athens are alive and well. For example, the premise that 'the four keys to urban planning are the four functions of the city: dwelling, work, recreation [and] transportation[3] still determines the spatial logic of many 'planned' cities today, despite major changes in the way in which domestic life, labour relations, manufacturing, industry and technology are organized. The belief that pedestrian routes and automobile routes should follow separate paths' still dominates planning orthodoxy, prioritizing the needs of the private car despite the increased awareness of its negative impacts on sociability and sustainability. And the conviction that 'unsanitary slums should be demolished and replaced by open space' is the guiding principle of many planning regimes that struggle to find the space, land or money to provide decent homes for millions of new urban dwellers.

There is an authority (and simplicity) to the language of the Charter of Athens that reflects its technocratic origins. Steeped in the promise of the Modern Era and problem-solving ideologies of the 1920s and 1930s, the Charter adheres to a set of principles conceived by western professional elites in response to the prevailing conditions of the time.[4] A century ago cities were seen as the repositories of poverty, overcrowding and ill-health. High population densities in central city areas were to blame. 'Chaos has entered into the cities', the Charter declaimed, but it could be tamed by deploying a number of technical instruments and imposing a set of planning regulations.

Le Corbusier's 1922 Plan Voisin for Paris was the litmus test. Notoriously, he called for the 'death' of the two-sided corridor street,[5] replacing much of central Paris with stand-alone monofunctional residential or office blocks sitting in open parks. The Charter went further. It stipulated that 'high-rise apartments [be] placed at wide distances apart [to] liberate the ground for large open spaces', that 'roads should be differentiated according to their functions: residential streets, promenades, through roads, major highways, etc' and that 'heavily used traffic junctions should be designed for continuous passage of vehicles, using different levels'[6].

The combined effect of these apparently neutral technical propositions are the highly fragmented, starkly differentiated and, at times, sparsely populated 'planned' urban landscapes of the late 20th century and early 21st century city. A byproduct of the reduction in density of occupation and the removal of the street has been the erosion of the public realm. As a consequence, the potential for transactions and unplanned encounter has diminished, sucking the lifeblood out of city life and deadening everyday urban experience. What has resulted, nearly a century after the Charter's conception, is a pervasive and generic urban genre which indeed imposes a degree of order; but an inflexible and 'brittle' one that ultimately works against the potential of generating a sense of urbanity or cityness[7].

While the Charter ends with the exhortation that 'private interests should be subordinated to the interests of the community', evidence suggests that many of its principles have inadvertently supported the process of land speculation and increased segregation. For example, prescriptive zoning regulations, which determine the amount and type of development in specific urban districts, have been easily manipulated by lawyers, landowners and investors to maximize value and stifle competition (and, at times, facilitate corruption of malleable city officials). The adoption of major road programmes advocated by the Charter of Athens has led to the destruction of inconveniently located neighbourhoods, damaging the fragile ecologies of existing urban communities and opening up the potential for displacement and resettlement in peripheral areas without access to public transport and jobs. Ultimately the fixed model implied by the Charter has proven unable to adapt to changing circumstances over time, acting as a constraint to progress and change despite the recognition that 'the factors which govern the development of cities are ... subject to continual change'.[8]

A new urban condition

Not only have the urban conditions changed since the early 20th century, but so have the forces that shape the urban environment. While less than 20% of the world's population lived in cities in the 1930s when the Charter was being discussed, we are gradually moving to a planet inhabited principally by urban dwellers. By 2050, 75% of the world's population will be living in cities, with one third in slum conditions. Cities today consume over 60% of global energy and contribute to 75% of global C02 emissions. The exponential rise in urbanization and globalization, the transformative effects of new technologies, the implications of climate change and resource scarcity, and the profound increase in inequality have impacted the dynamics of urban growth. Yet we adhere to technical and spatial solutions that are not only outdated but have demonstrably failed to create liveable and sustainable cities. It is as if modern medicine were based on practices founded before the discovery of antibiotics and vaccines.

This paper argues that patterns of urbanization today require a reframing of the discourse and practice of planning, one that questions the very tenets of the Charter of Athens and challenges the value of anachronistic 'bottom-up vs top-down' models, so heavily rooted in western urbanism (aka Robert Moses vs Jane Jacobs).[9] It contends that the physical shape of cities, the form of their buildings and the spaces between them are instrumental to social and environmental equity, even though most planning and urban policy operates in a technical bubble that fails to engage with this dynamic. At a more practical level, evidence 'on the ground' suggests that much of the discourse on cities is trapped in a paradigm determined by urban professionals and policymakers, while everyday urban realities are being shaped by a very different set of informal processes and actors that are largely immune to planning and policymaking.

Unlike experimental scientists and creative thinkers, most planning and urban design experts seem unable to conceptualize spatial models capable of adaptation and change, at a time that city dynamics are both volatile and uncertain. Planning departments of municipal, metropolitan and central governments are highly regulated and risk-averse, preferring to work with anachronistic, uni-dimensional and rigid urban models conceived before World War II rather than search out new models that respond to the complex social and environmental exigencies of 21st century urbanization.

There are, of course, exceptions. The socially-led planning initiatives of Medellín and Bogotá in Colombia that integrate transport with community facilities like libraries and schools have transformed the dynamics of deprived inner-city neighbourhoods without resorting to tabula rasa solutions. The progressive policies of Copenhagen, Stockholm, Amsterdam, Berlin and Barcelona have made these cities more attractive to young urban dwellers, contributing to local economic growth while reducing their environmental footprint. And the centrally controlled city-states of Hong Kong and Singapore have introduced radical transport and housing programmes that have contained sprawl and optimized the efficiency of their urban footprints, boosting competitiveness and standards of living.[10]

Embracing incompleteness

The reflections offered in this paper are based largely on the analysis of projects, developments and initiatives in over twenty cities that have been the subject of research and direct involvement over the past decade.[11] Even a cursory review of the evidence suggests that formal planning processes and ready-made solutions (inspired by the Charter of Athens) have uniquely failed to capitalize on the potential of cities to improve quality of life and living standards. While international agencies like UN-Habitat rightly focus on 'urbanization as a transformative force',[12] UN-Habitat's most recent report underscores the fact that urban inequality and segregation are again on the rise, that density has dropped substantially and that urban sprawl had grown exponentially in cities across the world. Apart from failures in governance and investment regimes, it seems there is an inability on the part of the design and planning professions to cope with the type of radical and rapid urban change that define the precarious living, economic and environmental conditions of a large proportion of city dwellers.

The blunt planning instruments inherited from the Charter of Athens are rigid and formulaic. They fail to recognise time, uncertainty and complexity as instrumental components of urban churn. Yet some strands of current urban design practice and academia reflect a more nuanced understanding of processes of urban 'accretion and rupture' that define how cities are changing spatially. The renewed interest in incompleteness, retrofitting and complex growth indicates a desire for new urban models that do more than satisfy the short-term needs of the market and weak metropolitan governments more concerned with mayoral election cycles than long-term sustainability of their communities. They are engaged with understanding the complex interactions between spatial and social form in urban systems that eschew classification and over-simplification.[13]

It is in these environments, concentrated especially in Africa and parts of Asia, that the pace and scale of urbanization is most acute. According to UN-Habitat a third of the global urban population lives in 'slum-like conditions', and the slum challenge continues to be one of the faces of poverty in cities in developing countries. The proportion of slum dwellers in urban areas across all developing regions has reduced since 1990, but the numbers have increased gradually.[14] In both Mexico City and Mumbai, for example, the same number of people who today live in New York City, London and Paris and Berlin combined live and operate in informal and unplanned environments, without access to basic services or infrastructure. While the Charter of Athens literally dismissed the slum as unworthy of attention (except to replace them with open spaces), contemporary scholars and policymakers recognise their intrinsic value as repositories of human capital and ingenuity but argue as whether such negative terms as 'slums', 'favelas' or 'barrios' should be used at all to describe these informal settlements which – to a lesser or greater degree – concentrate poverty in physically deprived conditions.

In *Planet of Slums,* Mike Davis[15] is forthright in his accusation of what he considers an unacceptable human condition, while Doug Saunders[16] in *Arrival City* rejects the term 'slum' and its connotations of abjection, hopelessness and stagnation. As Ash Amin notes, Saunders finds 'even in these grimy and ill-serviced clearances a teeming populace with the rural skills and drive to get on and up: enduring adversity, mobilising entrepreneurship, working with others to form businesses, find work, make savings, build better homes, improve the fortunes of their children, send remittances home'.[17]

In *Shadow City,* Robert Neuwirth[18] rejects the term slum for its denigrating connotations, arguing that the residents of Rocinha in Rio, Sanjay Gandhi Nagar in Mumbai, and the gecekondular of Istanbul have over the years improved their neighbourhoods by investing in local environments and developing forms of 'associational life' that make the most of human potential. AbdouMaliq Simone's recent work on the dynamics of 'feral urbanism' in African and Asian cities vividly identifies practices of survival, collaboration and mutual support amongst the most precarious sectors of society.[19]

These accounts bring into sharp focus the apparent paradox of codependency between the formal economy and informal development in many global cities where homogeneous concentrations of 'placeless' capital often sit cheek-by-jowl with the vibrancy of informal neighbourhoods, providing cheap labour close to centres of power and production.[20] The social and political complexities raised

by such volatile associations partly explains the inability of the planning professions to come up with credible solutions of how to deal with these informal repositories of human capability and their juxtaposition to the formal city. As Rahul Mehrota has powerfully argued,[21] the temporal dimension is critical to understanding the dynamics of everyday social life in many cities of the developing world. For example, the multiple and temporary uses of public spaces in Mumbai—for cricket games, weddings, festivals—requires a far more open and non-deterministic environment than one which is specifically tied to a single functional use—the fundamental precept of the Charter's espousal of the 'functional city'.

The tabula rasa ('blank slate') approach to planning is predicated on the notion that problematic, unhealthy neighbourhoods should be demolished to make space for new development. This was not only espoused by the authors of the Charter of Athens but is often the preferred model of 'progressive' city leaders of the global South.[22] As Deyan Sudjic has noted, 'politicians love cranes[23] just as much today as in 1970s when Jane Jacobs fought her rear-guard action to protect New York from Robert Moses' demolition plans. Rebuilding anew is one of the enduring principles of the Charter of Athens informed by the desire to cleanse and heal 'sick' urban communities. Its physical manifestation appeals to landowners and investors who prefer the uncomplicated nature of zoning, land-use and density regulations, and the certainty that comes with 'big planning'. The spaces it produces are easier to regulate, but they also 'manage out' any possibility for the unpredictable and unexpected.

It is in these spaces that the interests of local politics and private capital often align; especially in contexts where corruption and favouritism are rife. The complex and messy process of 'urban retrofitting' of spaces and communities is far more difficult to implement than wholescale regeneration or building on greenfield sites. It requires an understanding of local conditions and subtle negotiation

with potentially problematic actors who—where democratic process allow—intercede and delay the complex process of construction and reconstruction. As Anaya Roy and Saskia Sassen have argued,[24] there is a complicit interaction between adopted typologies of urban form and the dynamics of local politics and erosion of democratic processes.

One of the critical aspects of contemporary urbanization that did not preoccupy the authors of the Charter of Athens is the stark difference in patterns of distribution of inequality. Today, 75% of the world's cities have higher levels of income inequalities than two decades ago.[25] All cities display some level of inequality. Some are more pronounced than others, depending on their national and regional contexts, and the level of economic development and informalization. What we are observing today, especially in cities of the developing world, is that social inequality is becoming increasingly segregated and spatialized.

In her observations on inequality in São Paulo, Teresa Caldeira has described a dual process of confrontation and separation of social extremes. The former is captured by the powerful image of the water-deprived favela of Paraisópolis in São Paulo overlooked by the expensive residential towers of Morumbi with swimming pools on each balcony. The latter Caldeira defines as a form of urbanization that 'contrasts a rich and well-equipped centre with a poor and precarious periphery. The city is made not only of opposed social and spatial worlds but also of clear distances between them. Since these imaginaries are contradictory—one pointing to the obscene neighbouring of poverty and wealth and another to a great distance between them—can both represent the city?'[26]

These imaginaries translate into distinct urban realities. Designers, developers, investors and policymakers are faced with increasingly tough choices as to how to intervene within changing urban physical and social landscapes. How do you maintain the DNA of the city when it undergoes profound transformations? Who is the city for? How do you reconcile public and private interests? Who pays and who gains? The city planners of London, Paris, Barcelona, Hamburg and New York are grappling with the same questions as the urban leaders of African, Latin American and Asian cities, even though the levels of deprivation and requirements for social infrastructure are of a different order of magnitude. Yet, the design and planning solutions—often imported via international professional offices and consultants—offer remarkably similar solutions whose roots can be traced back to mid-20th century.

Many metropolitan areas in fast-growing economies are undergoing rapid, violent change. Mumbai's attempts to redevelop Dharavi, India's largest slum located on valuable land near the centre, with large commercial and housing blocks replacing the fine urban grain of one of the city's most sustainable communities, raises the spectre of 1960s 'slum clearance' programmes that devastated the social life and urban structure of so many European and American cities. In Dharavi, as elsewhere, the proposed design solutions to replace slums are 'pure' Charter of Athens in their generic form and impact.

This is what Ash Amin has aptly described as 'telescopic urbanism', a form of intervention that relies on top-down and rapid implementation of buildings and spaces which have little to do with the scale, texture and fabric of existing neighbourhoods and communities but fit neatly into ownership patterns and political boundaries. Superblocks and ground-scrapers that turn their backs on streets and alleyways; housing, commercial or leisure enclaves disconnected from their contexts are the hallmarks of this new urbanism founded on old modernist principles enshrined in the Charter of Athens. Keller Easterling's astute observations on the collusion between emerging typologies of the 'free-zone' and the vested interests of global corporations and nation states adds a fresh perspective on the negative social impact on these new forms

of urban development.[27]

Urban life from above

While scholars, planners and architects continue to debate the connections between democracy and urban form, most would agree that time and appropriation are critical to the creation of a sense of collective identity.[28] We know how difficult it is to create an 'instant city', with the overlaying complexities of urban life that Richard Sennett so accurately defines in his defence of the 'open' city and critique of 'brittle' urbanism that is resistant to social and temporal change and exemplified by realities of New York's Battery Park City, London's Canary Wharf or Paris' La Defense.

This phenomenon is not new, nor is it exclusive to the modern age. Many ideal towns built throughout the ages suffer from the same blandness and one-dimensionality. Filarete's unbuilt concept of the star-shaped city of Sfozinda—the very first ideal city imagined for the ruling Sforza family in 15th century Milan—and Scamozzi's geometrically charged defence machine of Palmanova display an imposed order designed to keep in check the messiness of the medieval city. Several centuries later Ledoux developed 'the' ideal model of working town for the Royal Saltworks at Les Salines de Chaux: a perfect closed urban system, incapable of modification or tinkering, not to mention tolerance of workers' unrest.

Le Corbusier and other modernist architects adopted equally definitive models to restructure European cities in the early 20th century. Common spatial characteristics which found their way into the Charter of Athens included crisp three-dimensional drawings (usually axonometrics) of institutional, residential or business districts, neatly separated by multi-level traffic systems and open space corridors. The first opportunity to realise the modernist urban project came with Lucio Costa and Oscar Niemeyer's new capital of Brasilia. Designed in 1956 as a symbol of the new independent state of Brazil, the city became the standard

bearer of functionalist planning principles. Despite its many architectural merits, as an urban system it is suspended in aspic, unable to respond to the messy requirements of the everyday and the contingent, where urban life has grown organically beyond the city's edges.

Yet, other less formal but nonetheless 'planned' ordering systems seem to have stood the test of time, adapting to economic and political cycles in ways that have enriched the urban grain, creating greater density and complexity in the everyday urban experience. A quick look at any page of the A-Z map of London, for example, speaks of the accumulated narrative of time and space at the local and metropolitan level. There is something about the configuration of streets and spaces, the distorted urban grid criss-crossed by meandering, linear yellow high-streets, the large green or white gaps carved out by Royal Parks or redundant railway goods yards that signify 'Londoness'. You could never mistake them as being part of New York City or Hong Kong, Dubai or Mumbai. The iconography of the map reveals the layering of time and negotiation that marks a broadly organic process of urban change, reflecting London's resistance to centralized planning.

In a similar fashion, the Nolli plan of Rome, drawn in 1748, captures the porosity and permeability of a historically multi-layered city, where the interiors of public buildings (churches, palazzi, monuments) and the public spaces of the streets, alleyways and squares intersect to create a seamless, open and accessible system. This quintessential 'figure-ground' map[29] describes the democratic spatial DNA of city whose form has accumulated over time (under everything but democratic regimes).

New York and Barcelona provide other models of urban resilience. The 200-year old Manhattan grid,[30] a brutally honest piece of real estate subdivision carved out of earth and rock, has served the city well as New York grew from a small trading post to major port and manufacturing hub, and then on to become one of the world's top financial centres (with a few crises in between). The monumental, relentless pattern of streets arranged around 264 feet by 900 feet (80 m × 270 m) urban blocks conceived by the Commissioners' Plan of 1811 has supported everything from corporate headquarters, department stores and mansion blocks, to warehouses, industrial buildings and sweatshops. While Henry James condemned it a century ago as a 'primal topographic curse'[31] it is Rem Koolhaas' view that its two-dimensional form created 'undreamed-of freedom for three-dimensional anarchy'[32] that has proven to be correct.

The city of New York has densified, rethought its zoning, adapted to economic restructuring, become more mixed in parts, more homogenous in others. Warehouses have turned into lofts, factories into workplaces, railways have become walkways—but the grid has remained constant. The combination of building typologies and continuous porosity has allowed (not caused) the city to adapt to extremes of economic and social transition, establishing an endemic connection to the democratic process of change in North American culture and society over the last two hundred years, a lesson that seems not to have been learnt by the current generation of 'city fathers' of expanding city regions.

Building on the New York experience, the 19th century Catalan engineer Ildefons Cerdà not only bequeathed the term 'urbanism' but also created a spatial infrastructure of urban expansion which saw Barcelona through a period of extreme growth, violent repression by a fascist dictatorship and political rebirth after the death of General Franco in 1975. Inspired by concepts of public health, in 1859 Cerdà organised the plan of the extension of Barcelona (Eixample) around a grid of streets with chamfered corners that provided gas, sewers and public transport to the new city residents, cutting across the vested interest of landlords and property owners. While the Cerdà grid has been revised, modified and compromised—with land speculation leading to the infill of spacious internal courtyards

of housing blocks—it remains a robust armature for adaptation and change. Pasqual Maragall, Narcís Serra and Joan Clos, the socialist mayors who lead the city out its dark period of Francist repression, continually referred to the democratic role of the Eixample in underpinning both the city's capacity to resist and to come back. Like Manhattan, the openness of its street plan, the intensity of its street life and the resilience of its built forms and high connectivity have allowed the city to reinvent itself many times over.[33]

Overly dense inner city districts were opened up in the 1980s with small parks and squares providing identity and sense of place to the new and old residents; the 1992 Olympics kick-started a reconnection between the city and the sea, a late 20th century extension of Cerdà's original plan; and the derelict industrial area of Poble Nou is still today being transformed, rendered more dense and complex, with new buildings and facilities that broadly follow the original city plan. No need for new towns or smart cities here, just careful retrofitting and extension of an adaptable urban DNA.

Both New York and Barcelona reveal, in their own macro geometric order, a degree of resilience: an urban form that has adapted to the process of gradual accretion and democratic change without the need for 'telescopic urbanism' or brutal application of the Charter of Athens. In effect these cities have been retrofitted over time. While Robert Moses tried his best to plough new roads and freeways for the city's urban districts, the Manhattan Grid remains largely intact, just as Barcelona has been able to continually reinvent itself without losing sight of its own metropolitan identity. In a less demonstrative way, London has gone about its business of metabolic adaptation following an organic, un-planned path for the last centuries providing another model of resilient urban design.

Ever since the faithful reconstruction of the City of London (the original urban money machine) after the Great Fire of 1666—cel-

ebrating its 350th anniversary in 2016—the British capital has never had a formal order imposed upon it by kings, queens, commissioners or engineers. Despite growing from one to ten million in the space of a century (from the early 19th century to early 20th century), the Royal Parks and the River Thames continue to define the mental map of the world's first megacity, far more so than its confusing array of linear high-streets, landscaped squares and suburban terraces. Only Patrick Abercrombie's Green Belt of 1944, which has successfully constrained growth, can be said to have substantially determined London's urban form and distribution. Yet, behind this organic 'dis-order' lies a spatial structure, captured in the specificity of the A-Z map, of immense resilience that bends and bows in response to a very British cocktail of market pressures, collective ambition and sense of justice. Referring to the 18th century English urban tradition, the architectural historian John Summerson described this Anglo-Saxon compromise as 'quintessentially pragmatic … a coincidence of intent and circumstance,'[34] a sentiment, which to my mind, defines the socio-spatial dynamics 21st century London as much as it did two centuries ago.

A period of economic structuring, a change in political priorities, the effects of migration and global competiveness have all resulted in shifts and alterations but the core urban structure has remained intact. As Suzi Hall has noted, these urban structuring devices constitute a form of 'democracy in built dimensions, a common literacy which provides clarity without prescription, allowing enrolment through interpretation which absorbs epochal shifts and ultimately both recognize and absorb the small endeavour.'[35] It is through this smaller-scale urban lens that cities are showing signs of vibrancy and resilience, to which I now turn.

Urban life on the ground

On the ground, other dynamics seem to be at work. At the micro scale of the back-streets of Istanbul, São Paulo or Mumbai there is evidence of creative ingenuity which both fosters identity and promotes a form of inclusion amongst the most excluded. In effect, there is a negative correlation between the human potential to innovate (and survive) and the level of infrastructure provided by national and metropolitan governments or international agencies. It is this emerging architecture of contingency rather than representation, which I suggest, has a greater impact on the average Paulistano, Capetonian or Mumbaikar than any metropolitan urban policy or government plan will ever do.

Despite Cape Town being a relatively wealthy city, its black population still lives in largely segregated ghettoes in sub-standard conditions, many crammed together in flat, relentless expanse of tin shacks with low-quality and insecure public and shared transport, no easy access to jobs, primitive plumbing and sanitary facilities. As Edgar Pieterse has put it 'Cape Town is a highly differentiated and malleable city, always filled with almost endless promise, but also continuously undermined by a variety of constraints and pressures.'[36] As part of an award process to identify outstanding urban projects,[37] the selection panel was exposed to over 200 projects that built on the notion that improvement in the quality and experience of place is the gateway to urban opportunities and improved liveability in a city. Several projects simply occupied abandoned public land and transformed it into productive allotments in a city region where food security is a major concern. Others, like the 'Mothers Unite' initiative,[38] addressed the need to protect and feed the youngest and most vulnerable members of the community by creating an elegant encampment of second-hand shipping containers that created a safe haven and space of dignity for pre-school children and internal spaces for reading, learning, cooking and resting. The power of such a project is the galvanizing impact on local people who see that spatial action can and does pay dividends, a process that can be replicated across this—and other—cities where public institutions fail to provide a basic human service.

The most outstanding project, though, was the judiciously named Violence Prevention through Urban Upgrading (VPUU),[39] whose title says exactly what's in the tin. This is one of the most impressive 'urban acupuncture' projects I have seen anywhere in the world. Based in Cape Town's 'former' township of Khayelitsha, the project involves some strong and confident architectural interventions—well-designed, modern multi-storey beacon community buildings that stand out in a flat single-storey sprawling landscape, clear pedestrian routes that link the main residential areas to immensely popular rail stations, as well as play areas overlooked by homes and public buildings where children enjoy the outdoors unsupervised (a rarity in this violent neighbourhood). Together these interventions create a composite urban whole that literally transforms the sense of identity and well-being of the entire community, proving that careful attention to the quality of public spaces and mobility corridors, especially in the harshest environments, can dramatically change the experience and horizons of a neighbourhood. Most importantly, in the context of this paper, it is an initiative which both captures the 'cityness' of Khayelitsha by building on its spatial DNA and recognising that its success will be determined by its adaptation over time. A model example, in many ways, of a process of intervention through accretion rather than rupture that allows its constituents to forge new identities around the public spaces and institutions of the project. In the same settlement, the architect Joe Noero has experimented with a modular structure which provides a solid roof to self-build housing units that can be extended upwards and outwards in response to individual family's financial circumstances.[40]

Across the Indian Ocean in Mumbai, a different set of interventions have resulted in similar results. Here the winner of a previous version of the award went to a simple but significant project for a community toilet in one of the city's poorest slums. As Suketu Mehta, author of The Maximum City[41] and one of the panel judges notes '[I]t became a pretty disgusting place,

as you might imagine. Because it was everybody's property, it was nobody's … the local residents came up with a solution: they put a couple of rooms on top of the building housing the toilet, and made it into an educational centre. They planted flowers around the toilet. The community centre offered simple English and computer classes, and became a social centre for the neighbourhood. To get to the community centre, you had to pass the toilet, and so people started taking responsibility for the cleanliness of it; nobody wants to study computers on top of a filthy place. Now the structure was no longer just a toilet, to be resorted to only when your need was urgent.'[42] This simple architectural intervention—two rooms and an open space with flower beds—has become 'the' social focus for the community, a place of identity that allows children and mothers to connect and make something out of their lives. Similar stories emerge from the favelas of São Paulo or the barrios of Mexico City. As Suketu Mehta reminds us, the poorest Mumbaikars (or any of the residents of these global cities) see their city as a 'bird of gold', a place of fortune, where you can change your destiny and fly.

Hybrid urbanism: the London Olympics

While East London is not referred to by its residents in such romantic terms, the opportunities afforded to many of its residents may have been lifted by the government-led $15bn investment which funded the 2012 Olympic Games and its legacy ambitions. Building on its 'Londoness' rather than opting for some novel telescopic intervention or Charter-like typology, the Olympics planning approach is a thinly concealed attempt at curing one of the city's most enduring spatial inequalities: the deep imbalance between London's relatively wealthy western half and more deprived eastern fringes where the Games have been located. Few cities could have attempted such an ambitious social operation on the back of a sports event, and I would argue that the city's inherent spatial flexibility has played an important role in developing the relatively delicate intervention that may—over a long period of time of perhaps 20 or 30 years—lead to a more durable impact on its urban metabolism.[43] In this respect it is a hybrid example of urban innovation, where equal attention has been given to the overall spatial framework and its potential to adapt and absorb change at the smaller scale over time.

Despite the quantum of public money and the benefit of its unchangeable deadline, the Olympic project does not stand alone in its desire to re-balance London. It has simply accelerated the process by about half a century. Ever since the 1970s, government-led initiatives have been aimed at regenerating the Thames Gateway (located in East London), including the spatially isolated but economically successful Canary Wharf office complex (which has added 100,000 new jobs to London since the mid-1980s). The Olympics is part of this complex urban jigsaw, where private interests and public investment continue to piggy-back on each other, trying to bring new jobs, housing and infrastructure to a large swathe of the city that has suffered from chronic under-investment. But the outcomes of recent regeneration projects in East London has not been positive, with largely piecemeal and fragmented development, ghettoized housing enclaves that benefit from expensive riverside views but turn their backs on existing communities.

The Olympics project in London has at least been conceived in a different paradigm, one which starts with the intention of leaving behind a real 'piece of city', that connects the new with the old, and which over time will bring about sustained levels of social improvement to existing and new communities. It is an experiment of big planning that recognizes the need to adapt and change. While it is of course too soon to tell whether the results meet these ambitious targets (the Olympic Park and first housing units have only been occupied since 2014), the planning methodology embraced by the public authorities is founded on a far more open, less brittle urban design framework than similar projects of a similar

scale and urgency.[44]

Centred around Stratford, a typical down-at-heel yet versatile town centre with exceptional public transport connections, the wider Olympic area in the Lower Lea Valley encapsulates London's spatial DNA. Rows of neat terraced houses inhabited by diverse ethnic communities sit next to 1970s social housing blocks and run-down shopping streets with discount stores and fast-food outlets. A network of canals and waterways winds through a rough post-industrial landscape with redundant gas cylinders and empty railway sidings. Nearby, the streets are crowded with an increasingly cosmopolitan population made up of Asians, Africans, Caribbeans and a new influx of Eastern Europeans who mingle with traditional London-born residents. The actual site of the Olympic Park was for decades relatively isolated, occupied by what became redundant railway goods yards and a myriad of semi-industrial, storage and waste facilities including a massive white goods dump which contributed to the high pollution levels of the land.[45]

The Olympics 'urban' project is, in effect, a sophisticated grafting exercise that recognises the exigencies of time and space. Housing, office buildings and hotels have been erected where temporary facilities and sponsors' pavilions stood during the summer of 2012 but in a slow process that will take up to 30 years to complete – recognizing the limitations of the market take-up and the need to allow time to create community and identity in an area where there was none. Between 35% and 50% of all new housing built on the site will be affordable, in line with current London policy, while up to 10,000 jobs have already been created by the new Westfield Shopping centre (not an Olympics initiative) and the conversion of the International Broadcast Centre into a data and technology cluster for new businesses named Here East. University College London and other central London educational institutions are joining the Victoria & Albert Museum, the Smithsonian and a major dance centre in a new 'cultural quarter'[46]

close to the transport connections, new housing, sports facilities and schools as well as the attraction of the Queen Elizabeth II (Olympic) Park. There is evidence that job creation has increased and deprivation has decreased quite substantially in some parts of the area since 2012,[47] even though accusations of displacement and gentrification continue to fuel debates on the long-term legacy of the project.

With over 35 new bridges, footpaths and links, the urban design of the Olympic Legacy plan is a topological distortion of London's spatial structure which has at least the potential of stitching this formerly disconnected site back into the intricate web of East London. In my view, the flexible urban armature is already demonstrating resilience by allowing smaller-scale initiatives, temporary structures and local activities to inform how the overall picture will involve. It is, perhaps, an example of planning by accretion, rather than rupture, that provides a framework for growth without being overly prescriptive, building on London's Londoness just as the Manhattan grid and Cerdà's example interpreted and shaped the dynamics of change in New York and Barcelona.

It is not by chance that KCAP, the original masterplanners of the London Olympics project designed the urban diagram for the regeneration of the former docks of the mercantile city of Hamburg in Germany. In many ways it represents the antidote to Charter of Athens ideology and typology. HafenCity's dense urban structure simply extends and intensifies the grain of the older city, with buildings and landscapes of a confident contemporary nature. Work, living, leisure and learning are completely interspersed amongst the buildings—both in plan and in section. Despite being implemented by the municipal authorities, HafenCity's top-down delivery agency has succeeded in creating a normal, fine-grained urban extension to a city that has to cope with high-levels of migration and associated integration. In so doing, the project has succeeded in attracting private investment to construct housing and offices, but has secured government support for educational and cultural buildings that constitute the public grain of this new urban neighbourhood in Hamburg. The spatial and the political are interwoven in ways that can absorb change and indeterminacy.

The London Olympics and HafenCity are not alone in imagining an urban future that attempts to integrate rather than segregate. Many recent examples exist in Holland, Germany and Scandinavian countries where the urban form has been designed to create frameworks of cohesion that bring people from different backgrounds and diverse activities together. For Suketu Mehta what matters is 'not that everyone is included. It's that no-one is excluded. It's not that you'll get invited to every party on the beach. It's that somewhere on the beach, there's a party you can go to.'[48] The spatial dimension in this equation is critical. It is the loss of porosity and complexity which Richard Sennett has identified as the critical characteristic of contemporary urban malaise kickstarted by the Charter of Athens. In his words: 'I don't believe in design determinism, but I do believe that the physical environment should nurture the complexity of identity. That's an abstract way to say that we know how to make the Porous City; the time has come to make it.'[49]

Conclusion

The distance between the intimacy of the Mumbai communal toilet or the violence prevention plans in the township of Khayelitsha and the mega-scale of the London Olympics or Hamburg's HafenCity could not be greater. Yet, they are witnesses to the fine-grained process of urban churn that is at work in these large global cities. This paper has argued that both small-scale interventions and metropolitan order play their part in structuring social cohesion and engendering a sense of urban democracy. They provide opportunities for people in cities to make the most of their circumstances, either by making small improvements that punch well above their weight in terms of quality of collective life or through flexible and resilient open spatial networks—urban retrofitting

—that optimize democratic potential of their urban residents.

Both forms of urban intervention afford a degree of adaptability that is intrinsic to the process of societal change. They understand the importance of incompleteness and recognize the role of time in making cities feel urban. Neither were envisaged nor encouraged by the rigid spatial instruments promoted by the Charter of Athens over 80 years ago. The lessons from small-scale acupuncture projects are that they have the potential to foster—rather than negate—capacity building and social cohesion. The lessons from flexible large-scale metropolitan plans are that a malleable urban framework lends itself to a process of gradual adaptation and accretion, which allows change without causing rupture of our fragile spatial and social urban fabric.

80 years on from the certainties of the Charter of Athens, it is the role of urban planning and design professions to reframe the contemporary debate about cities, accepting indeterminacy and embracing incompleteness. It is the responsibility of agencies like UN-Habitat to firmly place the options for national and metropolitan governments on the table, challenging the design and planning professions, landowners and investors to rethink the ways our cities are shaped. One of the key legacies of Habitat III should be to mark a paradigm shift away from the rigidity of the technocratic, generic modernist model we have inherited from the Charter of Athens towards a more open, malleable and incremental urbanism that recognizes the role of design and space in making cities more equitable.

1 After its fourth meeting held in Athens in July 1933, the leading figures of CIAM (Congress Internationaux d'Architecture Moderne) boarded the SS Patris to cruise the Mediterranean and draft a set of design principles for the functional city. The original document, known as 'the Charter of Athens' which included Observations and Resolutions was redrafted by Le Corbusier and published in different versions after World War II. References in this paper are from: The Congress Internationaux d'Architecture Moderne (CIAM), (1933) La Charte d'Athenes or The Athens Charter, Trans J. Tyrwhitt. Paris, France: The Library of the Graduate School of Design, Harvard University (1946)

2 Van Es, E. Harbusch, B. et al (eds), Atlas of the Functional City: CIAM 4 and Comparative Urban Analysis, THOTH Publishers, gta

3 CIAM, op cit (1933) Ref 35: 'All residential areas should be provided with sufficient open space to meet reasonable needs for recreation and active sports for children, adolescents and adults. Ref 36: Unsanitary slums should be demolished and replaced by open space. This would ameliorate the surrounding areas. Ref 62: Pedestrian routes and automobile routes should follow separate paths. Ref 76: The four keys to urban planning are the four functions of the city: dwelling, work, recreation (use of leisure time), transportation.'

4 CIAM, op cit (1933) Ref 73. 'Although cities are constantly changing, their development proceeds without order or control and with no attempt to apply contemporary town planning principles, such as have been specified in professionally qualified circles'.

5 Le Corbusier, 'Il faut tuer la "rue-corridor"…' (1930)

6 CIAM, op cit (1933) Recommendations 29, 61 and 63

7 Sennett, R. 'The Open City', in (eds) Burdett, R, and Sudjic, S. 'The Endless City', London (2008) and Sassen, S. "Cityness in the Urban Age," Urban Age Bulletin 2 (Autumn 2005)

8 CIAM, op cit (1933) Ref 83. 'The city should be able to grow harmoniously as a functioning urban unity in all its different parts, by means of preordained open spaces and connecting links, but a state of equilibrium should exist at every stage of its development'.

9 Koolhaas, R., 'Whatever Happened to Urbanism?', in Koolhaas, R. and Mau, B., S, M, X, XL, Monacelli Press, (1994); Angotti, T., The New Century of the Metropolis: Urban Enclaves and Orientalism, Routledge (2012)

10 There is extensive literature on the successful urban retrofitting and improvement programmes in these and other cities: see, for example, Dávila, J D (ed) Urban Mobility and Poverty: Lessons from Medellín and Soacha, Colombia, Development Planning Unit, UCL and Universidad Nacional de Colombia (2013); Rieniets, T. et al (eds) The City as Resource: Texts and Projects 2005-

2014, Berlin: Jovis Verlag (2014); Flaoter, G. Rode, P. and Zenghelis, D. Copenhagen: Green Economy Leader Report, LSE Cities (2014)

11 Much of the research has been carried out at LSE Cities, an international centre based at the London School of Economics, and through the Urban Age programme, both directed by the author and Philipp Rode (see www.lsecities.net). Findings of the research are summarised in Burdett, R. and Sudjic, D. (eds) The Endless City, London, Phaidon (2008) and Burdett, R. and Sudjic, D. (eds) Living in the Endless City, London, Phaidon (2011)

12 State of the World's Cities, Urbanization and Development: Emerging Futures, United Nations Human Settlements Programme, Nairobi, Chapter 2 (2016)

13 For example, the 10th International Architecture Exhibition of La Biennale di Venezia, Cities, Architecture and Society, directed by the author in 2006 focussed on the social consequences of rapid urbanization and the 15th International Architecture Exhibition of La Biennale di Venezia of 2016, Reporting from the Front, directed by Alejandro Aravena highlights the importance of incomplete urban and architectural systems; see also: Aravena, A. Elemental: Incremental Housing and Participatory Design Manual, Hatje Cantz, Berlin (2016); Mehrotra, R. and Vera, F. Ephemeral Urbanism: cities in constant flux, Arc-en-Reve, Bordeaux (2016); Christiaanse, K. and Baum, M. City as Loft: Adaptive Reuse as a Resource for Sustainable Urban Development, gta Verlag Zurich (2012); Sassen, S. Who Owns the City?, Guardian Cities (November, 2015)

14 State of the World's Cities, Urbanization and Development: Emerging Futures, United Nations Human Settlements Programme, Nairobi, chapter 1 (2016)

15 Davis, M. Planet of Slums: Urban Involution and the Informal Working Class London: Verso (2006)

16 Saunders, D. Arrival City, Pantheon Books, New York (2010)

17 Amin, A. 'Telescopic Urbanism and the Poor', City, Volume 17, Issue 4 (2013)

18 Neuwirth, R. Shadow Cities, Routledge, New York (2005)

19 Simone, A. Jakarta, Drawing the City Near, University of Minnesota Press (2014)

20 Sassen, S., The Global City: New York, London, Tokyo Princeton University Press (2001)

21 Mehrota, R. 'Negotiating Static and Kinetic Cities', in Hussyen, A. (ed) Other Cities, Other Worlds, Duke University Press (2008)

22 The new 'Mumbai 2020 Urban Vision' developed by McKinsey and Company and commissioned by the municipal authorities of Maharashtra, for example, suggests that all slums will be replaced by affordable social housing by 2020 (ref)

23 Sudjic, D, The Edifice Complex: How the Rich and Powerful and Their Architects Shape the World, Penguin, London (2007)

24 Roy, A. The Land in Question, Urban Age (2014); Sassen, S., Who Owns the City?, Guardian Cities (November 2015)

25 State of the World's Cities, Urbanization and Development: Emerging Futures, United Nations Human Settlements Programme, Nairobi (2016), The Widening Urban Divide, Chapter 4

26 Caldeira, T. 'Worlds Set Apart', LSE Cities (December 2008): https://lsecities.net/media/objects/articles/worlds-set-apart/en-gb/

27 Easterling, K. Designing Infrastructure, in Burdett, R., Hall, S., (eds) Handbook of Urban Sociology, SAGE, London, (2017, forthcoming)

28 Virilio, P. Open Sky, London: Verso (2000); Wacjman, J. 'Life in the fast lane? Towards a sociology of technology and time', The British Journal of Sociology, Volume 59, issue 1, pp 59-77, (March 2008); Hall, S. City, Street and Citizen: The measure of the ordinary, London: Routledge (2012); Mehrotra, R. 'The Kinetic City' in Architecture in India since 1900, Mumbai: Pictor (2011)

29 Rowe, Colin; Koetter, Fred: Collage City, The MIT Press (1984)

30 Ballon, H., The Greatest Grid: The Master Plan of Manhattan, 1811-2011, Columbia University Press (2012); Kimmelmann, M., 'The Grid at 200: Lines That Shaped Manhattan', The New York Times (2 January 2012) http://www.nytimes.com/2012/01/03/arts/design/manhattan-street-grid-at-museum-of-city-of-new- york.html

31 James, H., New York Revisited, 1904, Franklin Square Press (revised edition 2008)

32 Koolhaas, R., Delirious New York: A Retroactive Manifesto of Manhattan, (first edition 1978) Monacelli Press (revised edition 1994)

33 Rowe, P., Civic Realism, The MIT Press (1999)

34 Summerson, John., Heavenly Mansions and Other Essays on Architecture, London, Cresset Press, p 103, (1949)

35 In conversation with Suzi Hall, Lecturer in Sociology and Research Fellow, LSE Cities, London School of Economics (October 2012)

36 Pieterse, E. 'The Deutsche Bank Urban Age Award Jury Statement', in Cityscapes Cape Town: African Centre for Cities (2012)

37 The Deutsche Bank Urban Age Award, see: https://www.alfred-herrhausen-gesellschaft.de/en/urban- age/urban-age-award-2014.htm. The author was a jury member from 2007 to 2014.

38 The Mothers Unite project was the winner of the 2012 Deutsche Bank Urban Age Award, see http://www.dbuaaward.net/page/Winner

39 http://www.vpuu.org/page.php?page=6#40

40 Joe Noero, http://www.noeroarchitects.com/urbanxchanger/

41 Mehta, S. The Maximum City: Bombay Lost and Found, New York: Knopf (2004)

42 Mehta, S. 'Bird of Gold', in Burdett, R. and Sudjic, D. (eds) Living in the Endless City, London: Phaidon, p106 (2011)

43 The author was Chief Adviser to the Olympic Delivery Authority (the government agency responsible for the delivery of the London 2012 Games) and an adviser to the London Legacy Development Corporation (the Mayoral body responsible for the future development of the area occupied by the summer Olympic and Paralympic Games)

44 The 2008 Beijing Olympics or the 2004 Athens Olympics have seen the construction of new facilities and infrastructures, but with little evidence of a lasting social, economic and spatial impact compared to the planning of the 1992 Barcelona Olympics and its Olympic Village which strongly influenced London's legacy-led design approach.

45 Many local commentators have criticized the top-down of the Mayor of London and the Olympic Delivery Authority in employing compulsory purchase orders (eminent domain) to relocate local businesses. See, in particular: Sinclair, I., Ghost Milk: Calling Time on the Grand Project, Penguin (2011)

46 Recently published images of the project have created some debate on the urban quality and vitality of the proposals for a new cultural district, see: Moore, R., London Olympicopolis: the design we might've had https://www.theguardian.com/artanddesign/2016/aug/21/london-olympicopolis-arts-quarter

47 https://www.gov.uk/government/uploads/system/uploads/attachment_data/file/414658/London_2012_Olympics_0315.pdf (2015)

48 http://www.theguardian.com/cities/2015/nov/30/beyond-maximum-cities-booming-party-ny-rio-mumbai

49 http://www.theguardian.com/cities/2015/nov/27/delhi-electronic-market-urbanist-dream

A CONVERSATION
RICHARD SENNETT AND JOAN CLOS

Part 1: London-Barcelona by Skype, Friday 19 August 2016

Richard Sennett:
How much do you think the problems of cities can be solved by cities themselves and how much can they be solved by nation states?

Joan Clos:
Historically the city came first, but since the emergence of the modern state, after the French Revolution, the state has taken the lead on many functions that were previously local. Cities are no longer able to do many things for themselves. Often only national legislation gives them the power to raise taxes or change their own rules and regulations. All countries are now constituted by nation states with overall legislative authority through their parliaments. The power of local authorities is now a delegated one. With the end of the tradition of city-states, a new pact is needed between the state and local government.

Richard Sennett:
There is a discussion about whether post-Brexit Europe will find a new kind of vigour of collaboration through networks of cities that will replace nation states. Do you think
that the Global South has to rely for solutions to urban problems more on the nation state than the Global North?

Joan Clos:
That is still speculative, because the legitimacy of the European Union comes from its national membership. It is difficult even for the European Parliament to establish effective policies. No state has yet given up its authority or disappeared and none of them has agreed to more than a limited degree of delegation to municipalities.

Richard Sennett:
That is what we are debating: whether one way forward for the European Union is a more political and economic union between cities, rather than integration at the national level.

Joan Clos:
But cities in Europe don't exist independently of their governments. This was the proposal of Romer: for the cities of the world to have their own independent charters.

I have thought very much about the proposal of Romer because we, in Barcelona, for many years, were asking for the recovery of the Charter of Barcelona. It was only Madrid and Barcelona that had special charters that delegated to them a small amount of capacity for tax collection and establishing the general plan and its regulations. We thought that finally someone understood how important it is for cities to have the capacity to establish their own legislation, their own rules, and their own regulations. But this has not happened. There are still only a few such examples, for example in the United States. I would say that as complex and problematic as Catalan or Scottish independence would be, for Barcelona or Glasgow to secure their own independence would be even more difficult.

Richard Sennett:
When New York City recovered from its bankruptcy it was sending so much more tax revenue to the state (the province) and the national government than it was getting back in services that

How would you like UN-Habitat to speak about cities, about getting nations to take seriously the need for urban policy?

In developing countries there is a need to strengthen the institutional capacity to act as soon as possible [...] The national government [is] the 'final actor' [that] is often in a position to [improve urbanization]...[by] strengthen[ing] the local authority and mak[ing] public local power legitimate.

National governments need to become fully aware of their responsibility for the quality of urban outcomes.

there was a whole movement for independence.

Joan Clos:
In the case of the nascent states in the South, the jealousy of central governments to retain power is still greater. They are even less prone to accept dissidence than states in the North.

Richard Sennett:
What can the role of UN-Habitat be in helping nations set urban policy?

Joan Clos:
First, national governments need to become fully aware of their responsibility for the quality of urban outcomes. In many developing countries, the central government is not fully aware of its impact on the quality of urbanization. This is particularly problematic where urbanization is taking place the fastest. It is true that some outcomes are unexpected; they arise from emerging conditions and only appear once people are living together. Nevertheless, the central government remains critical for certain outcomes such as the finan-

cial unity of the country. Remember that in the eighteenth century many cities still printed their own money. Only in the twentieth century did the United States create the Federal Reserve. It also established the security policy, the welfare policy, the energy policy and many others. Currently, the prevalent geopolitical order is based on the legitimacy of the nation state, and this demands a pragmatic and reinforced collaboration between state and city to address the emerging issues. Security, economic policy, health, education, social services are shared responsibilities between central and local governments and cannot be addressed without their mutual cooperation.

Richard Sennett:
But what would you counsel as Executive Director of UN-Habitat, working directly with cities, to a national government?

Joan Clos:
This is what is elaborated in the New Urban Agenda. To begin with, we are counselling countries to establish a national urban

policy. [There] should be a national appraisal of what is going on in urbanization. The problem is that it is very typical of national governments to be organized sectorally. Because the ministries are divided by sector, the cities are often placed in one of the sectors. In many countries, cities fall under the interior ministry; in other countries, under the development ministry, the housing ministry, or the public works ministry. Those are the four main patterns. If you ask in a central government who is in charge of a city, you'll find immediately that it falls in one of those sectoral ministries. But the problem is that city governments—and some provincial governments—are typically horizontal rather than sectoral. Of course they also organize themselves by sectors, but the mayor or the governor is supposed to deal with whatever problems arise there. Eventually there are often conflicts of competence between different levels of administration. But if there is a disaster in the morning the mayor or the governor is expected to appear even if the nature of the disaster is not a part of their typical

Fig 113: The octopus city
© UN-Habitat

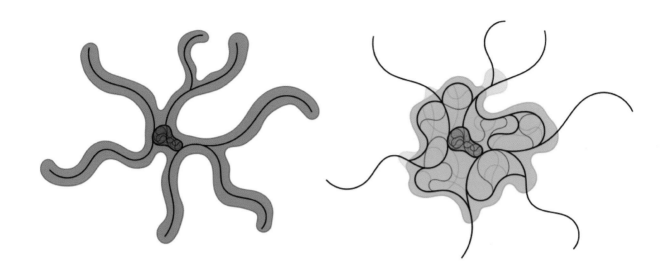

competencies.

Richard Sennett:
Back to what you want to do: how would you like UN-Habitat to speak about cities, about getting nations to take seriously the need for urban policy?

Joan Clos:
In developing countries, there is a need to strengthen the institutional capacity to act as soon as possible to improve urbanization. However, with limited capacity and resources, local authorities are not often able to address the problem adequately. But the national government, the 'final actor', is often in a position to do something about it: either to tackle the problem by itself, which is not recommended, or to strengthen the local authority and make public local power legitimate. The final outcome lies in the determination of who is in charge.

Richard Sennett:
You once described to me brilliantly the idea of the 'octopus city' when thinking about uneven development and how it works.

Joan Clos:
It is easier to build infrastructure—for example a motorway or water canal—than to urbanize effectively. Urbanizing effectively means addressing conflicts of interest—including, for example, land ownership, with a continuous and persistent methodology. In the last 30 to 40 years, countries and development banks have become more prone to financing motorways linking intermediate cities than investing in sound urbanization. They are more immediately financially rewarding. But there is also a lot of spontaneous urbanization around those transportation connections, which results in an 'octopus'-shaped spatial configuration. And the problem here is that you only create value in the immediacy of the infrastructure—the rest of the land between infrastructural lines is empty of value. In these areas there is no plotting, minimal or no public space, no street, and ultimately no urban value. This is a terrible lost opportunity. There should be no infrastructural development without a simultaneous

urban plan.

Richard Sennett:
The way I understand it, the moment there is a political side to it—the moment you say 'infrastructure first'—what you say is 'experts first.' That's what the Washington Consensus was about: development required a kind of expertise, which has to be imported from outside the city.

Joan Clos:
I would put it differently, because for me it is a question of priorities, not a question of denial that infrastructure is needed and that it can lead to improvement. But if you don't put the issue of urbanization first on the priority list you generate bad outcomes. It is not that I am against infrastructure; what I am against is doing infrastructure without attending to the urban plan. For example, the metros of Manhattan and Moscow are praised as being very efficient urban transport systems. But that is largely because they follow the lines of the streets, not the other way around. Now, even in New

153

Fig 114: Dharavi and Sion, Mumbai, India, 2007
© Bing Maps (Microsoft Product Screenshot reprinted
with permission from Microsoft Corporation)

It is easier politically to build infrastructure than to urbanize effectively

York, the expansion of the Second Avenue subway line is largely only possible because the public rights of way to do so already exist. It is a clear example of the plan preceding the infrastructure. In contrast, by putting infrastructure before a plan, the city is subjugated to the dictates of sectoral experts. The priority has been given to the infrastructure based on the belief that the infrastructure is going to deliver value. In reality, what happens is that usually the infrastructure provides much less value than urbanization. It's a mistake to put urbanization at the service of the infrastructure; it should be the other way around.

Richard Sennett:
The octopus city is also an effect of inequality. It is connecting richer rather than poorer areas, and it exacerbates poverty. What do you recommend as alternative ways to deal with urban inequality?

Joan Clos:
The welfare state has advanced in correcting and addressing the issue of poverty through national policies. The city tends to be too small of a unit to make all the transfers required to help the poor over the long term. The welfare state was first made possible because there was a pact between capital and labour to redistribute financial gains. That has been feasible at the national level, not at the city level. In cities charity has been possible, but this is a kind of self-sustaining familiar solidarity rather than a pact between capital and labour.

What do cities contribute to it? For me, urban planning induces and favours equality and solidarity. If it is well done there is enough public space for everybody, all the plots are connected to public space and you have a system that is big enough to avoid monopolistic control of the land. That is to say that cities can support welfare, but they are not ultimately responsible for it. No welfare state has been created ever by a city. In the United States now you have the problem of city bankruptcies, including that of Detroit, caused largely by the pension funds of municipal employees. In Europe, no city attempts to support its own pension fund—

solidarity is a national business, not a local one.

Richard Sennett:
Onto public space. Would you give a city the right to eminent domain?

Joan Clos:
The provision of public space is one of the fundamentals of urbanization. Unfortunately, there is a poor understanding of the value of public space in creating good urbanization. In a well-designed city, public space is around 60 or 70% of the land. 30% of street land, 20% of public spaces and parks, and between 10 or 20% of the land of public buildings like churches, hospitals, schools, museums and other public equipment. The "tradeable" bond is no more than 30 or 40% of the total. That factor is well understood in mature cities. Unfortunately, it is very difficult to sell to emerging cities.

Richard Sennett:
We need a profound change in how we think about public space. Public space is smaller, more informal, and

The city tends to be too small of a unit to make all the transfers required to help the poor over the long term.

needs a different kind of protection and generation than the way we thought about it in the twentieth century as something fixed, such as a park. I am for building little places in the streets or discrete corners for children to play. What are the techniques to create public spaces that work both in the developed and developing world? It takes a different kind of architectural understanding of public space. Public space is often much more messy, multi-use, or under-built so that people can use it in different ways at different times. What I am recommending is a post-Olmsted way of thinking about public space: public spaces somehow divorced from everydayness and protected as public. It has to be much more integrated into the dysfunctions and messiness of the city. I don't know where you stand on this. You know I'm an old anarchist.

Joan Clos:
I am in the pragmatic business of helping poor countries and cities to find political solutions that can provide results in a reasonable timespan. For me, the most import-

ant public spaces are the street and public parks. The street serves many purposes. We can go to Jane Jacobs to list all the contributions of the street to communal life. The problem is nowadays there is a generalized backward trend in the provision of street space.

Richard Sennett:
You don't think it is a question of physical design?

Joan Clos:
Yes, but it is even more important to address the fact that public space must be owned by the community—not the private sector—and governed by the local government. In fact, the local government originated out of the need to maintain public space. There was an autonomous organization of the neighbourhood to keep everything clean and tidy.

Richard Sennett:
We may disagree there. I think there are certain basic principles on how to make public space; basic prescriptions. For instance, green space never has a fence around it; it

is such a simple thing. People think this it is a trivial detail. You want to protect the plant, but not at all. If you have a public space, it is open to the public.

Joan Clos:
I agree, but when I tell them this, they respond, 'but I don't have police and I had twenty attacks during the last fortnight, so with your permission I am going to build a fence. And when I eventually find a solution to the problem of security, I will come back to your ideas.' Okay, build a fence if there is no other solution, but make it transparent. The city is a living organism that changes with time and where recipes are not of much interest. An ongoing conversation and dose of pragmatism are required. Also, a clear conviction about the fundamentals of urbanization. Populism is not a good practice if you want to build a decent city.

Coming back to the street, A well-planned city gives all plots access to the street, and this usually requires about 30% of the land area. The width of Roman streets was the

width of the chariot, two and a half to three meters; the main road was five or six meters. In Barcelona, you can move from the medieval streets of two meters or more to the streets of one thousand years later, which span five and a half meters, to the streets of the eighteenth century, which expanded to eight meters, the late eighteenth century, at 12 meters, and ultimately 20 meters with Cerdà's nineteenth-century plan.

Richard Sennett:
And you know why that is? Because he, for the first time, imagined unimpeded movement, like an artery and vein.

Joan Clos:
In Manhattan, it was also calculated as the width required to turn a chariot without having to reverse the horse. The grid of 20 meters has supported the car, which is a fantastic proof of flexibility of this public space. But now the post-Second World War street coming up after the tower in the park and Corbusier's poor interpretation has lost its proportion. It can be 60, 80,

100 or even 200 meters wide. If, in two millennia, we went from 3 to 20 meters wide, now let's go to 25. 25 is something that I can imagine working with. But I don't know how to create efficiency and equality where streets are 80 to 120 meters wide. Take Regent Street, for example, or Oxford Street, both in London—these are streets of human proportions. You can walk from one side to the other even if you are 80 years old; you don't die in the process.

Richard Sennett:
If you have a street of 20 meters wide, your peripheral vision registers as you move forward that there are sides to the street. When you have streets of 100 meters wide, it is a physiological thing. Your peripheral vision no longer registers a side. So the street loses a kind of focus, and you focus on the centre rather than on the whole. The wider the street, the less visual information people are taking in. There is a natural limit on how wide a street can be. It is the limit of the human body; it is peripheral vision. Beyond that the

amount of information that we can take in shrinks.

Joan Clos:
The new peripheral streets that we are seeing in the world should be the exception rather than the norm. As we return to a more humane urbanization, we need to recover the street so that its size is responsive to human needs.

Richard Sennett:
Saskia Sassen has contributed a paper to this discussion called 'Who owns the city?' She's demonstrated that most cities are owned by people who don't live there. It is a modern pattern of urbanization. It is true even in China. In a city like Shanghai, most of the owners are corporations and government entities that are not in Shanghai. So what are the means by which citizens can own their city? Is it a measure of regulations?

Joan Clos:
Well, clearly this can only be answered through politics. I worry when private property becomes so powerful that it doesn't allow for

Fig 117: Superblock in Barcelona, Spain

As part of the Urban Mobility Plan of Barcelona for 2013-2018, four pilot areas are testing the Superblocks (Superilles) model, which reduces the presence of cars in city centres. It is not to be confused with the term previously used to describe large city blocks lacking passage ways for cars and pedestrians. Here, nine-square city blocks have been closed to vehicular traffic, limiting speed to 10 km/h and turning curbside parking into underground parking, making the streetscape more pedestrian friendly.
© Agència d 'Ecologia Urbana de Barcelona

good organization. I am not against private property; it has served many purposes historically. The problem is that in practice, it becomes an absolute power. Sassen, in that sense, is presenting a case of unchallenged power in action. When people live in bad conditions because this issue of private property is not well addressed, there is an obligation on the part of the public power to take corrective measures. When addressing qualitative urbanization, we are always balancing the risks of public versus private property. In quite a number of national regulations, there is an absolute protection of the right to private property, and when this is the case, the quality of urbanization suffers severely. In the most modern constitutions a new practice is applied, recognizing the social responsibility of private property and allowing the development of legal tools to correct excesses.

Richard Sennett:
So your view is that in certain cases, expropriation, eminent domain— these techniques which violate the sanctity of private property—are legitimate. It's not a question of the ethics of the private realm, but of who owns it, that the public should own more. You and Saskia are on the same page. Saskia is arguing that the public should own more.

Joan Clos:
Expropriation in urban areas has a long history. We rightly criticize evictions when they are done without respect to legislation and without due process and proper compensation. The key is in the democratic quality of the institutions behind them.

Richard Sennett:
I agree. This is a key point for her, as it may be for you: the renewal of the notion of eminent domain, which is more politically acceptable than expropriation.

Fig 118: Congestion avoidance in São Paulo
© Tuca Vieira

Part 2: New York, Apartment of Richard Sennett, Thursday 22 September 2016

Richard Sennett:
I want to ask you about climate change—not so much about what it is, but about how it will particularly, in your view, affect cities.

Joan Clos:
Well, I think that we need to differentiate between two scenarios. One is the developed city, and the other is the developing city. Now, the developed city is a high emitter of CO2 and there is a profound need to review the developed city's urbanization in order to be able to provide a city that consumes less carbon—not necessarily less energy, but less carbon. I think that the big decision about the decarbonization of the economy will be made. I am optimistic. The economy could decarbonize rapidly, particularly since alternative energies can be put on the energy market relatively easily.

Richard Sennett:
This is practical.

Joan Clos:
This could be done in 10-15 years. The biggest reaction would be from the existing companies, infrastructure, utilities, et cetera, who may be afraid that the change in business model will jeopardize their investments. Nevertheless, I think that, electric mobility, for example, will come very soon to developed cities.

Richard Sennett:
Now what about for the less developed cities?

Joan Clos:
Cities in less developed countries are not yet emitting very much CO2. But they need development to improve their citizens' well-being, which probably means a large increase in energy use. They will also need to leapfrog carbon energy by using sustainable and renewable energy, for example solar, wind and geothermal. In many parts of the world, geothermal energy is highly available and relatively inexpensive. But in order to have energy for development they need infrastructure investment for sustainable energy. For example, the

grids are not there yet; there is still some kind of debate on whether the grid is necessary. I don't believe in advocating for poor societies a type of direct energy without a grid. I think that they have the right to have a powerful grid that uses renewable energy in order to have energy whenever they need it. The other question for them is as sufferers of climate change consequences. Because, of course, the problem of climate change is that most coastal cities are exposed to high risks and, on top of being exposed, they don't have the resources to react easily. They don't have the money to move the city two kilometres away from the risk areas. And that, then, is why this very important international debate is taking place: who needs to pay for the costs associated with the outcomes of the current model of the economy and its climate change-induced catastrophes?

Richard Sennett:
Henk Ovink and Jane Harrison argue that what unites rich and poor nations is the question of water, and that this will become the

159

The life of a city is cooperation,
a permanent cooperation.
It is what defines it.

kind of climate change that will put them together in a kind of crisis: in either its scarcity or abundance. As it was framed by these experts, it is a crisis of the commons. How do you get a kind of urban commons that deals with issues of climate?

Joan Clos:
Well, I think we must accept that in the city, to have a decent life, we require a lot of [public space]. The public land ends up being something between 60 and 70% of the total land of the city. This is very counterintuitive to the [thought] that the market is governing urbanization. What governs the quality of good urban life is the provision of public land.

And in that sense also...common services, because we know that common services such as the grid, ...water system, electricity, or even...telecommunications—all-these urban services are better served when they are managed in a manner that provides service to everyone at a very affordable price. In that sense, the life of a city is cooperation, a permanent coopera-

tion. It is what defines it. We are in a very artificial environment based on a lot of cooperation and a lot of common goods, because otherwise it is impossible. Because almost everything, even the productivity of the city, is based on the quantity of interrelations and information, on the flux of information between us.

Richard Sennett:
This takes us back to something you and I are preoccupied with, which is: at the level of government, can a city deal with a problem like water or scarcities of water? Don't we hop again from the urban to a non-urban level of governmentality and control? To actually deal with climate change in a city is a challenge. Can the city work as a kind of unit for political action?

Joan Clos:
Well, the city has a lot to do and to talk about. First, on the water issue: water is extremely related to energy, because if you have energy you can access water nearly every place in the world... We know how to manage energy and the related problem of scarcity of water. The

other—excess of water—is another question. Because the excess of water requires infrastructure, protection, and better urbanization—even to take advantage of the excess of water. But that can also be managed if you have resources, you can use hydropower to generate energy and to tame the water in order to avoid its coming into the city in an uncontrolled manner. I understand that there is a lot to be done in relation to water, but I think that water and energy are something that we are more or less on the verge of controlling. I am not pessimistic about that. I am more worried about the political arrangements of the city: its governance, how to manage inequalities, how to manage political conflict, how to manage diversity, how to manage even the animal spirits of our own condition as humans.

Richard Sennett:
[laughter] But this is quite interesting—in other words, unlike climate doomsayers, your notion is that technological problems posed by CO2 and by issues of water scarcity are ultimately not

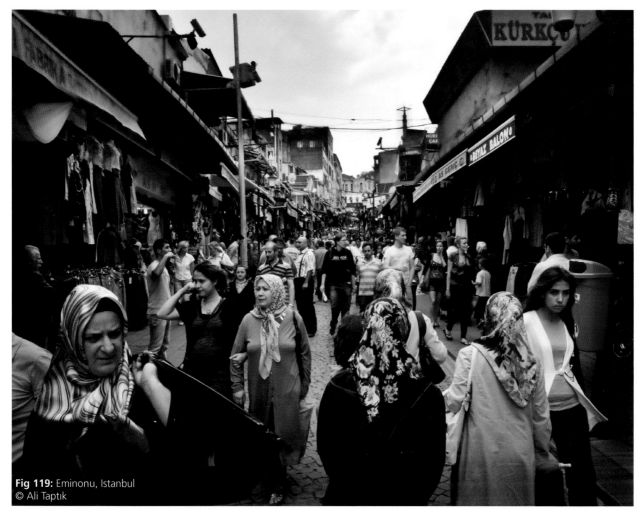

Fig 119: Eminonu, Istanbul
© Ali Taptık

technologically impossible, but the challenge is resources; political resources, economic resources.

Joan Clos:
...and to discipline the ones who make money with this agenda...

Richard Sennett:
[laughter] Yeah, yeah, of course...

Joan Clos:
...it's a very good business, and there is a lot of money generated with all these things, and I think that [it] is more difficult to fight against these powers than to deal with the thing...itself. But if we agree that we need to move speedily to a non-carbon economy, it's just a question of placing a tax on carbon and you will see that in 10 years or 15 years the creativity of society to adapt to the new financial and ecological environment. It is going to be very fast.

Richard Sennett:
It is a kind of a political melodrama that many environmentalists portray cities as doomed. It starts with Rachel Carson talking about

pollution as a problem which escapes political control.

Joan Clos:
No, what escapes political control are the big companies. Those are the ones who escape political control [laughter].

Richard Sennett:
Let me ask you in this regard the same thing about smart cities. Big companies are making lots of money selling smart city technology. How, in your view, do we bring smart city dimensions down to the everyday life of poorer people who don't have command over those kinds of resources?

Joan Clos:
The problem that I have with smart cities is that it is a very good name, trademark, but it is very generic and you can adapt the smart city concept to whatever you want to say. You cannot advocate the contrary, which is a stupid city. We all agree that the city should be smart, but when it is so generic it doesn't add a lot. It doesn't say much. When there are a lot of

people who centre the smart city on communications technology that is more specific. [But] I don't like this focus only on technology. I would say that a smart city is the one that has the right rules and regulations. Digitalization is changing human life. But this comes out of the creativity of the people in doing innovative things with the technology. It is not that the technology dictates whatever the people should do. The process is fortunately out of control in a positive manner.

Richard Sennett:
That's one side of it.

Joan Clos:
Yes, the other side is that information technology doesn't need support from the public sector. It sells very well. If you look at telecommunications companies, they are doing very well. It is not the same as public housing companies. You need to incentivize public housing. But the public sector does not need to incentivize telecommunications, other than perhaps to ensure that everybody has access. But as the business is so productive,

The question is not the technology itself but its use, its purpose. This is when politics come to the debate.

I am more worried about the political arrangements of the city: its governance, how to manage inequalities, how to manage political conflict, how to manage diversity...

that should be taken care of by the sector itself.

Richard Sennett:
I must say, I slightly disagree with you. When I think about a good smart city, I think about the example of community budgeting, not using a google map. To do that, actually the programs that are there for collective budgeting use big data sets. The traffic is less important than equity in doing budgeting. The programs for that are of very poor quality. And there is no economic incentive to make those programs. For that, you need a city to invest, but that kind of technology is not being developed.

I had another striking instance of this when I was doing a book on labour in the digitized labour force. I saw that most of the programmes were oriented towards a kind a Marxist nightmare, orienting productivity, second by second of the workforce, through these monitors. There are very few good quality programmes that allow workers in different places to cooperate together from different places, which is a form

of productivity. It implies action from the bottom up rather than control from the top down. There is no investment in that. Google tried some very primitive programs but they abandoned them afterwards. So I'm not sure that the communications industry is going to really develop smart technologies that are democratic. There is no money in it.*

Joan Clos:
Well, there is no profit out of it.

Richard Sennett:
When I do these technology studies, it makes me an old-fashioned Marxist more and more.

Joan Clos:
[laughter] In medicine, we can extrapolate the condition when [we] have a technology or a medication that works. It's good for humanity. Then there is a second derivative: you need to make sure that it will reach everybody. If you have something that works against diabetes, then that is good for humanity, like telecommunications, for instance. But then when the problem of

democracy and redistribution comes up, this good is distributed to the ones who can afford it.

Richard Sennett:
To take the medical analogy back to the city—how can we make uses of smart city technology an advantage to everybody in the city? I'm thinking of a very simple example, that of bicycles and self-driving cars. If you drive a bicycle, a simple technology with great ecological and biological benefits, what do you care about the fact that the city has spent vast quantities of money on self-driving cars?

Joan Clos:
That's a good example. You can have a lot of information technology in driverless cars and you can have a lot of technology in electrical bicycles, for example. Even at the same level of sophistication, the function of the same technology is very different if you apply it to one model of transportation or another. Then, the question is not the technology itself but its use, its purpose. This is when politics come to the debate.

Fig 121: Public space in Santa Marta, Colombia
© UN-Habitat / Alessandro Scotti

Richard Sennett:
We never escape.

Joan Clos:
And we shouldn't. It is right that we never escape.

Richard Sennett:
In your view then, it is a double issue for the smart city. How do we make it more democratic and how do we make it more egalitarian in its distribution of resources? Those are both political dimensions.

Joan Clos:
Yes, but those are always the political dimensions of any issue in the city.

Richard Sennett:
That's true. Very true.

Joan Clos:
It is like that for technology, education, health, pension systems, et cetera. The human quality of good urbanization is the ability to address this question: the democratic quality applied to every factor of the city, not just to one. Technology arrives and new technologies will

arrive. Perhaps in five years we will have a new technology that now we cannot imagine. And again, the problem of distribution of the technology will be the same problem. Then the question for me is this permanent effort to make the city a just place, a place where every innovation is not owned by a minority and denied to the rest, or used by a minority only to make more money.

Richard Sennett:
Do you—not as an intellectual, but as a politician—do you then have an image in your mind of how to make cities more democratic? Is there some kind of guiding principle that has been guiding you as a politician?

Joan Clos:
Yes, I think that the most innovative experimentations with forms of democracy are usually in cities, because in cities there are a lot of people together. Even if nobody cares about the quality of democracy, we need to deal with everyday conflicts. Without knowing, we are exploring new

forms of democracy. In the city, you always see phenomena here and there where people find their own arrangements, which can have a profound sense in terms of exploring and advancing new solutions. For example, take the new collaborative economy, which is now emerging spontaneously in many places; it has not been designed by the government. It has emerged from the fact that you have a house or a car that you don't need all the time, and it occurs to you that you can perhaps share it at a good price with others. These kinds of new things are, by the way, very motivating for young people, because they see in these kinds of inventions the possibility of a new narrative, a new epic, a new moral; ethical behaviour. I think that this comes from the extreme capacity of urbanization to genuinely create natural experiments. Some of them succeed and they continue; some of them fail, because they have mistakes. We should be very wise in listening to the noise of the street and see what is emerging, because democracy is in dire straits. Democracy needs a profound

review. Formal democracy is going through difficult days.

Richard Sennett:
We are speaking in New York City, on the eve of something that may be the end of formal democracy. The reason that the city prompts these experiments is that it shoves together the differences it contains. You don't get much experimentation in a community in which people are isolated from one another. Yet the noise comes from the conflicts of these differences colliding, sometimes agreeing, sometimes disagreeing. Some scientists think about natural experiments which are not controlled, but purposefully open-ended. Something comes out of that kind of experiment that does not come out of a hypothesis-testing experiment.

Joan Clos:
I agree totally. The emerging goods of the city, the ones that appear without design, the ones that are unexpected, are in many occasions the most interesting ones. Any design, like evolution, doesn't pursue a theological design; social interaction has this capacity to generate unpredictable outcomes. This is very interesting, because I want to believe that we are not living in a deterministic world. I want to think that we have a little bit of free will, that we have something like ethics, and we can choose a little bit. And then, the fact that some of the emerging conditions of the city at least…look indeterministic for is me is very good news. I celebrate that.

Richard Sennett:
Well, it comes back to a basic principle about the difference with The Charter of Athens and what we discuss now. The Charter of Athens was one where you had a tight fit between form and function, whereas what we are doing is something in which, by its prescription, you may get surprising results.

Joan Clos:
Yes, it can be totally surprising. I celebrate the unpredictability of the future.

Richard Sennett:
That means a different kind of city planning. Less regulation? More enablement?

Joan Clos:
Well, less regulation and more enablement, which are conducive to increasing communication between people. It shouldn't be a type of urban planning with big frontiers between neighbourhoods. I understand what you mean by the lack of prescription, but also the lack of prescription can bring you to an urbanization of motorways which divide. So, lack of prescription, yes, but it can have varying results.

Richard Sennett:
Well, a lack of controlled outcomes.

Joan Clos:
The concept that urbanization is a project for which you design the beginning and the end is wrong, because cities are living organisms and the city itself needs to digest the programme of urbanization. It is not that you provide a template. This is why, for example, when you are in Chandigarh, you have the feeling of too much prescription in a unidirectional way. Or in Abuja—

165

The concept that urbanization is a project for which you design the beginning and the end is wrong...

perhaps the intention was good but it is out of place, because communities that like to live together are separated by huge avenues.

Richard Sennett:
Right, so the model of urban planning that you subscribe to is experimental. Some experiments can involve abrasion and conflict and a kind of destruction of something that was planned at the beginning. That implies a very different kind of government than the ones we have now, which are all about defining the beginning and the end and making the throughput meaningless. You are emphasizing the throughput rather than the end result.

Joan Clos:
Yes, the process is much more interesting. Of course, you cannot accept it if in the beginning the basics are wrong, at least technically. We are at a level at which we have enough information to avoid big mistakes. The problem is...when you have, for example, conflicts between the interests of the people and the success of the market. If

you go to real estate developers in many parts of the world, you'll see now that what sells well is a form of urbanization of about 4,000 inhabitants per km^2, or 45 inhabitants per hectare. But we know that th[is] densit[y is] too low, because the cost per capita of the services is too high. We need to go at least to densities of 10,000-15,000 inhabitants per km^2, or 120-150 inhabitants per hectare.

Richard Sennett:
That's my bottom line too.

Joan Clos:
But then the market has more difficulties selling this kind of urbanization than the sprawl one. Here there is a conflict. This is why the market shouldn't be left alone in the city, because the market is not a good urban planner.

Richard Sennett:
Let's expand this, it is important. One of the reasons why the market is a bad urban planner is that sprawl is more profitable than density. What are other ways in which the market is a bad urban planner?

Joan Clos:
Well, in the provision of public space. It is very difficult for the private owner to understand that the provision of public space is fundamental, and in fact generates private value. It is counterintuitive. Only in a very few places does the market understand that. The market operates at a smaller scale. The problem is then, who designs the street that will bring you from this neighbourhood to the other neighbourhood in an efficient manner? It is not the market, because the market is unable to predict the use of these common goods. It is a limitation that is not related the good or ills of the market; it is inherent to the condition of the market.

Richard Sennett:
So there would be a third reason why the market is a bad planner: because it can calculate risks, but not long-term benefits. Is that what you mean?

Joan Clos:
Yes, this is very clear! In fact, the market works better when it

Fig 123: Aerial view of Gaborone, Botswana
© Martin H, CC BY 2.0

doesn't plan the city; when there is a real government who plans the city. In the interest of making sure that you can move from here to there, you can provide affordable services for everybody. The market, for example in New York, works very well. There are some billionaires doing business in New York. But the market has not designed the streets of New York.

Richard Sennett:
If people read this, you will become a hero to people under 30 and not so heroic to people over 30 in New York. For a certain age group in cities, neoliberalism is seen as a solution to cities' problems.

Joan Clos:
What a mistake.

Richard Sennett:
I want to talk about this thing we both care about, which is the adaptation to the city. How do people evolve in the city?

Joan Clos:
Well, the city is an artificial environment that we humans have created

in the last 10,000 years. And it seems that in this century, most of us are going to live in this artificial environment we have created. And we know now by cognitive sciences [and] neurology, that we as humans adapt to the environment. The environment changes us. I am very interested in this because I come from the medical profession. How does this environment change us? I wonder not only how we change the environment, how we create the city and how the city creates or recreates us. In terms of neuron connectivity, the exposure that a child of six months has in kindergarten with lots of kids, noise…going through the streets, the exposure to stimuli is immensely higher than in rural areas. I was born in and spent a good part of my youth in rural areas. There was not much noise, there were not many people. I am sure that people who grow up in the city are different physiologically as well. I think that is relevant, because in the city people learn social skills. You learn to share—even when you walk in the street, you do so without pushing the other. You learn to behave and deal with conflicts without fighting

on every occasion; without the need to submit to the alpha male or whomever else is in command. Of course we have created the city, but what we haven't thought enough about is how the city is recreating us.

Richard Sennett:
I couldn't agree more with you. I would put it in a slightly different way. I think that what people do in the city is they learn how to deal with complexity. The more they become skilful in dealing with complex situations, the less threatened they become by the expanded way of letting more things in, in the process of being able to feel that they can manage it. This notion of becoming, that living in the city is a skill is something we see neurologically, we see sociologically. We also see it psychologically that people who have for instance lived in very complicated environments for long periods of time, are less anxious about the difference, the appearance of a new kind of stranger in the city. You have the skill to feel like a manager that can cope. So there is the appearance of

Fig 124: Nehru Place, Delhi, India
© Muhammad Yawar

something is less anxiety-provoking.

It's based on a phenomenon, which is not my discovery but that of Leon Festinger, about what he calls the management of cognitive dissonance. He noticed when he put pigeons in very complex situations, when things were not clear and they were kept in cages for long period of time, they didn't become crazy—just the reverse. They gradually became very able pigeons, adapted. Their hormonal levels that measure anxiety sunk. They weren't happier pigeons, but they were pigeons that no longer felt this constant threat. And I have a little of that feeling when I watched the Pegida group in Germany protest against all these Muslim refugees. One group of them was asked by a clinician, 'Well, how many Muslims do you know?' 'Oh, I wouldn't live near Muslims.' That's the Festinger notion, they would've been less threatened if they were actually in this very complex situation. I think it applies more broadly across the board. It certainly applies in the United States, racially. When people grow up in multiracial neighbourhoods, *they are much calmer about other forms of difference, because they learn that skill.*

Joan Clos:

Yes, in the past we used to say that that was 'civilization.' What is true, perhaps, in this conversation, is the physical effect that urbanization has on our bodies, on our mental structure, on our brain.

Richard Sennett:

Yes I think that's new now. It was just taken for granted for instance by Simmel, when he wrote about crowds. When you're in the midst of a crowd...you're physiologically overstimulated. The whole notion is that you want to reduce the stimulation to complexity. Now we know that is broadly not true. And I think what you said is true cognitively, and it has a social knock-on effect as well. This suggests less bordered, more compact, and more mixed-in uses in the composition of cities. In other words, it argues for more disorder; that disorder can make one smart.

Joan Clos:

Yes, you learn more from disorder. The definition of the city that I like most is the definition that says that the city is the place where you find what you're not looking for. It is the serendipity, the margin condition, the creativity inherent to urbanization. Interestingly enough, the cities that other social animals build...tend to be built by instinct; something that is written in the genetic code of bees or termites, for example. In this case, all habitats are equal. You open one and you know that the next is going to be the same. But the city is totally different. Although we are social animals, we don't build our cities by instinct. We build our cities by negotiation, by political interaction; not by instinct. And the city changes us; the bee is not changed by the beehive. But we are changed by the city.

Richard Sennett:

Absolutely, it is a theoretical problem of what is called the meme. You learn how to do something, but somebody else has to learn it again. It is not a simple mimetic function; we learned that a hundred years ago, so if I follow

168

We have created the city, but what we haven't thought enough about is how the city is recreating us.

that tradition it will have the same effect. And to me, one of the puzzles about, for instance, how to make a street that evolves in two or three centuries, is whether the forms of it allow people to relearn certain kinds of social behaviours.

Jan Gehl said that you can be very specific about this: if you have a street with lots of perforations, people in time will learn to be looking to people on the side. What was made in the street, the street with many doorways, openings, people coming and going, can be relearned and relearned; whereas a street with only a few entrances doesn't allow the sense of a re-learnable form to emerge. It is a very interesting thing for a planner: what allows people to learn the same environment from generation to generation.

Joan Clos:
In a continuation of this idea, for example, in the case of Barcelona, the Roman street, which has been there for 2,000 years—you can walk across the intersection of the Cardo and Decumanus. But

the use now is very different. We reinvent the use of...form in every generation. There is a capacity for interaction with whatever form we need to deal with, except if it is out of human proportions. A street that has 200 meters of width never will be reinterpreted, because there is no human proportion; but a street of 5 or 20 or 25 meters—in three generations they are going to make use of these human-proportioned designs with their own technology; their own vision. Here the limit is a kind of human proportion.

Richard Sennett:
This is exactly what Jan Gehl believes. There are certain human skills you can use. There are certain basic urban forms which allow people to go through the process we are talking about, and we're not building those today. They can be specified. If you have streets that are too wide, you don't have a learning environment.

Joan Clos:
There should be a permanent dis-course between all of us: sociology, anthropology, history, architec-

ture… This is one of the marvels of the city. It is not a finished project. It is not a beehive.

Richard Sennett:
That is very important. It is not a beehive. Can you talk a little about how this experience of running UN-Habitat has changed your ideas about cities?

Joan Clos:
What I have learned is that urban-ization is very diverse. It happens at very different levels of development and wealth. And now, by the way, most urbanization is happening in societies of between 500 dollars per capita and 2,000 dollars per capita—very low in the process of development, and without much social capital. And the city that grows in such an environment tends to become very unequal and conflictual. In order to help, you need to go back to the basics. There is no magic solution, no silver bullet that can provide improve-ments.

I see, for example, the 'new towns' movement everywhere. People

*Can you talk a little about how this
experience of running UN-Habitat
has changed your ideas about cities?
What have you gained from running
this organization for six years?*

What I have learned is that
urbanization is very diverse.
It happens at very different levels of
development and wealth.

Fig 125: Exclusive suburban gated community in Johannesburg, South Africa, 2015
© Matthew Niederhauser and John Fitzgerald with support from the MIT Norman B. Leventhal
Centre for Advanced Urbanism

think that by designing and building a new town, they are going to be a city, a community. This is a mistake, even if it is well intended. It tends to produce monsters. You lose a lot of time, money, and legitimacy. The government that supports it loses legitimacy. This kind of mistake arises from a lack of attention, a lack of professionalism and a naive approach to urbanization. It can create dangerous things. It is not an innocent mistake.

I think that there is a need to go back to the fundamentals of urbanization. Because I think that in the twentieth century, with the arrival of the car, with the Charter of Athens, well-intended as it was, and the market control of urbanization, we have lost a little bit the fundamentals of urbanization. This is what I have learned.

I didn't pay attention when I was Mayor of Barcelona. Of course, I was mayor of a city that had the Cerdà plan from the nineteenth century and I didn't care about the efficiency of the street, about moving people from one

neighbourhood to another, as it was there for free. But you go to places and see how much money can be uselessly spent on projects that, with a little bit of insight, you can see will fail. This is what has transformed me in a bold and perhaps radical way, and made me impatient with the mistakes of urbanization. Because there is no need to make these mistakes, if we come back to the basics, such as good regulations and financial design, because urbanization costs money. You cannot do good urbanization with a little bit of financial design or physical or urban design. I think that this is the problem that I have learned. I took for granted that everybody understood urbanization when I was Mayor. Because in Barcelona, everybody talks about urbanization. This is a common conversation, about this street or the other. A single street corner can inspire a discussion that lasts for three months! But I go to other places in the world, where there is no conversation about urban design.

[U]rbanists alone cannot change

the future of humanity—urbanization is not the only factor in societal well-being, but society seems to have forgotten that urbanization is still one of the most important factors. I think that we have lost the appreciation of how, when you do it well from the beginning, urbanization is actually quite easy to do well.

Richard Sennett:

There are very complex things you can say about the environment, but in the end there are these very basic issues of equity, engagement, learning...all of them don't require universities doing super planning. They are there. I must say that one of the reasons we have made the city such a hard problem is because we delegitimize urbanites from being involved in it. In a certain sense, urbanism includes ways of delegitimizing the populus. In ancient Greek times, very few people really knew about building cities. They built wonderful cities. Romans knew more as engineers, but they were still comparably rudimentary to nowadays, and their cities worked better.

The author of the city is a little bit more diffuse. It is a collective changing over time, including different generations.

Joan Clos:
Roma had its Cloaca Maxima, and how many cities in Africa don't have the main collector for the sewage? But if it was done 2,000 years ago, one would expect humankind to understand that it is easy to do, that it can be done, and that it is not going to expose you to external debt.

Richard Sennett:
So for you, these last six years have been a return to basics?

Joan Clos:
Yes, and to value how important the basics are. The most important thing is to go back to basics in terms of urbanization—the basic principles that humanity has learned during the 7,000-8,000 years of urbanization, which are not very complex, but must be there. And it's not a recipe, but some kind of containment. It is not about losing the mind in exotic things. Because this is not useful for the majority of people. Going back to basics allows you first to reach everybody. Then, if there are some

spurs of exoticism, you can allow it. What I like about the Cerdà plan is that it provides a scenario for a lot of people, and that it doesn't contradict th[e] value of Gaudí's funny, out-of-mind, [and] in a sense useless projects. They become additions. As Mayor I was confronted with this question. How far do you allow the eccentricity of the project, which tends to become a manifestation of someone's ego—either the author, or the owner of the building—to go?

Richard Sennett:
There should be some of that but it is not a general model.

Joan Clos:
This is what has killed Potsdamer Platz. You need to find the equilibrium.

Richard Sennett:
As a teacher, I always believed something like that: that the model for making a city is not the best work of art or the best work of architecture in it. In Venice for instance, it is wonderful that we have all those wonderful churches,

but what makes the model of a city is not the Redentore. I think the principle for this, is to try and find the kinds of forms that are workable every day. We are not based on a model of a perfect object, or a wonderfully complex object. I don't think 'starchitects' are very good guides, with exception of Rem Koolhaas, to what a city should be. I don't think that the High Line here is a model for growth. I don't think Gaudí could ever be considered as a model for making a city. The art of making a city has different formal principles: in urbanism there is no avant-garde.

Joan Clos:
And it has more authors.

Richard Sennett:
Everybody is an author.

Joan Clos:
The author of the city is a little bit more diffuse. It is a collective changing over time, including different generations.

BIBLIOGRAPHY

1.1: Growing differences in population dynamics require focus- and speed-differentiated approaches to good urbanization

Background paper:

United Nations, Department of Economic and Social Affairs, Population Division. *World Population Prospects: The 2015 Revision, special tabulations.* New York: United Nations, 2015.

Sources for illustrations:

Department of Economic and Social Affairs. *Data and charts for UN Habitat Regions.* New York: United Nations, 2016.

United Nations. *World Urbanization Prospects, 2014 Revision.* New York: United Nations, 2014.

1.2: A massive loss of habitat is accelerating and driving; new flows of migration

Background paper:

Sassen, Saskia. "A massive loss of Habitat, New drivers for Migration," in *Sociology of Development*, Vol. 2, Number 2, pgs. 204-253. Oakland: The Regents of the University of California, 2016.

Other references:

Ackerman, Spencer, Tom Dart, Daniel Hernandez, and David Smith. "Immigration Activists Condemn US Deportation Asylum Seekers." The Guardian. January 4, 2016. Retrieved January 10, 2016. https://www.theguardian.com/us-news/2016/jan/04/immigration-activists-condemn-deportations-asylum-central-america.

"Adrift at Sea." 2015. Straits Times. Retrieved January 11, 2016. http://www.straitstimes.com/asia/se-asia/malaysian-pm-najib-orders-search-and-rescue-operation-for-migrants-adrift-at-sea.

AFP. "Five Police Killed by Turkish Militants in Turkey's Southeast." The Guardian. September 16, 2015. Retrieved January 13, 2016. http://www.ngrguardiannews.com/2015/09/five-police-killed-by-kurdish-militants-in-turkeys-southeast/.

AFP. "Southeast Asia Migrant Crisis." Reposted on The Citizen. Retrieved January 11, 2016. http://www.citizensrw.org/index.php/guest/newsStoryDetails/33.

Albert, Eleanor. "The Rohingya Migrant Crisis." CFR Backgrounder, Council on Foreign Relations. 2015. Retrieved January 10, 2016. http:// www.cfr.org/burmamyanmar/rohingya-migrant-crisis/p36651.

Alhamad, Karam, Vera Mironova, and Sam Whitt. "In Two Charts, This Is What Refugees Say About Why They're Leaving Syria Now." Washington Post. September 28, 2015. Retrieved January 11, 2016. https://www.washingtonpost.com/news/monkey-cage/wp/2015/09/28/in-twocharts-this-is-what-refugees-say-about-whythey-are-leaving-syria-now/.

Alund, Aleksandra, Branka Likic-Brboric, and Carl-Ulrik Schierup. "Migration, Precarization and the Democratic Deficit in Global Governance" in *International Migration* Volume 53, Issue 3, pgs. 50–63. John Wiley & Sons Ltd on behalf of International Organization for Migration, 2014.

Ambrogi, Thomas E. "Goal for 2000: Unchaining Slaves of National Debt." National Catholic Reporter. March 26, 1999. http://natcath.org/NCR_Online/archives2/1999a/032699/032699a.htm.

Amen, Mark, and Barry Gills. "Globalization and Crisis." In special issue: *Globalizations,* Volume 7, No. 1-2. 27 April, 2010.

Amin, Ash. *Land of Strangers.* Cambridge: Polity Press, May 14, 2012.

Anseeuw, Ward, Liz Alden Wily, Lorenzo Cotula, and Michael Taylor. *Land Rights and the Rush for Land: Findings of the Global Commercial Pressures on Land Research Project.* Rome: International Land Coalition, 2012.

AP. "Deportations in Mexico up 79% in First Four Months of 2015." The Guardian. June 11, 2015. Retrieved May 12, 2016. http://www.theguardian.com/world/2015/jun/11/deportations-mexico-central-america.

AP. "Despite Border Crackdown in Ethiopia, Migrants Still Risk Lives to Leave." The Guardian. August 25, 2015. Retrieved January 11, 2016. http://www.theguardian.com/global-development/2015/aug/25/despite-border-crackdown-ethiopia-migrants-risk-lives.

Archibold, Randal C. "On Southern Border, Mexico Faces Crisis of Its Own." New York Times. July 19, 2014. Retrieved May 12, 2016. http://www.nytimes.com/2014/07/20/world/americas/on-southern-border-mexico-faces-crisis-of-itsown.html?_r=3.

Arrighi, Giovanni. *The Long Twentieth Century: Money, Power, and the Origins of Our Times.* New York: Verso, 1994.

Barney, Keith, Margarita Benavides, Michael DeVito, Dominic Elson, Marina France, Alain Karsenty, Augusta Molnar, Phil Shearman, Carlos Soria, and Petro Tipula. *Large Acquisition of Rights on Forest Lands for Tropical Timber Concessions and Commercial Wood Plantations.* Rome: International Land Coalition, 2011.

Bello, Walden. *Deglobalization: Ideas for a New World Economy.* London: Zed Books, 2004.

Beneria, Lourdes, and Shelley Feldman. *Unequal Burden: Economic Crises, Persistent Poverty, and Women's Work.* Boulder: Westview Press, 1992.

Borras, Saturnino M., Jr., Jennifer C. Franco, Cristobal Kay, and Max Spoor. *Land Grabbing in Latin America and the Caribbean Viewed from Broader International Perspectives.* New York: United Nations, 2011.

Borras, Saturnino M., Jr., Ruth Hall, Ian Scoones, Ben White, and Wendy Wolford.

"Towards a Better Understanding of Global Land Grabbing: An Editorial Introduction," in *Journal of Peasant Studies*, Volume 38, No. 2, pgs: 209–16. New York: Taylor & Francis, 2011.

Borwick, Summer, Mark Brough, Robert D. Schweitzer, Jane Shakespeare-Finch, and Lyn Vromans. "Well-being of Refugees from Burma: A Salutogenic Perspective," in *International Migration*, Volume 51, No. 5, pgs: 92–105. 2013.

Bradshaw, York W., Claudia Buchmann Sershen, Laura Gash, and Rita Noonan. "Borrowing against the Future: Children and Third World Indebtedness," in *Social Forces*, Volume 71, No. 3, pgs: 629–56. 1993.

Brautigam, Deborah, and Tang Xiaoyang. *African Shenzhen: China's Special Economic Zones in Africa.* Cambridge: Cambridge University Press, 2011.

Buechler, Simone. "Deciphering the Local in a Global Neoliberal Age: Three Favelas in São Paulo, Brazil." in *Deciphering the Global: Its Scales, Spaces, and Subjects*, pgs. 95–112. Edited by Sassen, Saskia. New York: Routledge, 2007.

"Buying Farmland Abroad: Outsourcing's Third Wave." The Economist, May 21, 2009. Retrieved April 12, 2016. http://www.economist.com/node/13692889.

Byerlee, Derek, Klaus Deininger, Jonathan Lindsay, Andrew Norton, Harris Selod, and Mercedes Stickler. *Rising Global Interest in Farmland: Can It Yield Sustainable and Equitable Benefits?* Washington DC: World Bank, 2011.

Chishti, Muzaffar, and Faye Hipsman. "Dramatic Surge in the Arrival of Unaccompanied Children Has Deep Roots and No Simple Solutions." Migration Policy Institute. June 13, 2014. Retrieved April 12, 2016. https://www.migrationpolicy.org/article/dramatic-surge-arrival-unaccompanied-children-has-deep-roots-and-no-simple-solutions.

Cockburn, Patrick. "Refugee Crisis: Where Are All These People Coming from and Why?" The Independent. September 7, 2015. Retrieved January 11, 2016. http://www.independent.co.uk/news/world/refugee-crisis-where-are-all-thesepeople-coming-from-and-why-10490425.html.

Colchester, Marcus. *Palm Oil and Indigenous Peoples in South-East Asia.* Rome: International Land Coalition, 2011.

Cotula, Lorenzo. *The Outlook on Farmland Acquisitions.* Rome: International Land Coalition, 2011.

De Schutter, Olivier. "How Not to Think of Land Grabbing: Three Critiques of Large-Scale Investments in Farmland," in *Journal of Peasant Studies*, Volume 38, No. 2, pgs: 249–79. 2011.

Foo, Wen, and Simon Scarr. "Asia's Migrant Crisis." Reuters Graphics. 2015. Retrieved January 10, 2016. http://graphics.thomsonreuters.com/15/rohingya/index.html.

Frank, Andre Gunder. *Sociology of Development and Underdevelopment of Sociology*. Stockholm: Zenit, 1969.

Frank, Andre Gunder. *Re-Orient: Global Economy in the Asian Age*. Berkeley: University of California Press, 1998.

Friis, Cecilie, and Anette Reenberg. "Land 176 Grab in Africa: Emerging Land System Drivers in a Teleconnected World." in *GLP Report No. 1.*. Copenhagen: Global Land Project International Project Office, 2010.

Galeano, Eduardo H. *Open Veins of Latin America: Five Centuries of the Pillage of a Continent*. New York: Monthly Review Press, 1997.

Gecker, Jocelyn. "Asia's Migrant Crisis: Who's Going to Friday's Summit, and Where Do They Stand?" Globe and Mail. May 28, 2015. Retrieved January 13, 2016. http://www. theglobeandmail.com/news/world/asias-migrantcrisis-whos-going-to-fridays-summit-and-wheredo-they-stand/article24659168/.

Haffner, Jeanne. *The View from Above: The Science of Social Space*. Boston: MIT Press, 2013.

Hall, Ruth. "Land Grabbing in Africa and the New Politics of Food." Future Agricultures, Policy Brief 41. June, 2011. Retrieved April 13, 2016. https://assets.publishing.service. gov.uk/media/57a08abfed915d3cfd0008fa/FAC_Policy_Brief_No41.pdf.

Hampshire, James. "Europe's Migration Crisis." in *Political Insight*, Volume 6, No. 3, pgs: 8–11. 2015.

Harvey, David. *The New Imperialism*. Oxford: Oxford University Press, 2003.

Hiskey, Jonathan, Mary Malone, and Diana Orces. "Violence and Migration in Central America." Latin American Public Opinion Project Insight Series. Washington, DC: USAID, 2014. Retrieved January 11, 2016. http://www.vanderbilt.edu/lapop/insights/IO901en.pdf.

Huffpost Miami. "Isabel Muñoz Captures Immigrant Experience in 'La Bestia' at CCE Miami (Photos)." Huffington Post. May 17, 2012. Retrieved January 10, 2016. http://www. huffingtonpost.com/2012/05/15/isabel-munoz-ccemiami-beast_n_1518697.html.

International Development Association (IDA) and International Monetary Fund (IMF). "Heavily Indebted Poor Countries (HIPC) Initiative and Multilateral Debt Relief Initiative (MDRI)—Status of Implementation." September 15, 2009. Retrieved May 10, 2016. http://www.imf. org/external/np/pp/eng/2009/091509.pdf.

International Monetary Fund (IMF). *Household Credit Growth in Emerging Market Countries*. Washington DC: International Monetary Fund, 2006.

International Monetary Fund (IMF). *Global Financial Stability Report: Containing Risks and Restoring Financial Soundness*. Washington DC: International Monetary Fund, 2008.

International Monetary Fund (IMF). *Factsheet: Debt Relief under the Heavily Indebted Poor Countries (HIPC) Initiative*. Washington DC: International Monetary Fund, 2009.

International Monetary Fund (IMF). *Poverty Reduction Strategy Papers (PRSP)*. Washington DC: International Monetary Fund, 2009.

International Monetary Fund (IMF). Fact sheet: *Poverty Reduction Strategy in IMF-supported Programs*. Washington DC: International Monetary Fund, 2015.

International Monetary Fund (IMF). *Financial Soundness Indicators (FSIs)*. Washington DC: International Monetary Fund, 2015.

International Monetary Fund (IMF). *Vulnerabilities, Legacies, and Policy Challenges: Risks Rotating to Emerging Markets. Global Financial Stability Report*. Washington DC: International Monetary Fund, 2015.

International Monetary Fund (IMF). "Factsheet: Debt Relief under the Heavily Indebted Poor Countries (HIPC) Initiative." Washington DC: International Monetary Fund, 2016. Retrieved May 10, 2016. http://www.imf.org/en/About/Factsheets/Sheets/2016/08/01/16/11/Debt-Relief-Under-the-Heavily-Indebted-Poor-Countries-Initiative.

Jubilee Debt Campaign. "Debt and Women." 2007. Retrieved January 10, 2016. https:// www.actionaid.org.uk/sites/default/files/doc_lib/ debt_and_women.pdf.

Jubilee Debt Campaign. "Angola." 2012. Retrieved January 10, 2016. http://jubileedebt.org.uk/countries/angola.

Kahn, Carrie. "Mexican Crackdown Slows Central American Immigration to U.S." All Things Considered. NPR. September 12, 2014. Retrieved April 12, 2016. http://www.npr.org/sections/parallels/2014/09/12/347747148/mexican-crackdown-slows-central-american-immigration-to-u-s.

Kanupriya, Kapoor, and Amy Sawitta Lefevre. "SE Asia Vows to Rescue 'Boat People'; Myanmar Seizes Migrant Vessel." Reuters. May 29, 2015. Retrieved January 11, 2016. http://www. reuters.com/article/us-asia-migrants-us-idUSKBN0OE05T20150529.

Kingsley, Patrick. "It's Not at War, but Up to 3% of Its People Have Fled. What Is Going On in Eritrea?" The Guardian. July 22, 2015. Retrieved January 11, 2016. https:// www.theguardian.com/world/2015/jul/22/eritrea-migrants-child-soldier-fled-what-is-going.

Kingsley, Patrick. "Refugee Crisis: Apart from Syrians, Who Is Traveling to Europe?" The Guardian. September 10, 2015. Retrieved January 11, 2016. https://www.theguardian.com/world/2015/sep/10/refugee-crisis-apart-from-syrians-who-else-is-travelling-to-europe.

Koslowski, Rey, and David Kyle. *Global Human Smuggling: Comparative Perspectives*.

Baltimore: Johns Hopkins University Press, 2001.

Land Matrix. *Land Matrix Newsletter*. November, 2015. Retrieved January 13, 2016. http://www.landmatrix.org/media/filer_public/95/1c/951c640e-3cda-4a0b-821c-3c5142b901b7/7365_up_ispa_land_matrix_newsletter_261115.pdf.

Land Matrix. "Dynamics Overview." Land Matrix. 2016. Retrieved January 13, 2016 (continuously updated). http://www.landmatrix.org/en/get-the-idea/dynamics-overview/.

Land Matrix. "Land Matrix: The Online Public Database on Land Deals." Land Matrix. 2016. Retrieved January 13, 2016. http://www.landmatrix.org/en/.

Laub, Zachary. "Authoritarianism in Eritrea and the Migrant Crisis." CFR Backgrounder. Council on Foreign Relations. November 11, 2015. Retrieved January 11, 2016. http://www.cfr.org/eritrea/authoritarianism-eritrea-migrant-crisis/p37239.

Lehrer, Brian. "NYC Immigration Commissioner: New Task Force to Help Unaccompanied Minors." The Brian Lehrer Show [radio program], WNYC. 2014. Retrieved January 10, 2016. http://www.wqxr.org/story/nyc-immigration-commissioner-new-task-force-help-unaccompanied-minors/.

Longhi, Vittorio. "Refugees: Ask the EU to Stop Funding the Eritrean Dictatorship!" Change.org. 2014. Retrieved January 9, 2016. https://www.change.org/p/free-eritrea-support-democracy-prevent-the-exodus-and-further-deaths-at-sea.

Lucas, Linda E. *Unpacking Globalization: Markets, Gender, and Work*. Kampala: Makerere University Press, 2005.

Maldonado-Torres, Nelson. "On the Coloniality of Being." in *Cultural Studies*, Volume 21. No. 2, pgs: 240–70. 2007.

Mark, Monica. "Boko Haram's 'Deadliest Massacre': 2,000 Feared Dead in Nigeria." The Guardian. January 10, 2015. Retrieved January 13, 2016. http://www.theguardian.com/world/2015/ jan/09/boko-haram-deadliest-massacre-baga-nigeria.

Marx, Karl. *Capital. Vol. 1*. London: Penguin Classics, 1992.

Mignolo, Walter. "Delinking: The Rhetoric of Modernity, the Logic of Coloniality, and the Grammar of De-coloniality." in *Cultural Studies*, Volume 21, No. 2, pgs: 449–514. 2007.

Moraga, Jesus Fernandez-Huertas, and Hillel Rapoport. "Tradable Refugee-admission Quotas (TRAQs), the Syrian Crisis and the New European Agenda on Migration." in *IZA Journal of European Labor Studies*, Volume 4, No. 1, pgs: 11–23. 2015.

Movimiento Migrante Mesoamericano. "El calvario de los niños migrantes en transtion por Mexico: Human Rights Watch." March 31, 2016. Retrieved May 10, 2016. https://movimientomigrantemesoamericano.org/2016/03/31/el-calvario-de-los-ninos-migrantes-en-transito-por-mexico-human-rights-watch/.

Organization of American States. "IACHR Expresses Concern over Mexico's Southern Border Plan." Press release. June 10, 2015. Retrieved May 10, 2016. http://www.oas.org/en/iachr/media_center/preleases/2015/065.asp.

Oxfam International. "Oxfam International Submission to the Heavily Indebted Poor Country (HIPC) Debt Review." Policy Paper. April, 1999. Retrieved January 10, 2016. http://policy-practice.oxfam.org.uk/publications/oxfam-international-submission-to-the-heavily-indebted-poor-county-hipc-debt-re-114964.

Pascaud, May. "Is Mexico Doing the US's Dirty Work on Central American Migrants?" PRI. June 23, 2015. Retrieved May 10, 2016. https://www.pri.org/stories/2015-06-23/mexico-doing-us-s-dirty-work-deporting-central-american-migrants.

Putzel, Louis, Samuel Assembe-Mvondo, Laurentine Bilogo Bi Ndong, Reine Patrick Banioguila, Paolo Cerutti, Julius Chupezi Tieguhong, Robinson Djeukam, Noël Kabuyaya, Guillaume Lescuyer, and William Mala. "Chinese Trade and Investment and the Forests of the Congo Basin: Synthesis of Scoping Studies in Cameroon, Democratic Republic of Congo and Gabon." Working paper. Bogor: Centre for International Forestry Research, 2011. Retrieved April 13, 2016. https://www.cifor.org/library/3501/chinese-trade-and-investment-and-the-forests-of-the-congo-basin-synthesis-of-scoping-studies-in-cameroon-democratic-republic-of-congo-and-gabon/.

Quijano, Anibal. "Coloniality of Power, Eurocentrism and Latin America." in Nepantla: Views from the South, Volume 1, No. 3, pgs: 533–80. 2000.

Rahman, Aminur. "Micro-credit Initiatives for Equitable and Sustainable Development: Who Pays?" in World Development, Volume 27, No. 10, pgs: 67–82. 1999.

Robinson, William I. A Theory of Global Capitalism: Production, Class, and State in a Transnational World. Baltimore: Johns Hopkins University Press, 2004.

Robinson, William I. Latin America and Global Capitalism: A Critical Globalization Perspective. Baltimore: Johns Hopkins University Press, 2008.

Robinson, William I. Global Capitalism and the Crisis of Humanity. New York: Cambridge University Press, 2014.

Safa, Helen Icken. The Myth of the Male Breadwinner: Women and Industrialization in the Caribbean. Boulder: Westview Press, 1995.

Sassen, Saskia. The Mobility of Labor and Capital. Cambridge: Cambridge University Press, 1988.

Sassen, Saskia. Guests and Aliens. New York: New Press, 1999.

Sassen, Saskia. Territory, Authority, Rights: From Medieval to Global Assemblages. 2nd, rev. ed. Princeton: Princeton University Press, 2008.

Sassen, Saskia. "Two Stops in Today's New Global Geographies: Shaping Novel Labor Supplies and Employment Regimes." in American Behavioral Scientist, Volume 52, No. 3, pgs: 457–96. 2008.

Sassen, Saskia. "Global Finance and Its Institutional Spaces." in The Oxford Handbook of the Sociology of Finance, pgs: 13–32. Edited by K. Knorr-Cetina and A. Preda. Oxford: Oxford University Press, 2013.

Sassen, Saskia. "When Territory Deborders Territoriality." Territory, Politics, Governance 1(1): 21–45, 2013b.

Sassen, Saskia. Expulsions: Brutality and Complexity in the Global Economy. Cambridge: Belknap Press of Harvard University Press, 2014.

Sassen-Koob, Saskia. "Recomposition and Peripheralization at the Core." in Contemporary Marxism, Volume 5, pgs: 88–100. 1982.

Sirkeci, Ibrahim, Deniz Eroglu Utku, and Pinar Yazgan. "Syrian Crisis and Migration." in Migration Letters, Volume 12, No. 3, pgs: 181–92. 2015.

Sisci, Francesco. "Libya's Refugee Crisis Is Europe's Biggest Challenge; Is Partition the Only Answer?" Asia Times. September 30, 2015. Retrieved January 11, 2016. http://www.atimes.com/libya-refugee-crisis-is-europes-top-challenge-is-partition-the-only-answer-sisci/.

Sladkova, Jana. "Stratification of Undocumented Migrant Journeys: Honduran Case." International Migration. December 22, 2013. http://onlinelibrary.wiley.com/doi/10.1111/imig.12141/full.

South Asia Terrorism Portal. "Fatalities in Terrorist Violence in Pakistan, 2003–2016." 2016. Retrieved January 11, 2016. http://www.satp.org/satporgtp/countries/pakistan/database/casualties.htm.

Tinker, Irene. Persistent Inequalities: Women and World Development. New York: Oxford University Press, 1990.

Toussaint, Eric. "Poor Countries Pay More under Debt Reduction Scheme?" TWN (Third World Network). July, 1999. Retrieved May 12, 2016. http://www.twn.my/title/1921-cn.htm.

Tribune Wire Reports. "Another Boat Found at Sea as Rohingya Refugee Crisis Deepens." Chicago Tribune. May 13, 2015. Retrieved January 13, 2016. http://www.chicagotribune.com/news/nationworld/ct-rohingya-refugees-20150513-story.html.

Tuckman, Jo. "Mexico's Migration Crackdown Escalates Dangers for Central Americans." The Guardian. October 13, 2015. Retrieved May 12, 2016. http://www.theguardian.com/world/2015/oct/13/mexico-central-american-migrants-journey-crackdown.

UN Conference on Trade and Development (UNCTAD). World Investment Directory. Vol. 10. Africa. New York: United Nations, 2008.

UN Conference on Trade and Development (UNCTAD). Investment Report: Transnational Corporations, Agricultural Production and Development. New York: United Nations, 2009.

UN Conference on Trade and Development (UNCTAD). World Investment Reports. New York: United Nations, 2015.

UN Development Programme (UNDP). A Time for Bold Ambition: Together We Can Cut Poverty in Half. Annual Report. New York: UNDP, 2005.

UN Development Programme (UNDP). Human Development Report, 2007–2008. Annual Report. New York: UNDP, 2008.

UN Development Programme (UNDP). Human Development Report 2014. Annual Report. New York: UNDP, 2014.

UN Development Programme (UNDP). Human Development Report 2015. Annual Report. New York: UNDP, 2015.

UN High Commissioner for Refugees (UNHCR). "Facts and Figures about Refugees." 2015. Retrieved January 11, 2016. http://www.unhcr.ie/ about-unhcr/facts-and-figures-about-refugees.

UN High Commissioner for Refugees (UNHCR). "2015 UNHCR Country Operations Profile—Pakistan." New York: United Nations, 2015. Retrieved January 11, 2016. http://reporting.unhcr.org/node/2546#_ga=2.214884639.944278614.1513199010-877870612.1513199010.

UN High Commissioner for Refugees (UNHCR). "2015 UNHCR Subregional Operations Profile—East and Horn of Africa." New York: United Nations, 2015. Retrieved January 11, 2016. http://reporting.unhcr.org/node/38.

UN High Commissioner for Refugees (UNHCR). "World at War: UNHCR Global Trends 2014." New York: United Nations, 2015. Retrieved January 9, 2016. http://www.unhcr.org/556725e69.html.

UN Inter-agency and Expert Group on MDG Indicators (IAEG). "The Millennium Development Goals Report." New York: United Nations, 2009. Retrieved April 13, 2016. http://www.un.org/millenniumgoals/pdf/MDG_Report_2009_ENG.pdf.

UN Office on Drugs and Crime (UNODC). "UNODC Homicide Statistics 2013." Global Study on Homicide. New York: United Nations, 2013. Retrieved January 13, 2016. https://www.unodc.org/gsh/en/data.html.

UN Statistics Division. "Debt Service as a Percentage of Exports of Goods and Services and Net Income." New York: United Nations, 2015. Retrieved January 9, 2016. http://mdgs.un.org/unsd/mdg/SeriesDetail.aspx?srid=655&crid=.

United Nations. Inter-agency and Expert Group on MDG Indicators (IAEG). http://mdgs.un.org/unsd/mdg/Host.aspx?Content-

=IAEG.htm.

U.S. Customs and Border Protection. "Southwest Border Unaccompanied Alien Children Statistics FY 2016." U.S. Department of Homeland Security. 2016. Retrieved January 10, 2016. http://www.cbp.gov/newsroom/stats/southwest-border-unaccompanied-children/fy-2016.

U.S. Customs and Border Protection. "Unaccompanied Children Encountered by Fiscal Year." U.S. Department of Homeland Security. 2016. Retrieved January 10, 2016. http://www.cbp.gov/newsroom/stats/southwest-border-unaccompanied-children/fy-2016.

U.S. Department of Homeland Security. "CBP Border Security Report, Fiscal Year 2015." U.S. Department of Homeland Security. December 22, 2015. https://www.dhs.gov/sites/default/files/publications/CBP%20FY15%20Border%20Security%20Report_12-21_0.pdf.

U.S. Department of State. "Targeting of and Attacks on Members of Religious Groups in the Middle East and Burma." Atrocities Prevention Report. March 17, 2016. Retrieved April 13, 2016. http://www.state.gov/j/drl/rls/254807.htm.

U.S. House Committee on Appropriations. "FY 17 Budget Hearing—U.S. Customs and Border Protection: Opening Statement as Prepared (Chairman Hal Rogers)." March 1, 2016. http://docs.house.gov/meetings/AP/AP15/20160301/104530/HHRG-114-AP15-MState-R000395-20160301.pdf.

Vanderklippe, Nathan. "In Transit to Nowhere: Rohingya Move from One Bleak Horizon to Another." Globe and Mail. May 28, 2015. Retrieved January 13, 2016. http://www.theglobeandmail. com/news/world/in-transit-to-nowhere-rohingya-move-from-one-bleak-horizon-to-another/article24624679/.

Van der Pijl, Kees. Handbook of the International Political Economy of Production. Edward Elgar. Cheltenham, 2015.

Von Braun, Joachim, and Ruth Meinzen-Dick. "Land Grabbing" by Foreign Investors in Developing Countries: Risks and Opportunities. Washington DC: International Food Policy Research Institute, 2009.

Wiener Bravo, Elisa. The Concentration of Land Ownership in Latin America: An Approach to Current Problems. Rome: International Land Coalition, 2011.

WOLA: Advocacy for Human Rights in the Americas. "Mexico Now Detains More Central American Migrants Than the United States." June 11, 2015. Retrieved May 10, 2016. https://www.wola.org/2015/06/mexico-now-detains-more-central-american-migrants-than-the-united-states/.

World Bank. "Increasing Aid and Its Effectiveness." Ch. 5 of Global Monitoring Report: Millennium Development Goals: From Consensus to Momentum. Washington DC: World Bank, 2005.

World Bank. Global Economic Prospects:

Economic Implications of Remittances and Migration. Washington DC: World Bank, 2006.

World Bank. Global Economic Prospects: The Global Economy in Transition. Washington DC: World Bank, 2015.

World Bank. Global Monitoring Report: Development Goals in an Era of Demographic Change. Washington DC: World Bank, 2015.

World Bank. "Intentional Homicides (per 100,000 People)." World Bank Database. Washington DC: World Bank, 2015. Retrieved January 10, 2016. http://data.worldbank.org/indicator/VC.IHR.PSRC.P5?order=-wbapi_data_value_2013+wbapi_data_value+wbapi_data_value-last&sort=desc.

World Bank. "Latin America and Caribbean." Poverty and Equity. Washington DC: World Bank, 2015. Retrieved January 10, 2016. http://povertydata.worldbank.org/poverty/region/LCN.

Yearwood, Edilma L. "Let Us Respect the Children: The Plight of Unaccompanied Youth." in Journal of Child and Adolescent Psychiatric Nursing, Volume 27, No. 4, pgs: 205–6. 2014.

Sources for illustrations:

Amnesty International. "Myanmar: open for business? Corporate crime and abuses at Myanmar copper mine." Amnesty International, 2015. Last consulted on 14 September, 2016. https://www.amnesty.org/en/documents/asa16/0003/2015/en/.

IDMC (Internal Displacement Monitoring Centre). "Pushed Aside - Displaced for development in India." IDMC, 2016. Last consulted on 13 September, 2016. http://www.internal-displacement.org/assets/publications/2016/201607-ap-india-pushed-aside-en.pdf.

The Land Matrix Global Observatory. "Web of transnational deals." The Land Matrix Global Observatory, 2016. Last consulted on 4 October, 2016. http://landmatrix.org/en/get-the-idea/web-transnational-deals/.

1.3: Large-scale urban land acquisitions could de-urbanize cities and undermine public control

Background papers:

Sassen, Saskia. "Who owns the city?" 2016.

Sassen, Saskia. Territory, Authority, Rights: From Medieval to Global Assemblages. 2008 2nd, rev. ed. Princeton: Princeton University Press, 2016.

Other references:

Acosta-Belen, Edna, and Christine E. Bose. Women in the Latin American Development Process. Philadelphia: Temple University Press, 1995.

Gorra, Vanessa, and Roel R. Ravanera. Commercial Pressures on Land in Asia: An Overview. Rome: International Land Coali-

tion, 2011.

Sassen, Saskia. Cities in a World Economy. 4th ed. Sage, 2012.

Sassen, Saskia. Expulsions: Brutality and Complexity in the Global Economy. Cambridge: Belknap Press of Harvard University Press, 2014.

Sassen, Saskia. Territory, Authority, Rights: From Medieval to Global Assemblages. 2nd, rev. ed. Princeton: Princeton University Press, 2008.

Data sources:

Cushman and Wakefield, Real capital Analytics, Oxford Analytics, World Economic Forum, Knight

1.4: Lack of access to water and the risks caused by an excess of water require a rethinking on the place and shape of future urbanization

Background papers:

Harrison, Jane. Waterbanks. 2016.

Ovink, Henk. Transformative Capacity of Resilience: Learning from Rebuild by Design. 2016.

Other references:

Adelana, S., Personal Communication, Department of Geology and Mineral Sciences, University of Ilorin, Nigeria.

Akudago, J., Kankam-Yeboah, K., Chegbeleh, L. and Nishigaki, M. "Assessment of well design and sustainability in hard rock systems of northern Ghana," in Hydrogeology J., Volume 15, pgs: 789-797. 2007.

European Environment Agency. Europe's Environment: The Dobris Assessment. European Environment Agency, 1995.

Garrity, Dennis, Director General of the World Agroforestry Centre, Personal Communication.

Gleitsmann, B., Kroma, M. and Steenhuis, T. "Analysis of a rural water supply project in three communities in Mali: Participation and sustainability," in Natural Res. Forum, Volume 31, pgs: 142-150. 2007.

Gou, J. "It is actually illegal in Colorado to collect the rain that falls on your home." Washington Post Online. March 24, 2015. https://www.washingtonpost.com/blogs/govbeat/wp/2015/03/24/it-is-actually-illegal-in-colorado-to-collect-the-rain-that-falls-on-your-home/.

Hallegatte S. et al. Nature Climate Change. September, 2013.
Hazelton, D. "The development of community water supply systems using deep and shallow well handpumps," in Report No. TT132/00: South Africa. Water Research Centre (WRC), 2010.

Hoekstra, A., The Water Footprint of Modern Consumer Society. Routledge, 2013.

Liu, S., Yang Y. et al. Liquid Assets IIIA;

Dongjiang Overloaded-2011 Dongjiang Expedition Report. Civic Exchange, 2012.

McDonald, R. et al. "Water on an Urban Planet: Urbanization and the reach of urban water infrastructure," in *Global Environmental Change,* Volume 27, pgs: 96-105. 2014.

McGuire, V. *Water-Level Changes in the High Plains Aquifer, Predevelopment to 2005 and 2003 to 2005.* Reston: U.S. Geological Survey, 2007.

Mekonnen and Hoekstra. "Four billion people facing severe water scarcity". Sci. Adv. 2016.

RELMA in ICRAF & UNEP. *Potential for Rainwater Harvesting in Africa: A GIS Overview.* 2005.

Siemens. "Facts, Trends and Stories on Integrated Mobility," in *Como – Issue 10.* 1993. Retrieved from https://www.siemens.com/content/dam/internet/siemens-com/customer-magazine/old-mam-assets/print-archiv/2/como/como-edition-10-13-en.pdf.

UNDP. *Human Development Report, 2007/2008*

UNEP. *ICRAF Report.* New York: UNEP. 2006.

UNEP/WAC Report released on November 13, 2006, at the UN Climate Convention talks in Nairobi, Kenya and quoted in UNEP press release: "Environment-Led Green Revolution Key to Future Food Security in Africa" (2009) and 'Africa's Potential to Boost Drinking Water Supplies and Agriculture Underscored in Report by UNEP and the World Agroforestry Centre" (2006).http://www.solutions-site.org/node/238.

World Bank. *Performance Audit Report No. 16511.* Washington DC: World Bank, 1997. United Nations. *World Water Development Report.* New York: United Nations, 2012.

Sources for illustrations:

"Surging seas: Sea level rise analysis". Climate Central. Last consulted on October 4, 2016. http:// sealevel.climatecentral.org.

Fountain, H. "Researchers link Syrian conflict to a drought made worse by climate change". NY Times, 2015. Last consulted on 19 September, 2016. https://www.nytimes.com/2015/03/03/science/earth/study-links-syria-conflict-to-drought-caused-by-climate-change.html?_r=0.

McDonald, R.I. et al. "Water on an urban planet: Urbanization and the reach of urban water infrastructure," in *Global Environmental Change*, Volume 27, pgs: 96-105. 2014.

SEDAC (SocioEconomic Data and Applications Centre). "Population Maps." SEDAC. Last consulted on 22 September, 2016. http:// sedac.ciesin.columbia.edu/maps/gallery/search?- facets=theme:population&facets=region:europe.

UNESCHO-IHE (Institute for water education). "Water footprints of nations." New York: UNESCO, 2004. Last consulted on 01 October, 2016. http://waterfootprint.org/media/downloads/Report16Vol1.pdf.

WRI (World Resources Institute). *Water Risk Atlas.* WRI, 2014. Last accessed on 28 September 2016. http://www.wri.org/resources/maps/aqueduct-water-risk-atlas.

1.5: If democracy is to survive it will have to resist internal populism and embrace external cooperation

Background paper:

W. Jamieson, Dale and Di Paola, Marcello. *Political Theory for the Anthropocene.* 2016.

Other references:

Bergson, H. *Creative Evolution.* Edited by K. Ansell-Pearson, M. Kolkman and M. Vaughan. London: Palgrave Macmillan, 1907/2007.

Crutzen, P. and Stoermer, E. "The Anthropocene", *in Global Change Newsletter*, Volume 41, pgs: 17–18. 2000.

Di Paola, M. "Virtues for the Anthropocene", in *Environmental Values,* Volume 24, pgs: 183–207. 2015.

Donaldson, S. and Kymlicka, W. *Zoopolis: A Political Theory of Animal Rights.* Oxford: Oxford University Press, 2011.

Driver, Julia. "Attribution of Causation and Moral Responsibility", in *Moral Psychology*, Volume 2, pgs: 423–439. Edited by W. Sinnott- Armstrong. Cambridge: MIT Press, 2007.

Gardiner, S. *A Perfect Moral Storm: The Ethical Tragedy of Climate Change.* Oxford: Oxford University Press, 2011.

Gosseries, A. "What Do We Owe the Next Generation?" in *Loyola of Los Angeles Law Review*, Volume 35, pgs: 293– 354. 2001.

Gosseries, A. "Nations, Generations, and Climate Justice," in *Global Policy*, Volume 5, No. 1, pgs: 96–102. 2014.

Gosseries, A. and González-Ricoy, I. *Institutions for Future Generations.* Oxford: Oxford University Press, Forthcoming.

Gosseries, A. and Meyer, L. *Intergenerational Justice.* Oxford: Oxford University Press, 2009.

Haidt, J. *The Righteous Mind: Why Good People are Divided by Politics and Religion.* New York: Pantheon Books, 2012.

Hale, T., Held, D. and Young, K. *Gridlock: Why Global Cooperation is Failing When We Need It Most.* Cambridge: Polity, 2013.

Heinzerling, L. "Statistical Lives in Environmental Law," *in Identified versus Statistical Lives: An Interdisciplinary Perspective*, pgs: 174-181. Edited by G. Cohen, N. Daniels and E. Nyal. Oxford: Oxford University Press, 2015.

Held, D. *Cosmopolitanism: Ideals and Realities.* Cambridge: Polity, 2010.

Held, D. and McGrew, A. *Globalization/Anti-Globalization: Beyond the Great Divide.* Cambridge: Polity, 2007.

Hibbard, K. A., Crutzen, P. J., Lambin, E. F., et al. "Decadal Interactions of Humans and the Environment," in *Integrated History and Future of People on Earth*, pgs: 341–375. Edited by R. Costanza, L. Graumlich and W. Steffen. Boston: MIT Press, 2006.

Hulme, M. *Why We Disagree About Climate Change.* Cambridge: Cambridge University Press, 2009.

Jamieson, D. *Reason in a Dark Time: Why the Struggle Against Climate Change Failed, and What It Means for Our Future.* New York: Oxford University Press, 2014.

Jamieson, D. and Di Paola, M. "Climate Change and Global Justice: New Problem, Old Paradigm?," in *Global Policy*, Volume 5, No. 1, pgs: 105–111. 2014.

Keohane, R. "Global Governance and Democratic Accountability," in *Taming Globalization: Frontiers of Governance*, pgs: 130–159. Edited by D. Held and M. Koenig-Archibugi. Cambridge: Polity, 2003.

Lepore, J. "Richer and Poorer. Accounting for Inequality." The New Yorker. 16 March, 2015. http://www.newyorker.com/magazine/2015/03/16/richer-and-poorer.

Marsh, G. P. *Man and Nature.* Washington DC: University of Washington Press, 2003/1864.

Shepard, M. *Sentient City: Ubiquitous Computing, Architecture, and the Future of Urban Space.* Boston: MIT Press, 2011.

Samuelson, W. and Zeckhauser, R. "Status Quo Bias in Decision Making," in *Journal of Risk and Uncertainty,* Volume 1, pgs: 7–59. 1988.

Steffen, W., Grinewald, J., Crutzen, P. and McNeill, J. "The Anthropocene: Conceptual and Historical Perspectives," in *Philosophical Transactions of the Royal Society A 369,* pgs: 842–867. 2011.

Stepan, A. and Linz, J. "Comparative Perspectives on Inequality and the Quality of Democracy in the United States," in *Perspectives on Politics*, Volume 9, pgs: 841–856. 2011.

Sternberg, E. *My Brain Made Me Do It: the Rise of Neuroscience and the Threat to Moral Responsibility*. New York: Prometheus Books, 2010.

Thompson, D. "Representing Future Generations: Political Presentism and Democratic Trusteeship," in *Critical Review of International and Political Philosophy,* Volume 13, No. 1, pgs: 17–37. 2010.

Tsebelis, G. *Veto Players: How Political Institutions Work.* Princeton: Princeton University Press, 2002.

Vitousek, P., Mooney, H., Lubchenco, J. and Melillo, J. "Human Domination of Earth's Ecosystems," in *Science,* 277(5325), pgs: 494–499. 1997.

Waldron, J. "The Dignity of Legislation," in *Maryland Law Review*, Volume 54, No. 2, pgs: 633–665. 1995.

Waters, C., Zalasiewicz, J., Summerhayes, C., et al. "The Anthropocene Is Functionally and Stratigraphically Distinct from the Holocene," in *Science* 351(6269), pgs: 137–138. 2016.

Wiland, E. "One Citizen, One Vote." What's Wrong? 2015. https://whatswrongcvsp. com/2015/08/12/one-citizen-one-vote/.

Zalasiewicz, J., Williams, M., Fortey, R., et al. "Stratigraphy of the Anthropocene," in *Philosophical Transactions: Mathematical, Physical and Engineering Sciences* 369(1938), pgs: 1036–1055. 2011.

Zalasiewicz, J., Waters, C. N., Williams, M., et al. "When Did the Anthropocene Begin? A Mid- Twentieth Century Boundary Level Is Stratigraphically Optimal," in *Quaternary International*. 2016. http://www.sciencedirect.com/science/article/pii/S1040618214009136.

Sources for illustrations:

Agiesta, J. and LoBianco, T. "Poll: Gun control support spikes after shooting." CNN. 2016. Last accessed: 2016. http://www.cnn.com/2016/06/20/politics/cnn-gun-poll/.

Amico, C. and Childress, S. "How loaded is the gun lobby?" PBS. 2015. Last accessed: 2016. http://www.pbs.org/wgbh/frontline/article/how-loaded-is-the-gun-lobby/.

Caldwell, L.A. "How the NRA exerts influence beyond political contributions." NBC News. 2016. Last accessed: 2016. http://www.nbcnews.com/storyline/orlando-nightclub-massacre/nra-s-political-influence-far-goes-beyond-campaign-contributions-n593051.

Elmqvist, T., Fragkias, M., Goodness, J., Güneralp, B., Marcotullio, P.J., McDonald, R.I., Parnell, S., Schewenius, M., Sendstad, M., Seto, K.C. and Wilkinson, C. "Urbanization, Biodiversity and Ecosystem services: Challenges and opportunities." Springer. 2013. Last accessed: October 7, 2016. http://www.springer.com/ us/book/9789400770874.

Friedrich, J. *CAIT climate data explorer*. CAIT, no date. Last accessed: 2016. http://cait.wri.org/.

Harmeling, S., Witting, M., Bals, C. and Kref, S. *Global Climate Risk Index 2011*. German Watch, 2010. Last accessed: 2016. http://germanwatch.org/klima/cri11.pdf.

McInnes, R.J. *Recognising wetland ecosystem services within urban case studies*. 2013. Last accessed: 2016. https://www.researchgate.net/publication/277683394_Recognising_wetland_ ecosystem_services_within_urban_case_studies.

Tasch, B. and Nudelman, M. "This map shows how much the refugee crisis is dividing Europe." Business Insider. 2016. Last accessed: 2016. http://www.businessinsider.com/map-refugees-europe-migrants-2016-2?r=UK&IR=T.

United States Senate. 2016. Last accessed: 2016. http://www.senate.gov/legislative/LIS/roll_call_lists/roll_call_vote_cfm.cfm?congress=114&session=1&vote=00321.

2.1: Good urbanization requires a three-decade time horizon, a focus on value creation, capture and sharing and a compact between all levels of government.

Background papers:

Bourdic, Loeiz and Kamiya, Marco. *The Economics of the 'Three-Pronged Approach' to Urbanization: Planned City Extension, Legal Framework, and Municipal Finance*. UN-Habitat, 2016.

Salat, Serge. *The Case for UN-Habitat Three-Pronged Approach*. Urban Morphology and Complex Systems Institute, 2016.

2.2: Open-system thinking and designing allow cities to evolve and change

Background papers:

Dall, Amica and Smith, Giles. *Public Space Design: The relationship between public space design and freedom*. 2016.

Sennett, Richard. *The Open City*. 2016.

Other references:

Allen, Marjory. *Planning for Play*. London: 1968.

Barttram, A. "The Edge of Recalcitrance," in *The Foundations of Playwork*. Bristol: 2008.

Gill, T. *No Fear: Growing up in a Risk Averse Society*. London, 2008.

Harvey, D. "Right to the City," in *New Left Review* no. 53. London: September – October, 2008.

Jacobs, S. "This is Water," in *Lobby*, No 2, Spring 2015. London: Bartlett School of Architecture, 2016.

Keats, J. *Letter to his brothers*, widely reproduced. December, 1817.

Lester, S., and Russell, W. *Children's Right to Play*. Working Paper No. 57. The Hague: 2010.

Molesworth, Helen and Erickson, Ruth. *Leap Before You Look: Black Mountain College, 1933–1957*. Edited by Molesworth, H. Boston: 2015.

Nicholson, S. "The Theory of Loose Parts," in *Studies in Design Education Craft & Technology*, Volume 4, No. 2. Stoke-on-Trent: 1972.

Vesely, D. *Architecture in the Age of Divided Representation*. Cambridge: 2004.

2.3: Contemporary urbanism provides the opportunity to set aside the blank slate for an ethic of cohabitation

Background paper:

Kaasa, Adam. *Cohabitation: Against the tabula rasa and towards a new ethic for cities*. 2016.

Other references:

Bauman, Zygmunt. *Modernity and the Holocaust*. Ithaca: Cornell University Press, 1989.

Campkin, B. *Remaking London: Decline and Regeneration in Urban Culture*. 2013.

Colomina, Beatriz. *Le Corbusier and photography*. Assemblage, 1987.

Davis, Juliet. "The making and remaking of Hackney Wick, 1870–2014: from urban edgeland to Olympic fringe," in *Planning Perspectives*, 31(3), pgs: 425-457. 2016.

Haffner, Jeanne. *The View from Above: The Science of Social Space*. Boston: MIT Press, 2013.

Kaasa, Adam. *Writing, Drawing, Building: The Architecture of Mexico, 1938-1964*. PhD Thesis. London School of Economics and Political Science, 2013.

"Moradores removidos dizem que não há clima de festa para Rio 2016". http://odia.ig.com.br/rio-de-janeiro/2016-08-05/moradores-removidos-dizem-que-nao-ha-clima-de-festa-para-rio-2016.html.

Wainwright, Oliver. "London's Olympic legacy: a suburb on steroids, a cacophony of luxury stumps." The Guardian. August 3, 2016. https://www.theguardian.com/artand-design/2016/aug/03/london-olympic-legacy-stratford-suburb-on-steroids.

Weizman, Eyal. *Hollow Land: Israel's Architecture of Occupation*. London: Verso Books, 2012.

Sources for illustrations:

Abegglen, Martin. *Bird view, Ribera, Barcelona*. 2012. https://flic.kr/p/cmcNoJ.

Consolidated Government Expenditure (%GDP), OECD

Heygate Leaseholders Displacement Map. last consulted on 7 October, 2016. https://www.google.com/maps/d/u/0/viewer?mid=1-_p4rJQDsMx3C6We2nB0Ft_7j-SM&hl- =en_US.

LSE Cities. *Transport and Social Equity: London Crossrail*. LSE Cities, 2013. Last consulted on 7 October, 2016. https://urbanage.lsecities.net/data/transport-and-social-equity-london-crossrail.

Public social expenditure across OECD countries, OECD

Social Expenditure as percentage of GDP and as percentage of Total General Government Expenditure in OECD Countries, OECD

2.4: Planning and design should operate at both metropolitan and neighbourhood scales and provide adaptable interventions that bridge social inequalities

Background paper:

Burdett, Ricky. *Space matters: reflections on the charter of Athens and contemporary urbanism*. 2016.

Other references:

Amin, A. "Telescopic Urbanism and the Poor", in *City*, Volume 17, Issue 4. 2013.

Angotti, T. *The New Century of the Metropolis: Urban Enclaves and Orientalism*. Routledge, 2012.

Aravena, A. and Iacobelli, A. *Elemental: Incremental Housing and Participatory Design Manual*. Berlin: Hatje Cantz, 2016.

Ballon, H. *The Greatest Grid: The Master Plan of Manhattan, 1811-2011*. New York: Columbia University Press, 2012.

Burdett, R. and Sudjic, D. (eds) *The Endless City*. London: Phaidon, 2008.

Burdett, R. and Sudjic, D. (eds). *Living in the Endless City*. London: Phaidon, 2011.

Christiaanse, K. and Baum M. *City as Loft: Adaptive Reuse as a Resource for Sustainable Urban Development*. Zurich: gta Verlag, 2012.

Dávila, J D (ed). *Urban Mobility and Poverty: Lessons from Medellín and Soacha, Colombia*. Development Planning Unit, UCL and Universidad Nacional de Colombia, 2013.

Davis, M. *Planet of Slums: Urban Involution and the Informal Working Class*. London: Verso, 2006.

Easterling, K. "Designing Infrastructure," in *Handbook of Urban Sociology*. Edited by Burdett, R. and Hall, S. London: SAGE, 2017 (forthcoming).

Flaoter, G. Rode, P. and Zenghelis, D. *Copenhagen: Green Economy Leader Report*. London: LSE Cities, 2014.

Hall, Suzanne. *Street and Citizen: The Measure of the Ordinary*. London: Routledge, 2012.

James, H. *New York Revisited, 1904*. New York: Franklin Square Press, 2008.

Kimmelmann, M. "The Grid at 200: Lines That Shaped Manhattan." The New York Times. 2 January 2012.

Koolhaas, R. *Delirious New York: A Retroactive Manifesto of Manhattan*. New York: Monacelli Press, 1994 (first edition 1978).

Koolhaas, R. "Whatever Happened to Urbanism?', in Koolhaas, R. and Mau, B., *S, M, X, XL*. New York: Monacelli Press, 1994.

Lin, John. "Umbrella urbanism: Hong Kong protests." The Architectural Review. October 28, 2014. Last accessed on 10 August 2017. https://www.architectural-review.com/rethink/viewpoints/umbrella-urbanism-hong-kong-protests/8671652.article.

Mehrotra, R. and Vera, F. *Ephemeral Urbanism: Cities in Constant Flux*. Bordeaux: Arc-en-Reve, 2016.

Mehrotra, R. "The Kinetic City" in *Architecture in India since 1900*. Mumbai: Pictor, 2011.

Mehrota, R. "Negotiating Static and Kinetic Cities," in Hussyen, A. (ed) *Other Cities, Other Worlds*. Durham: Duke University Press, 2008.

Mehta, S. "Bird of Gold," in Burdett, R. and Sudjic, D. (eds) *Living in the Endless City*. London: Phaidon, 2011.

Mehta, S. *The Maximum City: Bombay Lost and Found*. New York: Knopf, 2004.

Neuwirth, R. *Shadow Cities*. New York: Routledge, 2005.

Rieniets,T. et al. (eds). *The City as Resource: Texts and Projects, 2005-2014*. Berlin: Jovis Verlag, 2014.

Rowe, Colin and Koetter, Fred. *Collage City*. Boston: The MIT Press, 1984.

Rowe, P. *Civic Realism*. Boston: The MIT Press, 1999.

Roy, A. *The Land in Question*. London: Urban Age/LSE, 2014.

Sackman, Sarah. "The Occupy London result raises the thorny issue of property v protest." The Guardian. January 18, 2012. Last accessed on August 10, 2017. http://www.theguardian.com/commentisfree/libertycentral/2012/jan/18/occupy-london-eviction-freedom-expression-private.

Sassen, S. "Cityness in the Urban Age," Urban Age Bulletin, No. 2. 2005.

Sassen, S. *The Global City: New York, London, Tokyo*. Princeton: Princeton University Press, 2001.

Sassen, S. "Who owns our cities – and why this urban takeover should concern us all." Guardian Cities. 24 November 2015. https://www.theguardian.com/cities/2015/nov/24/who-owns-our-cities-and-why-this-urban-takeover-should-concern-us-all.

Saunders, D. *Arrival City*. New York: Pantheon Books, 2010.

Scola, Nancy. "One Lasting Occupy Effect: An Awareness of Private "Public" Spaces." Next City. 18 September 2013. Last accessed on 10 August 2017. https://nextcity.org/daily/entry/one-lasting-occupy-effect-an-awareness-of-private-public-spaces.

Sennett, R. "The Open City," in *The Endless City*. Edited by Burdett, R. and Sudjic, S. London: 2008.

Simone, A. *Jakarta, Drawing the City Near*. Minneapolis: University of Minnesota Press, 2014.

Sudjic, D. *The Edifice Complex: How the Rich and Powerful and Their Architects Shape the World*. London: Penguin, 2007.

Summerson, John. *Heavenly Mansions and Other Essays on Architecture*. London: Cresset Press, 1949.

United Nations Human Settlements Programme. *State of the World's Cities, Urbanization and Development: Emerging Futures*, Chapter 2. Nairobi: UN-Habitat, 2016.

Van Es, E. Harbusch, B. et al (eds). *Atlas of the Functional City: CIAM 4 and Comparative Urban Analysis*. Bussum: THOTH Publishers, 2014.

Virilio, P. *Open Sky 2008*. London: Verso, 2000.

Wacjman, J. "Life in the fast lane? Towards a sociology of technology and time," in *The British Journal of Sociology*, Volume 59, Issue 1, pgs: 59-77. March 2008.

2.5: UN-Habitat Sample of Cities shows that contemporary patterns of urbanization can reap greater benefits

Background paper and source for illustrations:

Towards an evidence-based urban agenda: 1) Monitoring World Urbanization Trends and Conditions with the Global Sample of Cities: 2) The Atlas of Urban Expansion--The 2016 Edition, 3) Layout Out Public Lands Before Development Occurs; 4) Keeping housing Affordable; 5) Making Regulatory Regimes Relevant and Responsive, Programme of research undertaken by UN-Habitat in collaboration with the New York University and the Lincoln Institute of Land Policy (2016), in preparation for the forthcoming *Atlas of Urban Expansion* (2016 Edition)

2.6: Integrative networks combine government-led and self-led approaches and expand the right to the city

Background paper:

Berrizbeitia, Anita. *Integrative Networks and Incremental Landscapes*. 2016.

Other references:

Cardona, Ignacio. *Arepa Arquitectura Ecología y Paisaje*. Alcaldía de Sucre, 2014. www.arepa.info.

De Soto, Hernando. *The Mystery of Capital, Why Capitalism Triumphs in the West and Fails Everywhere Else*, PGS: 32 – 34, New York: Basic Books, 2003.

Departamento Administrativo de Planificación Distrital. *Plan de Desarrollo Económico, Social y de Obras Públicas 1995-1998 Formar Ciudad*. Alcaldía Mayor de Santa Fé de Bogotá. Approved on 1 June 1995.

Echeverri, Alejandro et al. *Rehabitar la Montaña, Estrategias para un habitat sostenible en las laderas de Medellín*. Medellín: Universidad EAFIT, 2015. See also: Empresa de Desarrollo Urbano. 2004-2007. Alcaldía de Medellín. https://es.slideshare.net/Michel-Maya/rehabitar-la-montaa.

EDUMedellín/ modelo-de-transformacin-urbana-proyecto-urbano-integral-pui-zona-nororiental.

González Pachecho, Felipe. *MGP Arquitectos*. Bogotá: Alcaldía Mayor de Bogotá, 2000. http://www.mgp.com.co/.

Inter-American Development Bank. *Programa de Urbanizacao de Assentamentos*

Populares do Rio de Janeiro. Washington DC: IDB, 1998.

Jauregui, Jorge Mario. *Favela-Bairro Project*. 2000. http://www.jauregui.arq.br/.

Silva, Elisa. *Intervenciones de Espacios Públicos en Barrios del Municipio Sucre*. Caracas: Fundación Espacio, 2012. See also: *Oficina de Proyectos Especiales*. Caracas: Alcaldía del Municipio Sucre, 2012. https://www.plataformaarquitectura.cl/cl/02-238348/intervenciones-de-espacios-publicos-en-barrios-del-municipio-de-sucre.

Sources for illustrations:

Rockefeller Foundation. *Decision intelligence document*. Rockefeller Foundation, 2014. Last accessed: 2016. https://www.rockefellerfoundation.org/report/constrained-opportunities-in-slum-economies/.

Rojas, E. (ed.) *Building Cities: Neighbourhood upgrading and urban quality of life*. Inter-American Development Bank, 2010. Last accessed: 2016. http://www.iadb.org/wmsfiles/products/publications/documents/35132311.pdf.

2.7: Commons can compensate for public/private deficiencies if they achieve sufficiently large-scale application in cities

Background paper:

Bingham-Hall, John. *Future of Cities: Commoning and Collective Approaches to Urban Space*. 2016.

Other references:

Atelier D'Architecture Autogeree. http://www.urbantactics.org/.

Belfied, Andy. *Guardians of the Commo*. http://designingtheurbancommons.org/gallery/ guardians-of-the-common/.

Benkler, Yochai. *The Wealth of Networks: How Social Production Transforms Markets and Freedom*. New Haven: Yale University Press, 2006.

"Common land and village greens." Gov.uk. https://www.gov.uk/common-land-village-greens.

"Commoners of the New Forest." Forestry Commission England. http://www.forestry.gov.uk/forestry/infd-6a4kql.

Depani, Alpa and Randall-Page, Thomas. "Service Wash." http://designingtheurbancommons.org/gallery/service-wash/.

Designing for Free Speech. http://designingforfreespeech.org.

Dimitriou, O., Mrdja, D., Kyriakou, K., Twine, E., Szabó, V., Molna, I. "Rainbow of Desires." http://designingtheurbancommons.org/gallery/rainbow-of-desires/.

Federation of Cumbria Commoners. http://www.cumbriacommoners.org.uk/.

Harvey, David. *Rebel Cities: From the Right to the City to the Urban Revolution*. London:

Verso Books, 2012.

Hess, Charlotte. "Mapping the New Commons." Presented at The Twelfth Biennial Conference of the International Association for the Study of the Commons, Cheltenham, UK, 14-18 July. Libraries' and Librarians' Publications, 2008. http://surface.syr.edu/sul/25.

Konstantinos Lerias and Orestis Michelakis. *Commonstruction: A Manual for Radical Inclusivity*. http://designingtheurbancommons.org/gallery/commonstruction-a-manual-for-radical-inclusivity/.

Mactiernan, K., Greenway, K., Daish, L., Sutton, J., Hamilton, I., Boyle, G. and Rowe, M. "Reinventing the Lodge." http://designingtheurbancommons.org/gallery/reinventing-the-lodge/.

McGuirk, Justin. "Urban commons have radical potential – it's not just about community gardens." The Guardian. June 15, 2015. http://www.theguardian.com/cities/2015/jun/15/urban-common-radical-community-gardens.

Oldenburg, Ramon and Brissett, Dennis. "The Third Place," in *Qualitative Sociology* Volume 5, no. 4, pgs: 265–84. December, 1982.

Osorio, Angela and Basile, Chiara. "The School of Losing Time." http://designingtheurbancommons.org/gallery/the-school-of-losing-time-tslt/.

Ostrom, Elinor. *Governing the Commons: The Evolution of Institutions for Collective Action*. Boston: Cambridge University Press, 1990.

R-Urban. http://r-urban.net/en/.

Rodriguez, O., Edoja, C., Rowe, D., Sindlinger, E., Challinor, P., Mulholland, B. "Studley Commons." http://designingtheurbancommons.org/ gallery/studley-commons/.

Rogers, Ludovica. "Commons Economy Generator." http://designingtheurbancommons.org/gallery/commons-economy-generator/.

Sanciaume, L., Shahed, L., Brakspear, B. "Saturday Commoning Fever." http://designingtheurbancommons.org/gallery/saturday-commoning-fever/.

Stavrides, Stavros. "On Urban Commoning: The City Shapes Institutions of Sharing," in *Make_Shift City: Renegotiating the Urban Commons*, Berlin: Jovis, 2014.

Sync, C., Gant, E., Tolley, S., Case, R., Decker, A. "Carbonsync." http://designingtheurbancommons.org/gallery/carbonsync.

2.8: Planning without democracy or democracy without planning? How cities might have it both ways

Background paper:

Baiocchi, Gianpaolo. *Babies, Bathwater, Rising Sea-Levels, and Cities: Why Climate Change Calls for More Urban Democracy –*

and Not Less. 2016.

Other references:

Andrade, J. C. S., & de Oliveira, J. A. P. "The role of the private sector in global climate and energy governance," in the *Journal of Business Ethics*, Volume 130, No. 2, pgs: 375-387. 2015.

Barber, B. R. *If Mayors Ruled the World: Dysfunctional Nations, Rising Cities*. New Haven: Yale University Press, 2013.

Beck, U. "Climate for change, or how to create a green modernity?" in *Theory, Culture & Society*, Volume 27, No. 2-3, pgs: 254-266. 2010.

Bernauer, T. "Climate change politics," in *Annual Review of Political Science*, No. 16, pgs: 421-448. 2013.

Bulkeley, H. and V. Castán Broto. "Government by experiment? Global cities and the governing of climate change," in *Transactions of the Institute of British Geographers*, Volume 38, No. 3, pgs: 361-375. 2013.

Bulkeley, H. and K. Kern. "Local Government and the Governing of Climate Change in Germany and the UK" in *Urban Studies*, No. 43, pgs: 2237- 59. 2006.

Clark, N. "Geopolitics and the Disaster of the Anthropocene," in *The Sociological Review*, Volume 62 (S1), pgs: 19-37. 2014.

Cohen, Daniel Aldana. "Democracy or Eco-Apartheid." Centre for Humans and Nature. 2013.

Cohen, Daniel Aldana. 2016. "The Rationed City: The Politics of Water, Housing, and Land Use in Drought-Parched São Paulo," in Public Culture, Volume 28, (2):261–89.

Cohen, Daniel Aldana. "The Other Low Carbon Protagonists: Poor People's Movements and Climate Politics in São Paulo", in *The City is the Factory*. Edited by Miriam Greenberg and Penny Lewis. Ithaca: Cornell University Press, 2017.

Downey, L. *Inequality, Democracy, and the Environment*. New York: NYU Press, 2015.

Dryzek, J. S., & Stevenson, H. "Global democracy and earth system governance," in *Ecological Economics*, Volume 70, No. 11, pgs: 1865-1874. 2011.

Fahey, B. K. and Pralle, S. B. "Governing Complexity: Recent Developments" in *Environmental Politics and Policy, Policy Studies Journal*, Volume 44, pgs: S28–S49. 2016.

Floater, G., Rode, P., Robert, A., Kennedy, C., Hoornweg, D., Slavcheva, R. and Godfrey, N. "Cities and the New Climate Economy: The Transformative Role of Global Urban Growth," in *New Climate Economy*. Cities Paper 01. LSE Cities. London: London School of Economics and Political Science, 2014.

Giddens, Anthony. "The Politics of Climate Change: National Responses to the Challenge of Global Warming." in *Policy Network Paper*. London: The Policy Network, 2009.

Habitat III issue paper no. 18: Urban Infrastructure and Basic Services, Including Energy. New York: UN-Habitat, 2015.

Held, D. The Governance of Climate Change. Cambridge: John Wiley & Sons, 2011.

Heilbronner, Robert. An Inquiry into the Human Prospect. New York: Norton, 1975.

Heinrichs, D., K. Krellenberg, and M. Fragkias. "Urban responses to climate change: theories and governance practice in cities of the Global South," in International Journal of Urban and Regional Research, Volume 37, No. 6, pgs: 1865-1878. 2013.

Intermediary Cities, Building a New Urban Agenda. UCLG policy paper. New York: UN, 2014.

Jamieson, Dale. Reason in a Dark Time: Why the Struggle against Climate Change Failed—and What It Means for Our Future. Oxford: Oxford University Press, 2014.

Kern, K. and H. Bulkeley. "Cities, Europeanization and Multi-level Governance: Governing Climate Change through Transnational Municipal Networks," in JCMS: Journal of Common Market Studies, Volume 47, No. 2 pgs: 309-332. 2009.

Oreskes, N., & Conway, E. M. Merchants of Doubt: How a Handful of Scientists Obscured the Truth on Issues from Tobacco Smoke to Global Warming. New York: Bloomsbury Press, 2010.

Sennett, Richard. "Why climate change should signal the end of the state." The Guardian. October 9, 2014. https://www.theguardian.com/cities/2014/oct/09/why-climate-change-should-signal-the-end-of-the-city-state.

Shearman, D., Smith, J.W. The Climate Change Challenge and the Failure of Democracy. Westport: Praeger, 2007.

UCLG. Global Taskforce: Initial Recommendations Habitat III. UCLG, 2015.

United Nations. Report of the High Level Panel of Eminent Persons on the Post-2015 Development Agenda. New York: United Nations, 2013.

Urban Governance and Sustainable Development: CITIES ON THE AGENDA. DIIS. Copenhagen: Danish Institute for International Studies, 2016.

Wheeler, Stephen M. Planning for Sustainability: Creating Livable, Equitable and Ecological Communities. Routledge, 2013.

Wisner, B. and M. Pelling. Urban Disaster Risk Reduction: Cases from Africa. London: Earthscan, 2009.

World Bank. Cities and Climate Change: An Urgent Agenda. Washington DC: World Bank, 2010.

World Urbanization Prospects, the 2014 revision. New York: UN-Habitat, 2015.

Zimmerman, M. "How Local Governments have become a Factor in Global Sustainability," in State of the World 2014: Governing for Sustainability, pgs: 152-162. Worldwatch Institute. 2014.

Sources for illustrations:

Air quality index (AQI) basics. 2015. Last accessed in 2016. https://airnow.gov/index.cfm?action=aqibasics.aqi.

December weather for Beijing, BJ. 2015. Last accessed in 2016. https://www.wunderground.com/history/airport/ZBAA/2015/12/30/MonthlyCalendar.html?req_city=Beijing&req_state=&req_statename=Beijing&reqdb.zip=00000&reqdb.magic=4&reqdb.wmo=54511.

Fritz, A. "Beijing Chokes on Off-The-Charts Air Pollution as Thick Smog Settles Over Northern China." Washington Post. 2015. Last accessed in 2016. https://www.washingtonpost.com/news/capital-weather-gang/wp/2015/11/30/beijing-chokes-on-off-the-charts-air-pollution-as-thick-smog-settles-over-northern-china/?utm_term=.21d-32b3f23bb.

LSE Cities. Governing Urban Futures. Urban Age Conference, Delhi, India. November 14-15, 2014. London: LSE Cities, London School of Economics and Political Science, 2014.

Rode, P., Burdett, R. et. al. Technical study: Cities and the Green Economy. LSE Cities working paper. 2011.

Rode, P., Burdett, R., Pieterse, E., Zenghelis, D., Viswanathan, B., Tiwari, G., Lam, D. and Lu, X. "The Green Economy Report: Cities," in Towards a Green Economy: Pathways to Sustainable Development and Poverty Eradication. Edited by Sukdev, P. Geneva: United Nations Environment Programme, 2011.

Stanway, D., Chen, K., Rose, A., Busvine, D. and Richardson, A." Smog chokes Chinese, Indian capitals as climate talks begin." 2015. Last accessed in 2016. http://www.reuters.com/article/us-climatechange-summit-china-smog-idUSKBN0TJ0DG20151130.

"Towards a Green Economy: Pathways to Sustainable Development and Poverty Eradication." UNEP, 2011. Last accessed in 2016. http://web.unep.org/greeneconomy/sites/unep.org.greeneconomy/files/field/image/green_economyreport_final_dec2011.pdf.

Wessels, G., Pardo, C.F. and Bocarejo, J.P. Towards a World-Class Transit Oriented Metropolis. 2012. Last accessed in 2016. http://www.despacio.org/wp-content/uploads/2012/10/Bogota-21-english.pdf.

Research Meetings

Initial London Meeting, 11 February 2014
LSE Cities, London School of Economics and Political Science

Participants: Andy Altman, Ash Amin, Dominick Bagnato, Lindsay Bremner, Ricky Burdett, Joan Clos, Gunter Gassner, Adam Greenfield, Alejandro Gutierrez, Suzanne Hall, Eddie Heathcote, Adam Kaasa, Amanda Levete, Ana Moreno, Eric Parry, Philipp Rode, Joseph Rykwert, Saskia Sassen, Richard Sennett, Deyan Sudjic, Stephen Witherford, Austin Zeidermann

Democracy and Climate Change Workshop, 10 October 2014
Institute for Public Knowledge, New York University
Participants: Hillary Angelo, Dominick Bagnato, Gianpaolo Baiocchi, Ricky Burdett, Daniel Cohen, Filiep Decorte, Andrew Dobson, Jane Harrison, Stephen Holmes, Dale Jamieson, Colin Jerolmack, Eric Klinenberg, Michael Laver, Ana Moreno, Henk Ovink, Saskia Sassen, Richard Sennett, Matthew Skjonsberg, Emma Torres, David Turnbull, J. David Velleman

Informality Workshop, 22 October 2015
Centre for Advanced Urbanism, MIT
Participants: Dominick Bagnato, Alan Berger, Anita Berrizbeitia, Homi Bhabha, Gerald Frug, Maren Larsen, Rahul Mehrotra, Carles Muro, Balakrishnan Rajagopal, Adele Santos, Richard Sennett, Matthew Skjonsberg, Clay Strange

Design of the Public Realm Workshop, 4 December 2015
LSE Cities, London School of Economics and Political Science
Participants: Dominick Bagnato, John Bingham-Hall, Shumi Bose, Ricky Burdett, Amica Dall, Alexander Giarlis, Peter Griffiths, Suzanne Hall, Harriet Harris, Francine Houben, Adam Kaasa, Winy Maas, Suketu Mehta, Francesca Perry, Richard Sennett, Matthew Skjonsberg, Steve Tompkins, Stephen Witherford

Charter of Quito Workshop, 13 July 2016
The Splendid Hotel, Venice
Participants: Dominick Bagnato, Homi Bhabha, John Bingham-Hall, Ricky Burdett, Judit Carrera, Joan Clos, Amica Dall, Filiep Decorte, Liza Fior, Adam Kaasa, Jinlin Li, Rahul Mehrotra, Jean-Louis Missika, Philipp Rode, Saskia Sassen, Richard Sennett, Lars Stordal

INDEX

A

Abercrombie, Patrick: 145
Abuja: 165
access: 26, 28, 50, 53, 66, 68, 121,
    125, 127-129, 139, 142, 144,
    146, 161
    accessibility: 42, 59, 110, 119
    accessible system: 144
    access to basic services: 34, 142
    access to jobs: 146
    access to labour markets: 111
    access to public transport: 141
    access to the street: 156
    access to water: 3, 32-33, 160
    affordable access: 66
    equal access: 126
accountability: 22, 44, 66, 138
accounting: 63
accretion: 85-86, 88, 142, 145-147
acquisition: 3, 21-22, 26-28, 39, 54
    corporate acquisition: 49-51
action: 53, 57, 74, 97, 133, 135,
    143, 146, 158, 163
    climate action: 47, 134
    cooperative action: 129
    political action: 127, 160
    possibility of action: 53, 74
    public action: 55, 57, 111, 113
activity: 7, 93, 124
    biological activity: 93
    human activity: 3, 42
acupuncture: 88, 148
    urban acupuncture: 86, 121,
    146
adaptation: 40, 41, 70, 86, 88, 92,
    142, 145, 146, 148, 167
administration: 127, 152
    land administration: 66, 99
advocacy: 40, 92
Afghanistan: 18
Africa: 3-4, 6, 8-10, 16, 37-39
age: 10-12
    age distribution: 3, 10
    age structure: 10
agency: 43-44, 46-47, 75, 135,
    147
    agency presupposition: 46
    international agency: 142, 145
    loss of agency: 47
agglomeration: 104
    economies of agglomeration:
    110-111
    urban agglomeration: 14, 100-
    101
aging: 6, 11
agriculture: 7, 11, 18, 21
aid: 24
Aix-en-Provence: 92
Allahabad: 76
Amin, Ash: 143-144
Amsterdam: 50, 142
anarchy: 92, 144
Angel, Shlomo: 1, 4, 16, 53, 56,
    101-105, 108, 110, 114-115

approach: 40-41, 59, 94, 118, 126,
    128, 132, 169
    approach to planning: 143, 146
    consumption-based approach:
    124
    deliberative approach: 138
    systemic approach: 53, 58
appropriation: 53, 84, 131, 144
architecture: 78-79, 82, 85, 91, 94,
    126, 144-145, 169, 172
    architect: 80-81, 91, 93-94,
    146
    starchitect: 172
armature: 87, 118, 145, 147
Arrival City: 143
art: 53, 91, 94, 121, 126, 128, 172
    artists: 50, 130
Asia: 4, 6-7, 9-12, 16, 62, 106,
    109-110, 134, 142
assessment: 80
asset: 27, 32, 50-1, 62, 119, 126,
association: 7-8, 59, 127
Atlanta: 64
Atlantic Yards: 50
austerity: 97, 127
author: 78, 143, 146, 172
authority: 126, 141, 150
    jurisdictional authority: 136
    local authority: 96, 124, 130,
    151, 153
autonomy: 28, 47, 133, 138 (*see
    also* self-determination)

B

Baiocchi, Gianpaolo: 53, 132
Bangkok: 51
bank: 20, 141, 153
    banking: 20, 153
    water bank: 41
bankruptcy: 54-55, 150
Barcelona: 64-65, 84-85, 142-145,
    147, 150, 156-158, 169, 171,
    173
Barra Tijuca: 81
barrio: 143, 146 (*see also* informal
    settlement, slum)
Battery Park City: 84, 144
Bauman, Zygmunt: 78
Beck, Ulrich: 138
behaviour: 10, 75, 124, 164
Beijing: 50-51, 101, 135, 141
Beirut: 73, 93
benefit: 54, 129-130, 146
Berlin: 142
Berrizbeitia, Anita: 53, 116, 118,
    120
bicycle: 163
Bingham-Hall, John: 53, 124, 128
biodiversity: 33, 76
birth: 8, 11, 29, 92
    birth rate: 11
blank slate: 53, 78, 80-81 (*see
    also* tabula rasa)
block: 45

block size: 110
    superblock: 144, 158
    urban block: 126
Bogotá: 142
bombing: 78
bond: 155
border: 72-73, 93
    border condition: 73, 93
    borderline: 72, 93
borehole: 37
boundary: 22, 66, 72, 93, 139
    administrative boundary: 101
    municipal boundary: 139
    porous boundary: 53, 72-73
Bourdic, Loeiz: 53
Brasilia: 144
Brazil: 23, 45, 55, 122, 133, 144,
    162
Brexit: 150
Brittle City: 68-69, 91-92, 94
Brown, John Seely: 91
budgeting: 137, 163
building: 1, 25, 27-28, 39, 41,
    49-51, 57, 59, 68, 70, 78, 83,
    85-88, 91-92, 94, 112, 116,
    127-128, 130, 142-144, 146-
    48, 156, 169, 171-172
    apartment building: 28, 50-51
    high-rise building: 10, 20, 28,
    50, 141
    hotel: 26, 50, 87, 147
    luxury building: 28, 50-51
    multi-storey building: 86, 146
    office building: 26, 28, 50-51,
    87, 147
    public building: 29, 51, 86,
    118, 144, 146, 155
    urban building: 49
built environment: 51, 82
built-up area: 64, 100-104, 110
    contiguous built-up area: 100,
    104
Burdett, Ricky: 1, 10, 12, 53, 88,
    140
bureaucrat: 69, 92
    bureaucratic: 91, 137
    bureaucratic system: 69, 92
Burke, Edmund: 92
buying: 3, 26, 28, 49-51
by-law: 124

C

C40 Climate Leadership Group:
    135
Cairo: 51, 67, 70, 92, 117
Caldeira, Teresa: 143
Canary Wharf (London): 84, 124,
    144, 147
canopy: 120
capacity: 20, 29, 40, 41, 47, 49,
    51, 54, 59, 63, 66, 83, 99, 119,
    132, 136, 139, 145, 150, 153,
    164, 165, 169
    capacity building: 88, 148

96, 111, 116, 119, 124, 126,
128-131, 141, 143, 158-160,
163-164, 166, 168-169
mixed use: 28, 50, 59, 66
multiple use: 59, 156
reuse: 69, 130
single use: 84, 143
temporary use: 84, 143
urban use: 55, 104, 108
utopia: 82

V

value: 20-21, 35, 38, 50, 58, 92-
94, 122, 126, 141-143, 153,
155, 172
capture of value: 53-54, 58
creation of value: 53-54, 59,
99, 110, 129, 153
generation of value: 54, 58, 63,
166
increase in value: 54, 62, 126
value of land: 58, 62, 126
value of property: 26, 51, 62
private value: 166
redistribution of value: 58
reinvestment of value: 58
sharing of value: 53, 54, 62
van der Rohe, Mies: 93
Venice: 172
ventilation: 120
veto player: 3, 44-45
victim: 32, 53, 134
Victoria and Albert Museum: 147
violence: 18, 78, 80, 148
violence by police: 51
Violence Prevention Through Urban
Upgrading (VPUU): 86, 146
vision: x, 3, 53, 70, 76, 78, 83, 92,
94, 123, 137, 169
ecological vision: 76, 94
peripheral vision: 93, 157
visualization: 10, 41, 72
vitality: 91
vulnerability: 32, 134

W

walkability: 54, 111
wall: 29, 50, 72, 92-94, 131-132
cellular wall: 72, 93
Greek wall: 92
medieval wall: 72-73, 92-93
wall of a city: 72
wallof a town: 72, 92
porous wall: 53, 72-73, 93
Roman wall: 92
virtual wall: 29, 50
war: 19, 24-25, 33, 49, 78, 80-81,
97, 133, 141-142, 157
Spanish Civil War: 78
technology of war: 78
Washington Consensus: 153
water: 3, 11, 19-22, 32-37, 39, 41,
65, 102-103, 116, 118, 120,

143, 147, 153, 159-160
collection of water: 120, 122-
123
consumption of water: 35, 39
crisis of water: 33, 125
demand for water: 36, 39
distribution of water: 122
drinking water: 38
excess of water: 3, 32, 41, 160
extraction of ground water: 36-
37
fresh water: 35-36, 42
ground water: 33, 36-39
illiteracy related to water: 38-39
lack of water: 32, 41
locally-available water source: 39
potable water: 34, 41
remote water: 36, 39
right to water: 34, 138
stormwater runoff: 120
surface water: 33, 37, 39
water bank: 41
water footprint: 33, 36, 39
water scarcity: 32, 43, 160
water self-sufficiency: 39
water source: 37
water stress: 3, 34, 38-39
water supply: 33-34, 37-38,
116
wealth: 86-87, 97, 143, 146, 169-
170
wealth generation: 58
weather: 135
weather event: 33, 43
weather pattern: 41
welfare: 34, 44, 47, 99, 152, 155
welfare service: 96, 98
welfare state: 96-98, 155
welfare transfer: 97
wellbeing: 97
Western Asia and North Africa
(WANA, regional grouping): 6,
10-11, 114-115
wilds, urban: 120
work: 3, 29, 34, 46, 51, 70, 73,
75, 76, 82, 91-95, 99, 126,
128-129, 133, 141-143, 145,
147-148, 153, 156, 160, 163,
166-167, 172 (see also employment)
worker: 20, 51, 144, 163
low-wage worker: 29, 51
working class: 26, 49
World Bank: 21
World Health Organization (WHO):
37
World Trade Organization (WTO):
44

Y

Yangtze River: 10, 141
youth: 10-12, 58, 97, 167
unaccompanied minors: 18

Z

zone: 24, 29, 33, 40, 49, 51, 72,
92-93, 144
functional zone: 10, 141
zone of exchange: 93
zoning: 10, 59, 68, 85, 91-92, 143,
145
preemptive zoning: 69, 91
prescriptive zoning: 141